CHARISMATIC LEADERSHIP
in Organizations

D0169548

CHARISMATIC
LEADERSHIP
in Organizations

Jay A. Conger
Rabindra N. Kanungo

SAGE Publications
International Educational and Professional Publisher
Thousand Oaks London New Delhi

7-27-99

For information:

SAGE Publications, Inc.
2455 Teller Road
Thousand Oaks, California 91320
E-mail: order@sagepub.com

SAGE Publications Ltd.
6 Bonhill Street
London EC2A 4PU
United Kingdom

SAGE Publications India Pvt. Ltd.
M-32 Market
Greater Kailash I
New Delhi 110 048 India

Printed in the United States of America

Library of Congress Cataloging-in-Publication Data

Conger, Jay Alden.
  Charismatic leadership in organizations / by Jay A. Conger and
Rabindra N. Kanungo.
    p. cm.
  Includes bibliographical references and index.
  ISBN 0-7619-1633-4 (acid-free paper)
  ISBN 0-7619-1634-2 (pbk.: acid-free paper)
  1. Executive ability. 2. Leadership. 3. Organizational
effectiveness. I. Kanungo, Rabindra Nath. II. Title.
  HD38.2 .C658 1998
  658.4'092—ddc21   98-9003

98 99 00 01 02 03 10 9 8 7 6 5 4 3 2 1

Acquiring Editor:	Marquita Flemming
Editorial Assistant:	Heidi Van Middlesworth
Production Editor:	Diana E. Axelsen
Editorial Assistant:	Lynn Miyata
Typesetter/Designer:	Danielle Dillahunt
Indexer:	Trish Wittenstein

Contents

Preface

When we first set out to explore charismatic leadership in organizations a decade ago, there were but a handful of references concerning the topic. We felt very much like adventurers exploring a new land. Today, it is with a sense of surprise that we see how the field has flourished. The saying "let a thousand flowers bloom" would certainly be appropriate to describe how interest has unfolded. Given the growing attention to the topic, it seemed timely to introduce a book that would not only aim to integrate what we have learned to date but also would push our frontiers of knowledge further. We trust that readers will feel that we have succeeded in both of these objectives.

To understand scientifically a phenomenon as elusive as charismatic leadership, three vital steps must be undertaken. First, a conceptual or theoretical framework is needed that can adequately describe the phenomenon and at the same time strip away its surrounding aura of mystery for both management scholars and practitioners. Second, the framework must then be empirically validated through systematic investigation looking at the nature, causes, and consequences of charismatic leadership. Finally, after such validation efforts, the framework can and should be used to explain and predict charismatic leadership in actual observed cases in organizations. The first two chapters of this book are devoted to the first step. They explore how theory has developed over the past decade and specifically how our own theoretical framework has evolved. They close with a model of charismatic leadership in organizations. Chapter 3 looks at the second step— empirical validation. In this chapter, we examine a series of studies undertaken to test our theory and to develop a measure of charismatic leadership. These investigations confirm the validity of the model and have resulted in a reliable measure of what has heretofore been considered a highly elusive form of leadership. Chapters 4 through 6 are devoted to the third step—the explanation of charismatic leadership as observed in company case studies. Here we illustrate our framework using examples of business leaders as well as expand on our model. Our final two chapters look at the challenges facing the field—the liabilities of charismatic leadership and future areas of research. Although charismatic leadership is often known for its positive consequences, it has a shadow side that has been poorly explored. In Chapter 7, we begin to address this important gap in our knowledge. Finally, while interest has grown dramatically in the topic, some might say that we have only scratched the surface. Chapter 8 therefore looks at where future attention must be directed if we are to more fully understand the many dimensions of charismatic leadership. We also include a discussion of the challenges facing leaders in the upcoming century and why charismatic leadership is particularly well suited to address these.

In our writing throughout this book, we have both been guided by a belief that charismatic leadership is a critically important topic within the larger field of leadership studies, one deserving far greater attention than it has received in the past. We say this because charismatic leaders are often exemplars of the qualities we normally associate with leadership. For example, they can be remarkable change agents, able to reinvent entire organizations and societies. They are also superb examples of leaders who are master communicators and motivators. As such, they provide many important lessons for those who wish to lead others or for those who wish to study leadership. Paradoxically, these same leaders also provide us with lessons about the greatest dangers of leadership. Throughout history, certain charismatic leaders have proved themselves master manipulators and purveyors of evil. They have been responsible for the collapse of corporations and of nations. Given these two faces of this form of leadership, it is imperative that we learn as much about it as we can for the well-being of ourselves, our organizations, and our society. It is our hope, therefore, that this volume will stimulate continued inquiry into this potent source of leadership.

In writing this manuscript, we have been fortunate in having wonderful help. We especially want to thank Kim Jaussi and Gretchen Spreitzer for their review of our manuscript. Their comments have played an important role in improving this volume. We also want to thank Sanjay Menon and Purnima Mathur, who collaborated with us in conducting several of the validation studies reported in Chapter 3. They were instrumental both in helping us collect data and in analyzing it. Finally, we are especially grateful for the patience, fortitude, and skills of Deletha Gafford and Kristen Martin. They did a remarkable job not only of transforming our handwritten notes and script into text but also of managing the modern process of producing a book, one that has been assembled through e-mail messages and computer disks.

PART I

THEORY DEVELOPMENT

1

Evolution of the Field

It is a commonplace observation that leadership plays an important role in the creation, survival, growth, and decay of organizations. Considering its importance, numerous books and articles have been written on leadership (see, e.g., Bass, 1990; Yukl, 1994) during the past half century, yet social scientists and managerial scholars started to show a genuine interest in studying the phenomenon of charismatic leadership in organizations only during the past decade. In this introductory chapter, we will look at how research on charismatic leadership in organizations has evolved over this decade. When we wrote the book *Charismatic Leadership* (Conger & Kanungo, 1988b) in 1988, the field was still very young. We commented at the time:

> The topic has actually suffered from a serious lack of attention. To put its neglect into perspective, we turn to *Stogdill's Handbook of Leadership* (Bass, 1981), which is considered the reference book on leadership studies. Combing through the more than 5,000 studies included in the handbook, only a dozen references to charismatic leadership are to be found. This is an ironic and disheartening discovery given the profound impact of charismatic leaders. (p. 12)

More recently, this situation has begun to reverse itself. Today interest in charismatic leadership has blossomed. What is particularly surprising is the number of empirical studies that have appeared. Most of the academic work up to the publication of *Charismatic Leadership* had been largely theoretical in nature, with little empirical research. Today that situation has changed dramatically.

Several dozen empirical investigations of charismatic leadership in organizations have now been conducted. They have involved a wide range of samples such as middle- and lower-level managers (Bass & Yammarino, 1988; Conger & Kanungo, 1994; Conger, Kanungo, Menon, & Mathur, 1997; Deluga, 1995; Hater & Bass, 1988; Koene, Pennings, & Schrender, 1991), senior executives (Agle, 1993; Agle & Sonnenfeld, 1994; Conger, 1985, 1989a), U.S. presidents (House, Spangler, & Woycke, 1991), educational administrators (Koh, Terborg, & Steers, 1991; Roberts & Bradley, 1988; Sashkin, 1988), military cadets and leaders (Atwater, Camobreco, Dionne, Avolio, & Lau, 1997; Curphy, 1990; Howell & Avolio, 1993; Koene et al., 1991; Waldman & Ramirez, 1992), and students who were laboratory subjects (Howell & Frost, 1989; Kirkpatrick, 1992; Kirkpatrick & Locke, 1996; Puffer, 1990; Shamir, 1992, 1995). In addition, the subject has been explored using a wide variety of research methods. For example, there have been field surveys (Conger & Kanungo, 1992, 1994; Hater & Bass, 1988; Podsakoff, MacKenzie, Moorman, & Fetter, 1990), laboratory experiments (Howell & Frost, 1989; Kirkpatrick, 1992; Kirkpatrick & Locke, 1996; Puffer, 1990), content analyses of interviews and observation (Conger, 1989a; Howell & Higgins, 1990), and analyses of historical archival information (Chen & Meindl, 1991; House et al., 1991; Shamir, Arthur, & House, 1994).

What is more remarkable than this flowering of research is the relative uniformity of findings despite some differences in theoretical approaches. As Shamir, House, and Arthur (1993) have noted, findings across the board demonstrate that leaders who engage in the behaviors that are theorized to be charismatic actually produce the charismatic effects that theory predicts. In addition, many of these studies have shown that leaders who are perceived as charismatic receive higher performance ratings, are seen as more effective leaders than others holding leadership positions, and have more highly motivated and more satisfied followers than others in similar positions (e.g., see Agle & Sonnenfeld, 1994).

Given this new body of research, this chapter aims to trace the evolution of the field over the last decade. The goal is to identify both advances and remaining gaps in our understanding of charismatic leadership in organizations. We begin our discussion, however, by exploring the backdrop of changes in the business world that not only have served as catalysts for the growing interest but also have shaped how researchers have approached the subject.

Following this discussion, we will describe contributions since the late 1980s. When *Charismatic Leadership* was published in 1988, the field was in its infancy, and the existing body of research at that time could be broken down into three distinct clusters based on (1) behavioral dimensions of the charismatic leader, (2) the psychological characteristics or dispositions of charismatic leaders, and (3) the institutionalization of charisma. Today, our knowledge has deepened in these areas. In addition, several other topic areas have received some attention. These include the dimensions of (1) contextual factors, (2) succession and maintenance factors, and (3) the dark side of charismatic leadership. In the second section of this chapter, we will cover developments in all these areas.

BACKGROUND FORCES IN THE BUSINESS WORLD

To understand why the subject of charismatic leadership has grown in interest for organizational theorists, we must look at the world around us—a larger backdrop of global competition. The rise of Asian economic powers, such as Japan and the Little Dragons, as well as European players like Germany, shattered the market dominance of North American companies. This had a dramatic impact not only on industry but also, in turn, on research within business schools. In terms of the world of commerce, it forced many large corporations to reinvent themselves radically after enjoying several decades of what in hindsight appears to have been relative stability. As companies attempted to adapt, they discovered that the process of reinvention was extremely difficult. For example, rarely did company insiders possess the courage and change management skills needed to orchestrate large-scale transformations. The leadership talent necessary for such undertakings essentially was in short supply.

A second dilemma facing these organizations was employee commitment. In the midst of their change efforts, companies resorted to extensive downsizing as well as to new organizational arrangements such as flatter hierarchies and strategic business units. While often improving bottom-line performance, these initiatives took their toll on worker satisfaction and empowerment. In the process, the old social contract of long-term employment in return for employee loyalty was broken. The net result was disenfranchisement for many in the workforce. This occurred just at the moment when corporations were demanding ever greater performance and commitment from employees. For companies, the challenge became a question of how to orchestrate transformational change while simultaneously building employee morale and commitment—a seemingly contradictory endeavor.

These important events in the business world had a direct impact on the study of leadership. Because the majority of organizational scholars who studied leadership held positions within business schools, their attention turned to the role of leadership in addressing these twin challenges of transformational leadership and empowerment. They would also feel a need to explain why so many organizations had been slow to change and why turnaround efforts often were unsuccessful. To address these issues, researchers turned to a simple dichotomy: Managers and leaders were different.

Up to this point in time, leadership researchers had rarely drawn a clear distinction between the roles of leading and managing. The idea that leadership and management might stand for different phenomena or roles or personalities was novel. Not even in its selection of candidates for study had the leadership field discriminated between the two notions. Instead, it was assumed that anyone in a management position essentially was in a "leadership role." A consensus is emerging, however, among management scholars that the concept of leadership must be distinguished from the concept of supervision/managership for the purpose of developing future research agendas and addressing organizational challenges (Adler, 1997; House, 1995; Kanungo & Mendonca, 1996b; Zaleznik, 1990). In light of this, the earlier streams of leadership research conducted in the 1950s and 1960s at Ohio State University and the University of Michigan, identifying the task or initiating structure and the person or consideration roles of leadership, would today be reclassified as more managerial because of the activities on which they focused.

One of the first appearances of a distinction between leading and managing can be traced back to 1975. Abraham Zaleznik and Manfred Kets de Vries (1975) argued in a book titled *Power and the Corporate Mind* that there were two types of organizational leaders: the maximum man and the minimum man. In business, the maximum man was the creative institution builder, and the minimum man was the modern-day manager:

> [Maximum man's relationship to subordinates] is usually simple: He is their leader. At times he may be recognized practically on sight because of the glow of confidence his inner light gives him. He is charismatic, people are drawn to him by the power of his convictions and visions of reality. His presence inspires both dread and fascination; he evokes mystical reactions. . . . The minimum man is concerned with the opinion of his peers. He would rather have egalitarian

relations with men as brothers than be in the socially distant position of a father figure. He does not, therefore, lead public opinion, but follows it. (pp. 237-241)

Their notions of "maximum man" and "minimum man" were rooted in the work of the early American psychologist William James (1958), who had formulated a theory of personality types called the "once-borns" and the "twice-borns." The once-borns, James proposed, were individuals who experienced the flow of life as relatively straightforward from the time of birth. Their family life was harmonious and peaceful. The twice-borns experienced quite the opposite. They faced great struggles. Their lives were never easy, and unlike the once-borns, they could take little for granted. As a result, the two personalities developed not only very different perspectives on the world but also different expectations of achievement. The once-borns went on to become managers: "Managers perceive life as a steady progression of positive events . . ." (Zaleznik, 1990, p. 9). Leaders, on the other hand, were the twice-born personalities:

> Leaders are twice-born individuals who endure major events that lead to a sense of separateness, or perhaps, estrangement from their environment. As a result, they turn inward in order to reemerge with a created rather than an inherited sense of identity. That sense of separateness may be a necessary condition for the ability to lead. (Zaleznik, 1990, p. 9)

This theme of essential differences between managers and leaders would be further accentuated in the 1980s, when a group of organizational theorists initiated what would in essence become a new paradigm of leadership theory. At the core of this group was a small number of individuals (e.g., Bass, 1985; Bennis & Nanus, 1985; Conger & Kanungo, 1987; Kotter, 1988; Kouzes & Posner, 1987; Peters & Waterman, 1982; Tichy & Devanna, 1986), most of whom were examining executives and managers involved in transforming their organizations. Called the "new leadership school" by Bryman (1992) and the "neo-charismatic paradigm" by House (1995), these researchers constructed their notions of leadership around contrasts with the role of management. For example, Bennis and Nanus (1985) would argue:

> By focusing attention on a vision, the leader operates on the emotional and spiritual resources of the organization, on its values, commitment, and aspirations. The manager, by contrast, operates on the physical resources of the organization, on its capital, human skills, raw materials, and technology. . . . An

excellent manager can see to it that work is done productively and efficiently, on schedule, and with a high level of quality. It remains for the effective leader, however, to help people in the organization know pride and satisfaction in their work. (p. 92)

Kotter (1988) would argue similarly that the fundamental difference between leadership and management was that the former is concerned with activities that produce "constructive or adaptive change," whereas the latter is concerned with producing "consistency and order." Leadership focused on the long-term issues of the organization, whereas management attended to the short-term. Leadership acquired commitment to performance through empowerment, whereas management acquired it through contractual arrangements.

As a result of these new conceptualizations, we today conceive of the role activities of leading and managing as distinct (as outlined in Table 1.1). A person in a managerial position may have to execute administrative, supervisory, and leadership functions for the organization. Administrative functions involve the procurement and deployment of available resources to maintain the day-to-day operations of the organization. Supervisory functions require looking after the efficient and effective day-to-day utilization of human resources so as to accomplish previously set operational tasks and organizational objectives. Execution of both functions ensures the maintenance of standard job behavior on the part of employees. Thus, both administration and supervision are directed toward maintaining the status quo. Both aim to achieve short-term, operational objectives of the organization, primarily by using control strategies and tactics. The execution of these functions is the primary objective of "managership." Leadership functions, on the other hand, require an executive or manager to formulate long-term objectives for the organization that are novel and therefore different from the status quo. The essential characteristics of leadership become (1) challenging the status quo, (2) engaging in creative visioning for the future of the organization, and (3) promoting appropriate changes in followers' values, attitudes, and behaviors by using empowering strategies and tactics.

Distinguishing leading from managing, the new leadership school argued that the inability of North American corporations to adapt to a changing world could be traced back largely to organizations directed by too much management and too little leadership. A severe shortage of leadership talent, it was thought, was at the heart of the problem (Bennis & Nanus, 1985; Kotter, 1988). Although this position would be challenged by writers such as Nadler and Tushman (1990), who argued that the two roles needed one another in any change effort, this viewpoint continues to be popular. Among leadership researchers (e.g., Hickman,

TABLE 1.1 Distinguishing Leadership From Managership

Managership	*Leadership*
1. Engages in day-to-day activities: Maintains and allocates resources.	Formulates long-term objectives for reforming the system: Plans strategy and tactics.
2. Exhibits supervisory behavior: Acts to make others maintain standard job behavior.	Exhibits leading behavior: Acts to bring about change in others congruent with long-term objectives.
3. Administers subsystems within organizations.	Innovates for the entire organization.
4. Asks how and when to engage in standard practice.	Asks when and why to change standard practice.
5. Acts within established culture of the organization.	Creates vision and meaning for the organization and strives to transform culture.
6. Uses transactional influence: Induces compliance in manifest behavior using rewards, sanctions, and formal authority.	Uses transformational influence: Induces change in values, attitudes, and behavior using personal examples and expertise.
7. Relies on control strategies to get things done by subordinates.	Uses empowering strategies to make followers internalize values.
8. Supports the status quo and stabilizes the organization.	Challenges the status quo and creates change.

1990; Kotter, 1988; Yukl, 1994), however, it is widely believed that although it is useful to conceive of leadership and management as distinct roles, it is not helpful to view managers and leaders as distinct types of people: Individuals can and do embody both roles.

Interestingly, many of the proponents of this distinction between managing and leading were influenced profoundly by the writings of political scientist James McGregor Burns. In his 1978 book *Leadership*, Burns concluded that leaders could be separated into two types: the "transformational" and the "transactional." For the field of organizational behavior, these would be translated by researchers into the roles of leadership (transformational leadership) and management (transactional leadership).

For Burns, leadership at its essence can be distilled down to the notion of an exchange. Both the leader and the follower have something to offer one another. It is in the nature of what was exchanged that his model came into play. For Burns, transformational leaders offered a transcendent purpose as their mission—one that addressed the higher-order needs of their followers. In the process of achieving this mission, both the leaders and the led were literally transformed or actualized as individuals—hence the term *transforming*. As Burns explained, "The result of transforming leadership is a relationship of mutual stimulation and elevation that converts followers into leaders and may convert leaders into moral agents" (p. 4). At the other end of the spectrum is transactional leadership, by far the more common of the two forms. Transactional leadership is based on a relationship with followers that consists of mundane and instrumental exchanges: "The relations of most leaders and followers are transactional—leaders approach followers with an eye to exchanging one thing for another: jobs for votes, or subsidies for campaign contributions. Such [instrumental] transactions comprise the bulk of the relationships . . ." (p. 4).

Burns's conceptualization influenced the thinking of many scholars in the organizational leadership field. For example, Bernard Bass (1985) would build much of his model of transformational leadership for organizational leaders around Burns's ideas. In drawing the essential distinction between managing and leading, Bennis and Nanus (1985) referred back to Burns's notion of what was exchanged:

> Management typically consists of a set of contractual exchanges, "you do this job for that reward," . . . "a bunch of agreements or contracts." What gets exchanged is not trivial: jobs, security, money. The result, at best, is compliance; at worst, you get a spiteful obedience. The end result of the leadership we have advanced is completely different: it is empowerment. "Not just higher profits and wages . . . but an organizational culture that helps employees generate a sense of meaning in their work and a desire to challenge themselves to experience success." (p. 218)

Not so surprisingly, the core idea of leadership as an exchange had been around for some time in the organizational literature. For example, we find it central to the leader-member exchange (e.g., Graen & Cashman, 1975; Graen & Scandura, 1987), operant conditioning (Luthans & Kreitner, 1975; Podsakoff, Todor, & Skov, 1982; Sims, 1977), and path-goal models (Evans, 1970; House, 1971; House & Mitchell, 1974). In each, the relationship between the leader and led depends on a series of trades or bargains that are mutually beneficial and are maintained as long as the benefits to both parties exceed the costs (Bass, 1970). In Burns's terms, however, these exchanges are "transactional," not "transformational." Missing is the element of higher-order needs being met and the elevation of both the leader and led to a more evolved state of being. This was the critical contribution that Burns brought to the existing organizational theory. As a result, as Howell (1996) points out, the notion of leaders who manage meaning, infuse ideological values, construct lofty goals and visions, and inspire was missing entirely from this literature of leadership exchange. What is intriguing about the influence of Burns, then, is not so much the notion of leadership as an exchange but the idea that certain forms of leadership create a cycle of rising aspirations that ultimately transform both leaders and their followers.

In the 1980s, Burns's ideas would have great appeal to organizational theorists grappling with the twin issues of organizational change and empowerment. The model of the transformational leader spoke to both these issues. After all, these were leaders concerned about transforming the existing order of things as well as directly addressing their followers' needs for meaning and personal growth. On the other hand, the transactional dimensions came to be associated with management. This dichotomy separating the two forms into distinct roles of leading and managing, however, has not proved to be entirely accurate: Studies of leadership show leaders employing both transformational and transactional approaches.

At this point in our discussion, readers may be wondering how these ideas of managing versus leading and transformational versus transactional leadership bridge back to charismatic leadership. In a nutshell, many researchers postulated that charisma is an important attribute of leaders who serve in the change agent or transformational roles (Bass, 1985; Weber, 1947; Zaleznik & Kets de Vries, 1975). Others believed that charismatic leadership was the most exemplary form that transformational leaders could assume (Conger, 1989a; Conger & Kanungo, 1987). (As we shall argue, there is far more overlap between the two than there are differences.) If we wished to understand the role of leaders in organizational change, therefore, it might be wise to study the most outstanding examples.

In concluding this introductory section, we can say that the forces of an intensely competitive, global business world and the paradigms of "managing versus leading" and "transactional versus transformational leadership" not only serve as catalysts to study charismatic leadership but also shape how it was studied and described. For example, as we are about to see, the emphasis on the act of leading change encouraged a focus on the *behaviors* and *activities* of individuals who were actually leading. The focus on the exchange would promote thinking about the effect of leader behavior on *follower outcomes*. These early influential theoretical distinctions have clearly shaped what has been studied and what has not in the field of charismatic leadership in organizations.

CONTRIBUTIONS FROM THE FIELD
OF ORGANIZATIONAL BEHAVIOR

Any discussion of charismatic leadership in organizations must start with a particular German sociologist, Max Weber, who applied the term *charismatic* to leaders in the secular world. His typology of three types of authority in society (the traditional, the rational-legal, and the charismatic) established *charismatic leadership* as an important term to describe forms of authority based on perceptions of an extraordinary individual. (For a more in-depth discussion of Weber's contribution, see Conger, 1988, 1993.) In contrast to authority derived from traditions and rules that conferred legitimacy on individuals, the holder of charisma is

> set apart from ordinary men and is treated as endowed with . . . exceptional powers and qualities . . . [which] are not accessible to the ordinary person but are regarded as of divine origin or as exemplary, and on the basis of them the individual concerned is treated as a leader. (Weber, 1947, pp. 358-359)

Although Weber did not provide a tight theoretical model of this form of leadership, his writings (Willner, 1984) provide us with elements of the character and the course of charismatic leadership: the condition under which it typically arises (distress), one requirement for its maintenance (success), its likely outcome over time (institutionalization), and some of the means by which charismatic leaders exercise their authority (powers of mind and speech, heroism, magical abilities). Because of Weber's sociological perspective, however, the issues of personal attributes and relational dynamics between the leader and followers were largely overlooked. Organizational theorists would focus much of their attention on these particular gaps. Because there has been a tremendous amount written about Weber's contributions to the field of charismatic leadership (for example, see Bryman, 1992; Conger, 1993; Conger & Kanungo, 1987), we simply point out his role here and nothing more. It is interesting to note that although Weber's work spurred a great deal of interest in charismatic leadership in the fields of sociology and political science in the 1960s through the early 1980s, attention from these fields has since largely died out. Instead, the greatest current interest in the subject can be found among organizational theorists.

Our focus from this point on will center on the contributions made by organizational theorists. We will organize the existing research using a framework built around the following general dimensions: (1) the charismatic leader's behavior, (2) the followers' characteristics and dynamics, (3) contextual influences, (4) routinization and succession forces that institutionalize various outcomes of the leader-follower relationship, and (5) liabilities of charismatic leadership.

The Charismatic Leader's Behaviors

The greatest amount of both theoretical development and empirical research on charismatic leadership to date has been in the area of leader behaviors. This is due largely to the backgrounds of the researchers, most of whom have a strong behavioral orientation. Essentially, there are four groups of researchers who have carved out their own models—though each has a measure of overlap with the others in the attributes they identify. They are (1) Bernard Bass, Bruce Avolio, and their colleagues; (2) Jay Conger and Rabindra Kanungo, (3) Robert House, Boas Shamir, Jane Howell, and their colleagues, and (4) Marshall Sashkin. In this section, we will examine in depth the work of Bass/Avolio and House/Shamir/Howell. Our own research will be presented in the next chapter. We will discuss only briefly here the fourth model, proposed by Sashkin (1988) under the label of "visionary leadership," because it has not been the subject of extensive theory development. It was presented in our book *Charismatic Leadership* in 1988. Although his model has received limited research attention, it does highlight the importance of visioning behavior, a core element in charismatic leadership. Besides visioning behavior, Sashkin identified five other behaviors: (1) creating attention of others on key issues through unconventional and creative actions, (2) effective interpersonal communication, (3) demonstrating trustworthiness, (4) showing self-respect and respect toward others, and (5) taking personal risk.

Bass and Avolio:
Transformational Leadership

As noted earlier, Bass and, later, his colleague Avolio would build on Burns's notion of transformational leadership and develop a similar model for organizational leaders. As Bryman (1992, pp. 97-98) has pointed out, their model goes farther conceptually than Burns's original model. In his 1985 book titled *Leadership and Performance Beyond Expectations*, Bass conceptualized the transactional and transformational dimensions as separate, whereas Burns had defined them as two ends of a spectrum. For Bass, therefore, a leader could be both transformational and transactional. In addition, Bass was determined to more precisely identify the actual behaviors that these leaders demonstrated, whereas Burns was content with more of a "big picture" overview.

At the heart of Bass and Avolio's model of transformational leaders is the notion that these leaders are able to motivate subordinates to performance levels that exceed both their own and their leader's expectations. Transformational leaders accomplish this by raising the importance of certain goals, by demonstrating the means to achieve them, and by inducing subordinates to transcend their self-interests for the goals' achievement. In the process, these leaders also stimulate and meet subordinates' higher-order needs—for example, Maslow's (1968) self-actualization need—which in turn generates commitment, effort, and ultimately greater performance.

Bass and Avolio (1993) built their model of transformational leadership around four behavioral components of the leader: (1) charisma or idealized influence, (2) inspiration, (3) intellectual stimulation, and (4) individualized consideration. Charisma is a separate component and is defined in terms of both the leader's behavior (such as articulating a mission) and the followers' reactions (such as trust in the leader's ability) (Bass & Avolio, 1993). The emphasis, however, is on charisma's role in enabling the leader to influence followers by arousing strong emotions and identification with the leader. Identifying with the leader reduces follower resistance to change, while emotional arousal creates a sense of excitement about the mission. Bass (1985) argues, however, that charisma alone is insufficient for transformational leadership: "Charisma is a necessary ingredient of transformational leadership, but by itself it is not sufficient to account for the transformational process" (p. 31).

Although originally treated as a subfactor within charismatic leadership, the component of inspiration is designed to motivate. Much of this dimension centers around communication, in that the transformational leader "communicates high expectations, uses symbols to focus efforts, expresses important purposes in simple ways" (Bass, 1990, p. 22). Intellectual stimulation concerns the leader's provision of a flow of new ideas and perspectives that challenge followers to rethink old and conventional ways of approaching organizational tasks.

The fourth component of individualized consideration is similar to the early Ohio State notions of consideration. Providing encouragement and support to followers, assisting their development by promoting growth opportunities, and showing trust and respect for them as individuals are activities under this dimension. Its role is to bond the leader and the led and to build follower self-confidence and heighten personal development.

In Bryman's *Charisma and Leadership in Organizations* (1992), the methodological shortcomings of the Bass model have been well highlighted. Because both of the measures to capture transformational leadership (the Leadership Behavior Description Questionnaire [LBDQ] and the Multifactor Leadership Questionnaire [MLQ]) are based on subordinate ratings, there are potential problems of contamination by implicit leadership theories. Bass and Avolio, for example, discovered that descriptions of the transformational leader are significantly closer to subordinates' images of the ideal leader than descriptions of transactional leadership are. There are also issues of whether respondents' ratings of their leader's behavior are affected by their knowledge of the leader's effectiveness. In other words, perceptions of effectiveness may result in heightened attributions of leadership despite reality. There is little appreciation for contextual variables or differences, and partly as a result, the implications for situational differences under the model remain unexplored (Bryman, 1992, pp. 128-129).

In addition, Bryman (1992) points out that Bass's measure of charisma itself may be a bit flawed. For example, vision is treated as a component of inspirational, rather than charismatic, leadership. The bulk of the literature in the field, however, sees vision as a component of charismatic leadership. Furthermore, Max Weber believed that the basis for charismatic leadership was a perception by followers that their leader was *extraordinary*. At best, only 2 of Bass's 10 measurement items could be considered to convey this quality (Bryman, 1992, p. 130). Moreover, despite some modifications, the measure includes items that are a mix of both leader behaviors and follower effects. As such, it blurs the distinctions between the two. Yet it is crucial that we be able to separate out the effects of individual leader behaviors on specific follower outcomes.

As one might imagine, there also has been some confusion as to the essential differences between the Bass and Avolio transformational leadership model and other models of charismatic leadership. As Bryman (1992) notes, the Bass model is built around the leader who articulates a vision that excites followers and who engages in behaviors that build intense loyalty and trust. These dimensions overlap considerably with those postulated by charismatic leadership theories. This is especially true given that the role of charisma in the Bass model is very important. In their empirical studies (e.g., Avolio & Yammarino, 1990; Bass, 1985; Hater & Bass, 1988; Yammarino & Bass, 1990), the component of charisma generally has the strongest correlation of any of the model's dimensions with subordinates' ratings of leadership effectiveness and their own satisfaction. It is clearly the most influential. (A comparison of the Bass model with other charismatic theories is presented in the next chapter. Such a comparison reveals that, in essence, there is little real difference in behavioral components. In the literature itself, we also see the two terms used interchangeably, and sometimes authors describe them as one or even use the label "charismatic/transformational leadership"; for example, Avolio and Gibbons, 1988; House and Shamir, 1993; Hunt, 1991).

House and Shamir: Charismatic Leadership

In one of the field's earliest writings on charismatic leadership in organizations, Robert House (1977) published a book chapter titled "A 1976 Theory of Charismatic Leadership." It outlined not only the leader behaviors that were possibly associated with charismatic leadership but also certain personal traits and situational variables. In it, House argued that charismatic leaders could be distinguished from others by their tendency to dominate, a strong conviction in their own beliefs and ideals, a need to influence others, and high self-confidence. Through emotionally appealing goals and the demonstration of behaviors that aroused followers' own needs for achievement, affiliation, and power, the charismatic leader was able to motivate high levels of task accomplishment. In addition, House theorized that these leaders simultaneously communicated high performance expectations as well as confidence in their followers' ability to meet such expectations. These actions, in turn, enhanced follower expectations that their efforts would lead to accomplishments. Through role-modeling, charismatic leaders demonstrated the values and beliefs they wished for followers to endorse so that the mission would be successful.

Like most models in the early stages of theory development, House's had several important shortcomings. As Yukl (1994) notes, House's description of the influence process was rudimentary, especially in the light of the profound influence he argued that charismatic leaders had over their followers. Second, his theory was based largely around dyads—the leader and "the follower"— rather than collectives that are the basis of organizations. Finally, absent from his theory were certain components that would appear in later theories, such as the notion of self-sacrifice, unconventional behavior, and the use of nontraditional strategies and tactics (Conger, 1989a; Conger & Kanungo, 1988b).

Since that time, House and a series of colleagues (House & Howell, 1992; House & Shamir, 1993; House et al., 1991; Shamir et al., 1993) have made revisions to his earlier theory. The most important and significant revision was by Shamir and colleagues (1993) in an article titled "The Motivational Effects of Charismatic Leadership: A Self-Concept Based Theory." Focused on explaining the profound levels of motivation typically associated with charismatic leadership, they postulated that these motivational effects could best be explained by focusing on the self-concept of the followers. Citing supporting research (e.g., Csikszentmihalyi & Rochberg-Halton, 1981; Kinder & Sears, 1985; Prentice, 1987; Snyder & Ickes, 1985), they point out that as human beings we seek to establish and affirm a sense of identity for ourselves (known as the self-concept). What charismatic leaders do is tie these self-concepts of followers to the goals and collective experiences associated with their missions so that they become valued aspects of the followers' self-concepts.

In terms of details, their theory hypothesizes that charismatic leadership transforms follower self-concepts and achieves its motivational outcomes through at least four mechanisms: (1) changing follower perceptions of the nature of work itself, (2) offering an appealing future vision, (3) developing a deep collective identity among followers, and (4) heightening both individual and collective self-efficacy. The processes that Shamir and colleagues (1993) describe as producing these effects follow in the paragraphs below.

Charismatic leaders transform the nature of work (in this case, work meant to achieve the organization's vision) by making it appear more heroic, morally correct, and meaningful. They in essence de-emphasize the extrinsic rewards of work and focus instead on the intrinsic side. Work becomes an opportunity for self- and collective expression. The reward for individual followers as they accomplish mission tasks is one of enhanced self-expression, self-efficacy, self-worth, and self-consistency. The idea is that eventually followers will come to see their organizational tasks as inseparable from their own self-concepts.

To accomplish this change in perceptions of work, the charismatic leader uses several means. One of the most important mechanisms, as described by Shamir and colleagues (1993), is the leader's vision, which serves to enhance follower self-concepts through three paths. By offering an optimistic and appealing future, the vision heightens the meaningfulness of the organization's goals. Second, the vision is articulated as a shared one, promoting a strong sense of collective identity. Presumably, the vision is also unique, and by stressing that the vision is the basis for the group's identity, the charismatic leader distinguishes his or her followers from others and further encourages followers to transcend their individual self-interests for the collective's. Third, the leader's expression of confidence in followers' abilities to achieve the vision heightens their sense of self-efficacy. They come to feel capable of creating a reality out of what is currently a lofty and utopian set of ambitions.

Integral to the Shamir and colleagues' theory is the charismatic leader's ability to create a deep collective identity. As just noted, the shared vision is one of the principal means. In addition, the charismatic leader actively promotes perceptions that only by banding together can group members accomplish exceptional feats. Furthermore, the leader uses his or her own behaviors to increase identification with the collective through the deployment of rituals, ceremonies, slogans, symbols, and stories that reinforce the importance of a group identity. The significance of creating this collective identity is in the follower outcomes that it is able to produce. Specifically, the authors cite research (Meindl & Lerner, 1983) indicating that a shared identity among individuals increases the "heroic motive" and the probability that individual self-interests will be abandoned voluntarily for collective and altruistic undertakings. As a result, as charismatic leaders cultivate a collective identity in their followers' self-concepts, they heighten the chances that followers will engage in self-sacrificial, collective-oriented behavior. The group identification in essence strengthens the shared behavioral norms, values, and beliefs among the members. All of this ensures a concerted and unified effort on the part of followers to achieve the mission's goals.

Finally, Shamir and colleagues argue that charismatic leaders achieve their extraordinary levels of follower motivation by focusing their efforts on building follower self-esteem and self-worth. They accomplish this by expressing high expectations of their followers and great confidence in the followers' abilities to meet these expectations (Eden, 1990; Yukl, 1989). This in turn enhances the perceived self-efficacy of followers. From the research of Bandura (1986), we know that the sense of self-efficacy can be a source of strong motivation. For example, it has been shown that individuals with a high sense of self-efficacy are more willing to expend greater work effort and to demonstrate persistence in overcoming obstacles to achieve their goals. By also fueling a collective sense of self-efficacy, the charismatic leader feeds perceptions of the group that they together accomplish tremendous feats. In addition, when collective self-efficacy is high, members of an organization are more willing to cooperate with one another in joint efforts to realize their shared aims (Yukl, 1994).

In Shamir and colleagues' revised theory, what we see is a shift from House's earlier conceptualization, in which charismatic leadership was viewed more as a dyadic process, to one in which it is a collective process. As Yukl (1994) has noted, the recent theory also places more emphasis on the reciprocal nature of the influence process under charismatic leadership. For example, charismatic leadership is likely to be far more motivational when the leader chooses a vision that is congruent with the followers' own values and identities. Likewise, followers are more likely to select as their leader an individual who espouses their core values, beliefs, and aspirations, despite the fact that these may not always be clearly articulated by followers themselves.

In conclusion, on the dimension of leader behaviors, there has been considerable attention directed toward specific behaviors and activities such as

(1) vision, (2) inspiration, (3) meaning-making, (4) empowerment, (5) setting of high expectations, and (6) fostering of collective identity. These charac-teristics have now formed a standard "paradigm" for the field in that there is fairly universal agreement concerning their importance. The question, of course, remains: What have we overlooked? As we shall see shortly, other behavioral characteristics play important roles. We suspect there may be others that we have yet to identify.

Follower Characteristics and Dynamics

The topic of the followers of charismatic leaders is very poorly explored. There are few studies in this area, especially in business contexts. Earlier research on charismatic leaders by political scientists and psychoanalysts (e.g., Downton, 1973; Kets de Vries, 1988) proposed that the followers of charismatic leaders were more likely to be those who, because of an essentially dependent character, were easily molded and persuaded by such dynamic leaders. They were drawn to the charismatic leader because he or she exudes what they lack: self-confidence and conviction.

From a psychoanalytic viewpoint, the argument essentially goes that follow-ers are attempting to resolve a conflict between who they are and what they wish to become. They accomplish this by substituting their leader as their ideal, or in psychoanalytic terms, their ego ideal. Some psychoanalysts (e.g., Downton, 1973; Erikson, 1968) trace this type of need back to an individual's failure to mature in adolescence and young adulthood. Because of absent, oppressive, or weak parents, individuals may develop a state of identity confusion. Associating emotionally with the charismatic leader is a means of coping with this confusion and achieving maturity. Given that the leader is in essence a substitute parent and model, a powerful emotional attachment naturally is formed by followers. Wishing to garner the leader's attention and affection, followers enthusiastically comply with his or her wishes. The assumption underlying this scenario of follower-leader dynamics is that followers are fulfilling a pathological need rather than a healthy desire for role models from whom to learn and grow. There has been support for these dynamics in research on cults and certain political movements. For example, in a study of the charismatic religious leader Reverend Sun Moon, Lodahl (1982) discovered that followers had greater feelings of helplessness, cynicism, and distrust of political action, as well as less confidence in their sexual identity, than a sample of college students. Other studies (e.g., Davies, 1954; Freemesser & Kaplan, 1976; Galanter, 1982) found followers of charismatic political and religious leaders to have lower self-esteem, a higher intolerance for indecision and crisis, and more experiences of psychological distress than others.

These studies, however, were conducted almost entirely on populations of individuals who voluntarily joined movements and were often disaffected by society or elsewhere, in contexts of crisis where individuals are needy by definition. In the corporate world, the situation is somewhat different. For example, in a large corporation, the subordinate of a charismatic leader may not have voluntarily chosen to belong to that leader's unit. More commonly, bosses are hired or promoted into positions, and the subordinates are already in place. For subordinates, then, there often is little freedom to select who will lead them. Likewise, leaders may find themselves inheriting a staff of confident, assertive employees. In the case of entrepreneurial companies founded by charismatic leaders, followers may be drawn to such contexts because of the challenge and opportunity. They may be seekers of the risk and uncertainty associated with a new venture—quite in contrast to followers who are dependent seekers of certainty.

Given this, there is a second school of thought that theorizes that followers are attracted to the charismatic leader because of a more constructive identification with the leader's abilities, a desire to learn from him or her, a quest for personal challenge and growth, and the attractiveness of the mission. This, of course, is largely what the theories in the previous section argued. With Bass (1985), it is the opportunity to fulfill higher-order needs. In the theory of Shamir and colleagues (1993), it is an opportunity to have one's self-esteem, self-worth, and self-efficacy constructively enhanced.

Confirming these theoretical speculations, Conger (1989a) found in field studies of charismatic leaders in business that subordinates often described their attraction to the leader's qualities of self-confidence, strong convictions in the mission, a willingness to undertake personal risks, and a history of prior accomplishment. As a result, subordinates felt a sense of fulfilling their own potential as they met their leader's high expectations. In addition, as others have found (e.g., Avolio & Bass, 1988; Bass, 1985), the leader's vision offered attractive outcomes that were motivating in themselves. Conger, however, felt that simple identification and an attractive vision did not fully explain the commitment and motivation that followers demonstrated for their charismatic leaders.

Instead, as theory suggested, Conger discovered that the personal approval of the charismatic leader became a principal measure of a subordinate's self-worth. A dependency then developed to the point that the leader largely defined one's level of performance and ability. As Shamir and colleagues (1993) also noted, the leader's expression of high expectations set standards of performance and approval, while a continual sense of urgency and the capacity to make subordinates feel unique further heightened motivation. Taken together, these actions promoted a sense of obligation in followers to continually live up to their leader's expectations. As the relationship deepens, this sense of obligation grows. The leader's expression of confidence in subordinates' abilities creates a sense of duty and responsibility. Subordinates can validate the leader's trust in them only through exceptional accomplishments.

Over the long term, a dilemma naturally occurs for many followers. As the subordinates' self-worth is increasingly defined in their relationship to the leader, a precarious dependence is built. Without the leader's affirmation, subordinates can feel that they are underperforming and even failing. In addition, there are fears of being ostracized. As one subordinate explained to Conger (1989a),

> There's a love/hate element [in our relationship]. You love him when you're focused on the same issues. You hate him when the contract falls apart. Either you're part of the team or not—there's a low tolerance for spectators. And over a career, you're in and out. A lot depends upon your effectiveness on the team. You have to build up a lot of credibility to regain any ground that you've lost. (p. 133)

The dark-side dynamics of this dependence will be discussed further in a later section.

In conclusion, we do have some insights into follower dynamics, but generally, our knowledge here is limited in the sense that it is based on only a few case studies and theoretical speculation. This is one area in need of significant attention in the future.

Contextual Influences

Until very recently, interest in the role of context and situational factors has been limited. This is due largely to the backgrounds of those researching leadership. "Micro theorists" (those with a psychological or social psychological orientation) have dominated the field. Few researchers with a more "macro" or sociological perspective have been active in studying leadership. As a result, environmental or contextual investigations rarely have been applied to leadership studies outside the fields of political science and religion. Our knowledge in this area therefore remains poor, and what does exist is largely theoretical and speculative.

The most common speculation has been that periods of stress and turbulence are the most conducive for charismatic leadership. This argument is derived from the work of political scientists looking at charismatic leadership in political and religious contexts; see Cell (1974) and Toth (1981). Max Weber (1925/1968), for example, specifically focused on times of "crisis" as facilitating environments. The basic assumption is either that times of stressful change encourage a longing among individuals for a leader who offers attractive solutions and visions of the future or that charismatic leaders have an easier time promoting a transformational vision during times of uncertainty, when the status quo appears no longer to function (Bryman, 1992).

To date, the most important empirical study to examine situational factors in organizational contexts was conducted by Roberts and Bradley and reported in our volume *Charismatic Leadership* (1988b). Using a field study, they looked at a school superintendent who was perceived by her organization as a charismatic leader. In a later appointment to state commissioner of education, that perception of her failed to transfer. In Roberts and Bradley's search to explain why the individual's charisma did not transfer, they discovered several essential differences between the two contexts.

In terms of the organizational environment, the individual's first context, a school district, was one in crisis—confirming the hypothesis that crisis may indeed facilitate the emergence of charismatic leadership. In contrast, the leader's second context at the state government level was not in a similar state of distress. The public's perception was that the state's schools were basically sound and simply in need of incremental improvements. The individual's authority also differed in the two situations. As a superintendent, she had much more control and autonomy. At the state level as commissioner, quite the opposite was true. Her number one priority was political loyalty to the governor. She no longer possessed the freedom to undertake actions as she deemed necessary. Instead, they had to be cleared through the governor's office. Her relationships also were different. Whereas the district organization had been small, localized geographically, and with limited stakeholders, the situation at the state level was at the opposite end of the spectrum. The agency was far greater in size, complexity, and bureaucracy. The numerous committees and associations in which she had to participate meant that she had little time to build the deep, personal bonds that she had established at the district level. As a result, her impact at the state level was no longer personal, and perceptions of her as a charismatic leader did not materialize.

From the Roberts and Bradley study, we might conclude that context shapes charismatic leadership in at least two ways. First, an environment in crisis is indeed more receptive to leadership in general and is more likely to be open to proposals—common to charismatic leaders—for radical change such as those embodied in the superintendent's vision. Second, there are characteristics of organizations that influence an individual's latitude to take initiative and to build personal relationships, which in turn shape perceptions of charismatic leadership. More latitude for initiative on the job simply may result in more opportunities to demonstrate leadership. Closer proximity to followers may permit greater relationship building. The superintendent's position allowed the leader far more autonomy to act than did the commissioner's position. The superintendent's responsibilities were more geographically concentrated and involved a more limited number of stakeholders, which resulted in deeper working relationships at the district level and also inspired affection and trust in her leadership. These in turn heightened perceptions of her charisma.

With findings like Roberts and Bradley's in mind, we can think of the contexts of organizations as divided into an outer and an inner context (Pettigrew, 1987), the outer being the environment beyond the organization and the inner including the organization's culture, structure, power distribution, and so on. Using this simple framework, it is useful to divide our discussion around these two contextual dimensions. We will start with the external environment.

On the issue of whether crisis is the critical external condition, Conger (1993) hypothesized that there actually could be much more variability in environmental conditions than we might think. He argued that charismatic leadership is not necessarily precipitated by conditions of crisis and distress but also may be found in entrepreneurial environments. In earlier research looking at charismatic business leaders (Conger, 1989a), he found charismatic leaders who were entrepreneurs operating in environments not so much of crisis but of great opportunity, munificence, and optimism. Instead of crisis being the sole contextual condition, there may instead be at least two conducive environments, one demanding a major reorientation of the existing order because of a perceived state of distress and the other involving the emergence or creation of a new order based on a "munificence entrepreneurial" context. Both environments, however, share conditions of uncertainty.

In addition, Conger argued that more of an interplay exists between the leader and the context. In other words, context is not the key determinant, but rather the leader and the context influence one another, with the relative weight of each's influence varying from situation to situation. For example, Willner (1984) found that among charismatic leaders in the political arena, some were able to induce or create through their own actions the necessary contextual conditions of a crisis. Similarly, we might be able to find charismatic leaders who are able to foster perceptions of munificence and great entrepreneurial opportunity.

Conger also went on to propose that the more conducive the existing contextual conditions, the less the magnitude or the fewer the number of charismatic attributes required for a leader to be perceived as charismatic. Likewise, the greater the intensity or the number of "charismatic attributes" present in a leader, the less need would exist for the context to be characterized by extreme crisis or rich entrepreneurial opportunities. Given a wealth of charismatic attributes, the leader may be able to create such interpretations of the environment through his or her own actions. Such hypotheses are speculative and still in need of research attention.

Beyond these limited efforts focusing on the external environments of charismatic leadership, there has been only one major theoretical work focusing on contextual conditions *within* organizations that may influence charismatic leadership. Pawar and Eastman (1997) proposed four factors of organizations that might affect receptivity to transformational leadership (see also Shamir, House, & Arthur, 1993, p. 578).[1] The four factors that Pawar and Eastman have identified are

1. the organization's emphasis on efficiency versus adaptation,
2. the relative dominance of the organization's technical core versus its boundary-spanning units,
3. organizational structures, and
4. modes of governance.

Their model is built around the central notion that transformational and charismatic leadership is essentially about leading organizational change. A critical premise is that only organizations that are receptive to change are likely to respond to and aid leadership that offers a new vision, new values, and a collective identity. Using a series of ideal types, Pawar and Eastman attempt to differentiate between organizations that are more conducive to change and therefore to charismatic and transformational leadership and those that are not.

They begin with the notion that organizations are seeking one of two basic goals—efficiency or adaptation (Selznick, 1948). The challenge is that the goals of efficiency and adaptation have conflicting purposes, the former requiring organizational stability and the latter centered around change. In reality, as we know today, most business organizations are attempting both simultaneously, and this highlights one of the dilemmas of Pawar and Eastman's theory. It is built around idealized polarities that provide a simple elegance in terms of theory building but may not reflect the complexities of reality. Nevertheless, they hypothesize that an efficiency orientation requires goal stability and, necessarily, administrative management or transactional leadership to achieve its goals. During adaptation periods, on the other hand, the leader's role is to overcome resistance to change and to align the organization to a new environment through a dynamic vision, with new goals and values. They argue, therefore, that organizations with adaptive goals are far more open to transformational leadership. The authors caution, however, that although adaptive periods are more receptive to leadership, there must be a *felt need* by organizational members for transformation; otherwise, they may accept more administrative management.

The second of Pawar and Eastman's factors—the relative dominance of the technical core versus boundary-spanning units—refers to the fact that an organization's task systems are either more inwardly oriented or more externally oriented. In this case, Thompson (1967) had argued that organizations divide their task systems into two parts—a technical core that performs the work of input processing through the operation of technology, and boundary-spanning functions that interface directly with the external environment. Isolated from an ever-changing external world, the technical core develops routines and stability in how it approaches its tasks (Thompson, 1967). In contrast, the boundary-spanning functions are forced to adapt continually to environmental constraints and contingencies, and as a result can never develop highly standardized or routine approaches (Thompson, 1967). Depending on whether the technical core or boundary-spanning functions dominate, an organization will either be receptive to charismatic leadership or not. Pawar and Eastman postulate that organizations in which boundary-spanning units dominate over the technical core will be more open to transformational and charismatic leadership because they are more receptive to change. From our perspective, we can see exceptions to their theory on this dimension. It would seem to us that inventor-entrepreneurs or leaders with backgrounds in the technical core in particular could override this aspect of the Pawar-Eastman theory. On the other hand, successful adaptation of the organization to changing environments through the leadership role would, as Pawar and Eastman argue, more likely occur in contexts where the leader has extensive exposure to boundary-spanning units. Such exposure ensures a marketplace-shaped and -driven technical core.

The third factor that Pawar and Eastman propose draws on Mintzberg's (1979) typology of organizational structures. Mintzberg's five "ideal type" structures are (1) the adhocracy, (2) the simple structure, (3) the machine bureaucracy,

(4) the professional bureaucracy, and (5) the divisional structure. Of these five, only two are hypothesized by Pawar and Eastman to be conducive to transformational leadership—the simple structure and the adhocracy. Specifically, both are felt to be more receptive to organizational change through the development and promotion of a vision. In the simple structure, the leader or entrepreneur-leader is the source of the organization's vision, and commitment is facilitated by employee loyalty to the leader. In an adhocracy structure, the vision is developed through professionals who possess the power, knowledge, and willingness to work collectively (Mintzberg, 1979).

It is argued that the three other forms have internal forces that mitigate against an openness to innovative leadership. For example, the machine bureaucracy is dominated by standardized tasks and work processes. Senior managers are obsessed by a control mind-set, and lower-level managers are intent only on implementing operational directives from above. As such, there is little concern with innovation and change, which are potentially threatening to a tightly orchestrated status quo. In the professional bureaucracy, professionals dominate to such an extent that management is simply a support function and marginalized to the role of facilitation. In addition, the professionals in these systems are far less committed to the organization than to their own work and profession. As a result, a collective vision is unlikely to be developed by these self-centered professionals, nor by a marginalized group of top managers. The divisional structure, built around two layers in which a headquarters' operation governs quasi-autonomous divisions, also is not conducive. The focus of the corporate headquarters is to specify operational goals and to monitor the divisions' accomplishment of them. The divisions then are concerned with attaining operational goals. Pawar and Eastman argue that because divisional structures are concerned with operational goals, neither group is likely to show great interest in developing a vision. Although theoretically this argument might appear appealing, there have been instances of leaders of divisional structures who have been perceived as charismatic. Jack Welch of General Electric is certainly one of the more visible examples (Tichy & Sherman, 1993).

The final factor influencing receptivity to leadership in the Pawar and Eastman model is the mode of internal governance. They start with the assumption that membership in organizations is built around furthering individual members' self-interests (Burns & Stalker, 1961; Thompson, 1967). The aim of transformational and charismatic forms of leadership, however, is for followers to transcend their own self-interests for collective goals. Under Wilkins and Ouchi's (1983) three modes of governance (the market, the bureaucratic, and the clan), the nature of transactions between an organization and its members will differ. Under the market mode, transactions based on the exchange of commitments between the organization and its members are determined by market or price mechanisms. Because an external market shapes commitments, the organization has little incentive to socialize its members to defer self-interests. In the bureaucratic mode, a contract for commitments is built around employees accepting organizational authority in return for wages. The organization then monitors compliance through formal monitoring and exchange mechanisms. These become the devices that curb members' self-interests. Finally, under the clan mode, organizational members are socialized in such a way that their own interests and the organization's are aligned as one. In other words, employees still hold their self-interests, but they believe they can fulfill them through achieving the collective's interests. Cultural values and norms shape self-interests. Under the Pawar and Eastman model, it is the clan mode that is most receptive to transformational leadership, because it allows for a merging of individual self-interests with the collective's goals.

Despite apparent limitations and exceptions to their model, Pawar and Eastman are the first to raise in a significant way the intriguing issue of whether the internal organizational environment will be more or less receptive to charismatic leadership. In concluding this section, we can say that the role of context in charismatic leadership has enormous potential as an area of future investigation. It is clear from the limited research to date that charismatic leaders and their contexts are intertwined in a complex and intimate fashion. Beyond such simple insights and some theoretical speculation, we remain largely in the dark about this subject in terms of solid, research-based understandings.

Routinization and Succession

Max Weber was deeply intrigued about the manner in which the leader's charisma could be transformed into routines and other institutional vehicles that in essence "lived on" beyond the leader. In this way, the vitality and positive consequences of the leader's influence might be retained long after his or her departure. Weber believed, however, that charisma was essentially an unstable force. It either faded or was institutionalized (or, as Weber termed the process, *routinized*) as the charismatic leader's mission was accomplished: "If [charisma] is not to remain a purely transitory phenomenon, but to take on the character of a permanent relationship forming a stable community, it is necessary for the character of charismatic authority to be radically changed. . . . It cannot remain stable, but becomes either traditionalized or rationalized or both" (Weber, 1947, p. 364). He argued there were strong incentives on the part of charismatic leaders and their followers to transform their movements into more permanent institutions: "Usually the wish of the master himself and always that of his disciples . . . [is] to change charisma . . . from a once-and-for-all extremely transitory free gift of grace . . . into a permanent everyday possession . . ." (Weber, 1947, p. 236). With success, the followers began to achieve positions of authority and material advantage. The desire naturally arose to institutionalize these, so traditions and rules grew up to protect the gains of the mission.

Institutionalization is another area in which little research has been conducted in the organizational literature. We know almost nothing about the routinization of charismatic leadership. The only major study was conducted by Trice and Beyer (1986). They examined two charismatic leaders; in one case, charisma had routinized, and in another, it had not. The case of successful routinization was the charismatic founder of Alcoholics Anonymous, Bill Wilson. Early in the organization's life, the leader and his initial group of followers established (1) an effective administrative apparatus independent of the founder, (2) rites that diffused charisma among the members, and (3) written and oral traditions that sustained the leader's message over time. For example, the founder's message of how he overcame alcoholism was codified into a publication titled *Twelve Steps and Twelve Traditions* (Alcoholics Anonymous World Services, 1953). As Trice and Beyer (1986) note,

> These writings form the core of his personal testament to his followers. This extensive written testament provides AA with a well-articulated set of norms and behaviors to guide its members. His testament also provides members with reference points and comparisons to use in telling their own stories to one another. The activities of AA center around talk—and this talk frequently makes reference to the founder and his testament. (Alcoholics Anonymous World Services, p. 150)

In contrast, the charismatic founder of the National Council on Alcoholism left behind no important oral or written traditions. No in-depth biographies of her were produced, and her philosophy was never codified into a personal testament. As a result, mention of her and her ideas is today rare. Her charisma failed to routinize. Trice and Beyer (1986) concluded that five key factors were largely responsible for the successful institutionalization of charisma in the first case. They were

1. the development of an administrative apparatus separate from the charismatic leader that put into practice the leader's mission,

2. the incorporation of the leader's mission into oral and written traditions,

3. the transfer of charisma through rites and ceremonies to other members of the organization,

4. a continued identification by organizational members with the original mission, and

5. the selection of a successor who resembled the charismatic leader and was committed to the founder's mission.

In the case in which charisma did not routinize, these factors were largely missing.

From the standpoint of the business world, however, it appears that charisma is a relatively fragile phenomenon in terms of institutionalization. There are several examples from the management literature in which succession dilemmas prevented the routinization of charismatic leadership (e.g., Bryman, 1992, 1993; Conger, 1989a; Rose, 1989). The charismatic leaders in Conger's 1989 study have all since departed from their original organizations as a result of either promotions, moves to new organizations, retirement, or, in one case, death. From follow-up observation, it is clear that there is little indication of any significant routinization of their charisma in their various organizations. In a 1993 article, Conger noted that one of the group—an entrepreneur—was able to institutionalize some elements of his original mission, values, and operating procedures. That individual has since left his organization, and a few years ago it was acquired by a much larger firm, which has superimposed its own mission, values, and procedures. Today, there is little evidence of that initial routinization of the leader's charisma. The leaders in Conger's study who were acting as change agents in large, bureaucratic organizations had practically no long-term impact in terms of institutionalizing their charisma.

As Bryman (1993) argues, succession is one of the most crucial issues in routinization. When an organization possesses a charismatic leader, it creates what Wilson (1975) has called a "charismatic demand." The dilemma, of course, is that it is highly unlikely that a charismatic leader will be found to replace the original one. Although Bryman (1993) found one example in a study of a transportation company, such situations appear extremely rare. Instead, what often happens is that a charismatic leader is replaced by a more managerially oriented individual. Examples of this would be Steven Jobs, who was succeeded by John Sculley and Michael Spindler; the succession of Lee Iacocca at Chrysler by Robert Eaton (Bryman, 1993; Taylor, 1991); and Walt Disney's replacement by Roy Disney (Bryman, 1993; Thomas, 1976). Biggart (1989) does note that direct selling organizations often attempt to overcome succession problems by either promoting a national sales executive into the leadership role or "invest[ing] the mission in one's children" (p. 144). Looking at Amway and Shaklee, Biggart discovered that the founders' children assumed active roles in the company, in turn fostering a "charismatic presence." He also found, however, that their roles were largely bureaucratic and that the companies had done little to institutionalize the founders' charisma beyond the presence of their children. Given the enormous demands for continual adaptation formed by competition and strong needs to develop rational and formalized structures, many business organizations may simply not be conducive to long-term institutionalization of a leader's charisma.

Even if routinization were to be successful, it is no guarantee of continued success. As Conger (1993) noted, part of the dilemma is that successors may not possess the strategic skills and other abilities crucial to ensure the firm's future leadership. For example, although the retailer Wal-Mart apparently has institutionalized Sam Walton's values and operating beliefs, a critical issue is whether it can institutionalize his visionary insights into the world of retailing. Just as important, Walton's vision was most likely time-bound, so even if his strategic competence were to be institutionalized, it is the product of a specific era in retailing and therefore may be unsuitable for anticipating the industry's next paradigm shift. The original mission of a charismatic leader is highly unlikely to be forever adaptive.

Institutionalization of the leader's charisma in rites and routines also may not necessarily produce positive outcomes. Elements as simple as institutionalized rituals of the charismatic leader may themselves become counterproductive over time. Conger (1993) cited the example of IBM, which very effectively institutionalized many of Thomas Watson, Sr.'s values and traditions. Several of these would prove maladaptive only decades later. For example, Watson's original strong emphasis on sales and marketing would ensure that future company leaders were drawn from these ranks, yet such individuals were not always the most technologically savvy or visionary about marketplace shifts. The future price to be paid would be in terms of these senior leaders' failure to understand adequately the strategic importance of certain new technologies such as personal computers and software systems. A tradition of rewarding loyalty through internal promotions only aggravated the problem. It encouraged inbreeding around the company's worldview and simply reinforced notions of IBM's mainframe mentality and its arrogance. Even simple traditions would lose their original meaning and transform themselves into bureaucratic norms. For example, IBM's traditional corporate dress code of dark suits and white shirts is illustrative. This requirement was intended by Watson to make salespeople feel like executives. "If you dressed like an executive, you would feel like one," was

Watson's belief. The dress code did build pride in the early days of IBM. Many decades later, however, this norm would be transformed into a symbol of rigidity and conformity. It bureaucratized itself, as Weber would have guessed.

In conclusion, we have little knowledge about this crucial area of charismatic leadership. A limited number of case studies and no systematic longitudinal research have offered us at best tantalizing tidbits of insight. In addition, there are questions about the potential problems of institutionalization and whether positive aspects of charisma may routinize to the point that they become meaningless or bureaucratic procedures.

Liabilities of Charismatic Leadership

Although the literature generally has been highly positive about the effects of charismatic leadership in organizations, there has been some interest in the negative outcomes associated with this form of leadership. In *Charismatic Leadership*, Jane Howell (1988) proposed a simple, dichotomous model of socialized and personalized charisma that attempted to address this issue. In conjunction with Robert House (House & Howell, 1992; Howell & House, 1993), the theory was refined to propose a set of personality characteristics, behaviors, and effects that distinguished two forms of charismatic leadership.

Specifically, socialized charismatics are described as articulating visions that serve the interests of the collective. They govern in an egalitarian, non–self-aggrandizing manner, and they actively empower and develop their followers. They also work through legitimate, established channels of authority to accomplish their goals. On the other hand, personalized charismatic leaders are authoritarian and narcissistic. They have high needs for power, driven in part by low self-esteem, and hold goals that reflect their own self-interests. Followers' needs are played on as a means to achieve the leader's interests. In addition, these leaders disregard established and legitimate channels of authority as well as the rights and feelings of others. At the same time, they demand unquestioning obedience and dependence in their followers. While portraying these two forms as dichotomous, Howell and House do acknowledge that a charismatic leader might in reality exhibit some aspects of both the socialized and the personalized characteristics. This latter view is probably closer to reality than their ideal model, and two parallel scales (of varying degrees of intensity) of each might be more accurate. A leader might therefore embody degrees of both socialized and personalized characteristics.

Drawing on actual examples of charismatic leaders, Conger (1989a, 1990) examined those who had produced negative outcomes for themselves and their organizations. He found that problems could arise with charismatic leaders around (1) their visions, (2) their impression management, (3) their management practices, and (4) succession planning. On the dimension of vision, typical problems occurred when leaders possessed an exaggerated sense of the marketplace opportunities for their vision or when they grossly underestimated the resources necessary for its accomplishment. In addition, visions often failed when they reflected largely the leader's needs rather than those of constituents or the marketplace, or when the leader was unable to recognize fundamental shifts in the environment that demanded redirection.

In terms of impression management, charismatic leaders appear prone to exaggerated self-descriptions and claims for their visions, which can mislead their followers. For example, they may present information that makes their visions appear more feasible or appealing than they are in reality. They may screen out looming problems or foster an illusion of control when things actually are out of control. From the standpoint of management practices, there are examples of overly self-confident and unconventional charismatic leaders who create antagonistic relations with peers and superiors. Some, such as Steven Jobs of Apple Computer, are known to create "in" and "out" groups within their organizations, thus promoting dysfunctional rivalries. Others create excessive dependence on themselves and then alternate between idealizing and devaluing dependent subordinates. Many are ineffective administrators, preferring "big picture" activities to routine work. Finally, charismatic leaders often have a difficult time developing successors. They simply enjoy "center stage" too much to share it. To find a replacement who is a peer may be too threatening for leaders who tend to be narcissistic.

Daniel Sankowsky (1995) has written about the dilemmas of charismatic leaders who are prone to a pathology of narcissism. Although we will discuss his work in greater length in Chapter 7, we include a synopsis here. Specifically, he has proposed a stage model showing how dark-side charismatics implicate their followers into a cycle of exploitation. First, these leaders offer a grandiose vision and confidently encourage followers to accomplish it. Followers, however, soon find themselves in an untenable position. Because of their leader's optimism, they have underestimated the constraints facing the mission as well as the resources they need but currently lack. As a result, performance inevitably falls short of the leader's high expectations. Wishing to comply with their leader's wishes, however, followers continue to strive. Soon, their performance appears substandard as they fall behind. Although initially the leader will blame the outside world for undermining the mission, his or her attention eventually will turn to the followers. Conditioned to accept their leader's viewpoint and not to challenge it, followers willingly receive the blame from their leader. Reversal of the many benefits ascribed to charismatic leaders then occurs. Instead of building their followers' self-worth and self-efficacy, the leader gradually destroys them and creates highly dependent individuals.

In general, the liabilities of charismatic leadership also remain a neglected area of study in business settings. In Chapter 7, we will explore this subject in far greater detail. We can conclude, however, that there is a great need for longitudinal studies and in-depth case analysis to better understand whether many of the manipulative dynamics found in political and cult settings also can occur in business contexts. As we noted earlier, a crucial distinction is that "followers" in corporations often are not in a position to freely choose or self-select their leader. Their leader may be appointed by the organization, or employees themselves may be promoted or moved into the leader's work unit—not necessarily by choice. We cannot be certain, therefore, that the degree or intensity of psychological dependence on the leader is the same as in political or cult movements. It is most likely to be different.

CONCLUSION

In this chapter, we have taken a broad sweep through the field as it stands today. Much has changed over the last 10 years. During this time, our own work has evolved and deepened. In the chapter to follow, we offer a stage model of charismatic leadership based on our own research and contrast it to the three other behavioral models proposed by Bass and Avolio, House and Shamir, and Sashkin for the purpose of comparative assessment.

NOTE

1. Given our earlier arguments that transformational and charismatic forms of leadership overlap, we are concluding that their hypotheses apply to charismatic leadership as well. Pawar and Eastman propose that their theory applies to "leadership that spells out a vision that is in the interest of the followers and gets followers to accept it by raising them to a higher level in their need hierarchy" (Pawar & Eastman, 1997, p. 84).

2

A Model of
Charismatic Leadership

The previous chapter traced the intellectual journey that scholars have taken in trying to unravel the mysteries of charismatic and transformational leadership in organizations. Any model that describes and explains charismatic leadership, however, must place itself in a nomothetic network of leadership constructs. As a social and behavioral phenomenon, leadership manifests itself in various forms. The models we have been discussing are just several among many such forms. It is important, therefore, to see how they are related to other leadership constructs. Are they similar or quite different? The relationships can be seen by (1) defining charismatic leadership and identifying its boundaries, (2) describing the constructs and processes involved in charismatic leadership, (3) relating it to other forms of leadership, (4) identifying the antecedent conditions that facilitate the emergence of charismatic leadership, (5) identifying the consequences of such leadership for organizations, and finally, (6) operationalizing or developing measurement tools for capturing the phenomenon and its antecedents and consequences. In this chapter, we will propose a model of charismatic leadership that addresses each of these objectives. First, however, it is necessary to review briefly the general literature on leadership behavior so as to demonstrate where charismatic leadership fits in the overall leadership paradigm.

THE LEADERSHIP LITERATURE:
A BRIEF REVIEW

The examination of leadership as a group and organizational phenomenon has been the focus of both theoretical and empirical analysis for more than half a century (Bass, 1990; Yukl, 1994). Literally thousands of articles, papers, and books on the topic have examined and probed leadership from every conceivable angle. Social scientists of many persuasions, such as organizational theorists (e.g., Nadler & Tushman, 1990; Pfeffer, 1977), political scientists (e.g., Burns, 1978; Willner, 1984), psychoanalysts (e.g., Kets de Vries, 1994; Zaleznik, 1990), psychologists (e.g., Bass, 1990; Hollander & Offermann, 1990), and sociologists (e.g., Bradley, 1987; Roberts, 1985), have unintentionally contributed to the enigmatic nature of the leadership phenomenon. They have proposed various analytical frameworks and focused on different content and process aspects of leadership across a wide range of contexts. As a result, there are splinter theories of leadership with supporting empirical studies within each advocacy group. Very often, these multidisciplinary approaches have spoken different languages that are specific to their own disciplines and, sometimes, unintelligible to those in other disciplines. Their levels of analyses are equally diverse: behavioral and organizational, individual and interactional, process and structural.

The resulting incomparable analytical and empirical treatments (see, e.g., Chemers & Ayman, 1993; Conger & Kanungo, 1988a; Hunt, Baliga, & Peterson, 1988; Yukl, 1994) have provided conflicting evidence on the role of leadership in organizational and group performance. In turn, they have obscured rather than deepened understanding of leadership. Peter Dorfman (1994) uses a telling metaphor to describe the situation: "If we think of leadership research flowing as a stream, it flows in a meandering, intertwining, and constantly shifting manner" (p. 4). This state of affairs has created considerable difficulty for scholars at both the conceptual and empirical levels of study. At the conceptual level, it is difficult to develop comprehensive and integrative frameworks to understand the leadership phenomenon. At the empirical level, the ambiguity of research findings has led some to question the usefulness of researching leadership.

One should not infer from the preceding discussion, however, that past research explorations of leadership phenomenon have been totally fruitless. Similarly, it would be erroneous and unwise to deduce that research pursuits on the topic should be given up because the phenomenon is too complex and enigmatic. Rather, the remarkable complexity and the elusive character of the leadership construct must be seen as a challenge. Leadership—its behaviors and processes—forms an essential, if not the key, element in group and organizational processes. Understanding its nature greatly enriches our knowledge—especially for the social scientist whose task is to unravel the mysteries underlying such social phenomena. Similarly, for the world of management, distilling the essential ingredients of effective leadership has the potential to enhance organizational performance and promote more rewarding workplaces.

Our purpose here is not to get entangled in the controversy of whether it is feasible or even worthwhile to study the leadership phenomenon that eludes us from time to time. We believe that "the romance of leadership"[1] in groups and organizations and among both researchers and management practitioners is too strong to deny its legitimate status as a behavioral phenomenon to be captured and studied scientifically (House, 1988; Meindl, Ehrlich, & Dukerich, 1985). At the same time, we agree with House's (1988) assertion that critics who emphasize the futility of leadership research often "misrepresent the current state of leadership knowledge" and "underestimate the amount of knowledge produced to date" (p. 248).

Although we recognize the importance of existing knowledge and the need to continue scientific research on leadership, we do not intend to present here an exhaustive review of the enormous literature on the topic. Such reviews exist elsewhere (e.g., Bass, 1990; Yukl, 1994). Rather, the purpose of this chapter is to identify common assumptions and modal trends in leadership research and to seek answers to questions such as the following: What have we learned from the past leadership debates in the psychological or behavioral literature? On which issues is there the most agreement among researchers? Where does charismatic leadership fit within the existing literature and current leadership paradigms?

Given these types of questions, our objective over the next several pages is fourfold: first, to identify the commonly held assumptions underlying leadership theory and research; second, to indicate the modal orientations in leadership paradigms as reflected in the writings of behavioral scientists and in organizational behavior texts; third, to assess the limitations of the leadership paradigms of the 1940s through the 1970s; and fourth, to highlight the shift in focus from more conventional leadership parameters to the study of charismatic leadership, which had been largely ignored and underresearched by behavioral scientists. This fourfold analysis will provide the foundation for a behavioral model of charismatic leadership to be presented later in the chapter. Although research in leadership has encompassed many disciplines—such as anthropology, sociology, and political science—our focus will be restricted solely to leadership from the point of view of management and social and organizational psychology.

BASIC ASSUMPTIONS UNDERLYING
LEADERSHIP THEORY AND RESEARCH

The theoretical frameworks and investigative strategies that researchers adopt when they explore a behavioral phenomenon are to a large extent directed by their assumptions about that phenomenon. In fact, controversies and misunderstandings among researchers often can be traced to a failure to recognize that differences exist with respect to the implicit assumptions adopted in their different studies, hence the need to be as explicit as possible about one's assumptions. For this reason, before we identify the principal modal orientations in leadership research, we start by explicitly stating the assumptions commonly held among behavioral scientists about leadership.

First, researchers in social and organizational psychology have come to accept leadership as a group or organizational phenomenon. The phenomenon is observed as a *set of role behaviors* performed by an individual. Leadership occurs when the situation demands that the individual influence and coordinate the activities of a group or members of an organization toward the achievement of a common goal. This individual is called the "leader," and the focus on his or her behaviors characterizes a behavioral perspective on leadership.

Before the behavioral approach, leadership was viewed in terms of the "great man" or "trait" theory of leadership, which essentially proposed that the success of a leader could be attributed solely to his or her personality and physical characteristics without regard to manifest behavior in a given situation (Cowley, 1928). Numerous studies, however, failed to identify a set of traits common to all leaders. The trait approach was considered too simplistic an explanation (Dorfman, 1994). Thus, instead of studying leadership as a cluster of stable personality traits in isolation from their context, today we view leadership as a set of role behaviors by individuals in the context of the group or organization to which they belong. As Cartwright and Zander (1968) point out, leadership consists of actions such as "setting group goals, moving the group toward its goals, improving the quality of interactions among the members, building cohesiveness of the group, and making resources available to the group" (p. 304).

From this description of leadership follows the second assumption that leadership is both a relational and an attributional phenomenon. The existence of a leader depends on the presence of one or more followers and the kind of status or power relationship that develops between them. Leadership comes into being when followers perceive the leader's behavior in a certain way, accept the leader's attempt to influence them, and then attribute leadership status to that individual. Without the followers' perceptions, acceptance, and attributions, the phenomenon simply would not exist (Beckhard, 1996).

Third, it is commonly assumed that leadership can be studied in terms of its *contents* (or elements) and its *processes* (or relationships among the elements). The study of the content of leadership involves the identification of specific sets of leader role behaviors that serve to achieve the group's objectives through influencing the attitudes and behaviors of group members. The study of contents also permits us to identify the perceived attributes of leaders and the properties of followers and situations—such as the task, the social climate, and so on—that facilitate or hinder the manifestation of leadership. *Content* therefore refers to the types of leader role behaviors and to the presence of specific attributes of leaders, followers, and the situation.

By *leadership processes*, we refer to the types of social influence processes between the leader and the led, and the psychological dynamics underlying them. Thus, leadership implies the exercise of influence over others by utilizing various bases of social power, reinforcers, tactics, and so on as a means of eliciting the group members' compliance with certain norms and their commitment to achieving the group's objectives (French & Raven, 1959; Kelman, 1958; Sims & Lorenzi, 1992).

The distinction between content and process in leadership research leads to another assumption. This assumption is that to understand leadership phenomena, one must analyze the properties of the basic *leadership elements* and the major *relational processes* between them. The basic leadership elements are the leader, the followers, and the situational context. The major relational processes are the leader-follower influence process, the leader-context relational process, and the context-follower relational process (see Conger & Kanungo, 1988b, for this type of analysis of charismatic leadership).

This brings us to the final assumption. The role behaviors of a leader are intended to directly influence followers' attitudes and behavior within a group or organization. Thus, *leadership effectiveness* should be measured in terms of the degree to which a leader promotes (1) instrumental attitudes and behaviors that encourage the achievement of group objectives, (2) followers' satisfaction with the task and context within which they operate, and (3) followers' acceptance of their leader's influence. This last dimension of the leader's influence is often manifested through the followers' emotional bond with the leader, by their attributions of favorable qualities to him or her, by their compliance behaviors, and by their commitment to attitudes and values espoused by the leader.

Instead of employing the measures just described, leadership effectiveness, somewhat surprisingly, more often has been measured through group or organizational productivity (Yukl, 1994). Such productivity measures often are expressed in terms of objective indexes of return on investment, units produced, cost per unit, cost savings, and so on. These types of "end results" are not appropriate measures of a leader's influence or effectiveness. We say this simply because, as indexes of group or organizational productivity, no matter how objective they might be, they depend not only on the followers' instrumental behavior but also on available environmental resources, technology, and market conditions over which a leader has little control.

MODAL ORIENTATIONS IN LEADERSHIP PARADIGMS

In both social and organizational psychology, the modal orientation of the past leadership research has been to address three specific issues related to the constructs of the "leader" and "leadership effectiveness." A concern for understanding the leader led to the first research issue of identifying leader role behavior in groups. A similar concern for understanding leadership effectiveness led to the second and third research issues. Specifically, the second research issue dealt with identifying contingencies for leadership role behaviors by studying the interactions between role behaviors and the characteristics of followers and the situational context. The third issue focused on analyzing the underlying mechanisms of the leader-follower influence process itself. We will briefly discuss each of these three modal trends.

Leader Role Behavior

Early research studies aimed at identifying leader role behaviors analyzed small formal and informal groups in both laboratory and field settings. These investigations (Bales & Slater, 1955; Cartwright & Zander, 1968; Fleishmann, Harris, & Burtt, 1955; Halpin & Winer, 1957) converged on the thesis that leader role behaviors were functionally related to two broad group objectives: group maintenance and group task achievement. A group member in an informal group, or an appointed leader in a formal group, is perceived to be acting as a leader when he or she engages in activities that promote group maintenance and/or ensure the performance of tasks and the achievement of goals.

Following in this vein, later studies of supervision and leadership in organizations (Yukl, 1994) identified two major leadership roles: a consideration or people orientation (also known as the social role) and an initiating structure or task orientation (also known as the task role). The first role—that is, a consideration or people orientation—reflects the social-emotional side of leadership: "the degree to which the leader's behavior towards group members is characterized by mutual trust, development of good relations, sensitivity to the feelings of group members, and openness to their suggestions" (Andriessen & Drenth, 1984, p. 489). The second role—initiating structure in the group—reflects task-oriented leadership: "the degree to which a leader is bent on defining and structuring the various tasks and roles of group members in order to attain group results" (Andriessen & Drenth, 1984, p. 489). This two-dimensional approach greatly influenced management practice, as evidenced by the popularity of leadership training programs such as the management grid (Blake & Mouton, 1964), which sought to identify a manager's predominant orientation—whether it was a task or a social orientation.

A third leadership role dimension related to decision making was identified by the work of Lewin and his associates (Lewin, Lippitt, & White, 1939; Lippitt & White, 1947). These researchers studied autocratic and democratic leadership roles in groups and their impact on decision making and decision implementation. In providing direction, in problem solving, or in providing interaction opportunities for group members, a leader could implement such decisions by using the resources available among group members or by using the leader's own individual resources. In other words, a leader could choose to engage in either autocratic or participative behavior.

Research on these three role dimensions dominated the field from the 1940s until the 1980s. As will be discussed later in this chapter, such research ignored an important leadership task role, that of *formulating future goals* for the group or organizational members and *the means to achieving the goals* through influencing the members.

Contingencies of Leadership Effectiveness

The second research issue—identification of the conditions or contingencies for leader role effectiveness—also studied small groups in both laboratory and field settings. Expanding on the earlier constructs of a leader's social and task role behaviors, Fiedler (1967) and his associates (Fiedler & Chemers, 1982) suggested that these leadership roles are contingent on situational conditions for their effectiveness. They operationalized a model called high and low Least Preferred Coworker (LPC) as the two key leadership attributes (they closely resembled consideration and initiating structure or social and task roles). Fiedler's contingency model suggested that in certain situations with certain types of tasks, follower attitudes, and position power, low LPC leaders (or initiating structure behavior) would be more effective than high LPC leaders (or consideration behavior), and in other situations with different types of tasks, follower attitudes, and position power, high LPC leaders would be more effective than low LPC leaders. For example, in situations in which the task is highly structured, relations with subordinates are good, and the leader has substantial position power, the low LPC leader is the most effective. With good relations but an unstructured task and weak position power, the high LPC is more effective. In another contingency approach, Kerr and Jermiar (1978) identified two kinds of situational factors, referred to as substitutes or neutralizers of leadership influence on subordinates. Their "substitutes for leadership" specify a set of characteristics of followers, tasks, and organizational contexts that reduce or nullify the effects of relationship- and task-oriented leadership roles. For example, highly experienced subordinates or an unambiguous task might substitute for the need for leadership.

Building on Lewin's classic studies of autocratic and democratic leadership, one additional school of contingency theorists emerged. These researchers explored the effects of autocratic, consultative, and participative leadership behavior on the effectiveness of a leader in achieving group objectives. Their published findings in both the social psychological and organizational behavior literature (Coch & French, 1948; Likert, 1961; McGregor, 1960; Tannenbaum & Schmidt, 1958; Vroom & Yetton, 1973) suggested that the extent to which a leader involved followers in decision making was a critical factor in leadership role effectiveness. Using a continuum of styles from autocratic to consultative to participative, these researchers identified the appropriateness of each style depending on the situational characteristics of both task and follower attributes. For example, when a decision is important and subordinates possess relevant knowledge and information lacked by the leader, an autocratic decision would be inappropriate (Vroom & Yetton, 1973).

This line of research in task, group, and situational contingencies for the effectiveness of different leadership roles can be extended to investigate the nature of context and follower characteristics responsible for other leadership role behaviors, such as formulating future goals and developing leadership strategies and the tactics to achieve them.

Leader-Follower Influence Processes

The third research issue dealt with how and why leaders become effective in influencing their followers. The goal was to understand the underlying psychological mechanisms that explain the link between a leader's role behavior and the followers' compliance and commitment to achieving group or organizational objectives. Psychological mechanisms were explored from three different theoretical perspectives: (1) the bases of social power (Dahl, 1957; French & Raven, 1959), (2) the nature of social exchange (Blau, 1974; Hollander, 1979), and (3) the motivational dynamics (Evans, 1970; House, 1971; Luthans & Kreitner, 1975). We will discuss each below.

Exploring the reasons for leadership power and influence, Cartwright (1965) suggested that leadership effectiveness stems from the followers' perception that their leader possesses and controls resources that they value. Control over such resources forms the bases of power (Dahl, 1957) of all leaders. Most studies of leadership effectiveness using this perspective (e.g., Student, 1968), however, have used French and Raven's (1959) formulation of five kinds of resources that form the bases of social power—reward, coercive, legal, expert, and referent. The first three bases of social power are often assumed to stem from one's formal authority position within a group or an organization; hence, they are referred to as position power bases. The last two, expert and referent power bases, are considered as residing in the leader's personal and idiosyncratic ways of influencing followers; hence, they are termed personal power or idiosyncratic power bases. The use of personal power by a leader has an incremental influence on followers (Katz & Kahn, 1978) over and above the influence that results from the use of the leader's position power. This incremental influence on followers is reflected in the followers' performance beyond an organization's prescribed performance expectations.

Research on the nature of the incremental influence resulting from a leader's use of the personal power base did not receive adequate attention from scholars, who were mainly concerned with the effects of position power. Only recently, with a growing interest in charismatic and transformational leadership, has the role of the personal power base in influencing followers become a central issue.

The second theoretical perspective used to explain leadership influence makes use of social exchange theory (Blau, 1974) in human interactions. Leaders acquire status and influence over group members in return for demonstrating task competence and loyalty to the group. Hollander and Offermann (1990) call this type "a process-oriented transactional approach to leadership. . . . It emphasizes the implicit social exchange or transaction over time that exists between the leaders and followers, including reciprocal influence and interpersonal perception" (p. 181). Using this approach, Hollander (1958, 1986) has advanced the "idiosyncratic credit" model of leadership that explains why the innovative ideas of leaders gain acceptance among followers. According to this model, leaders earn these credits in the eyes of followers when they demonstrate good judgment. For example, if a leader's innovative proposal is quite successful, followers' trust in their leader's expertise is confirmed. In turn, followers become more willing to suspend their judgment and go along with the leader's innovative ideas. The more successes a leader has, the more credits he or she gains. A leader can then utilize such credits (which, in effect, represent followers' trust) to influence followers' compliance and commitment to innovative goals.

Finally, a leader's influence over followers also has been explained by analyzing the motivational processes governing follower satisfaction and performance. A path-goal theory of leadership was first proposed by Evans (1970) and later advanced by House (1971) using the expectancy theory of motivation to account for leadership effectiveness. According to House and his associates (e.g., House & Dessler, 1974; House & Mitchell, 1974), each of the four types of leadership role behavior (directive, achievement-oriented, supportive, and participative) influences followers by increasing the personal payoffs to them for group task accomplishments and "making the path to these payoffs easier to travel by clarifying it, reducing roadblocks and pitfalls, and increasing the opportunities for personal satisfaction en route" (House, 1971, p. 324). Similar motivational explanations for the effectiveness of various leadership activities have been suggested by Oldham (1976), who observed that leadership activities such as rewarding, setting goals, and designing job and feedback systems heighten followers' motivation. Other researchers (e.g., Podsakoff et al., 1982; Sims, 1977) have explained leadership effectiveness in terms of the behavior modification principles of contingent reinforcement. This approach to maintaining influence over followers also has been interpreted as a form of transactional leadership (Avolio & Bass, 1988).

In summary, these modal trends have led researchers to focus on three major leadership role dimensions: (1) a "people concern" that manifests itself in a relationship orientation and through activities that emphasize the leader's consideration and supportiveness; (2) a "task concern" that focuses on achievement and activities that emphasize initiating structure, goal setting, and facilitating task performance; and (3) a concern for making and implementing decisions that includes behavior such as facilitating interaction and implementing appropriate decision-making styles that range from autocratic and directive to consultative and participative. These specific role dimensions have been studied in situational contexts involving varied characteristics of three distinct elements: (1) tasks, (2) followers, and (3) groups and organizations. Most contingency theories of leadership consider these three elements as the possible contingencies for understanding leadership effectiveness.

Finally, the nature of the leader-follower influence process also is understood in terms of three theoretical perspectives: control over valued resources, social exchange processes, and motivational dynamics. During the last quarter of a century, leadership contingency models dealing with the three behavior dimensions, the three situational elements, and the three classes of explanations discussed above have dominated the scientific literature both in the East (Misumi, 1985; Sinha, 1984) and in the West (Fiedler, 1967; Heller, 1971; House, 1971; Vroom & Yetton, 1973).

LIMITATIONS OF EXISTING MODAL ORIENTATIONS

More recently, these earlier leadership models have been considered to be too narrow and sterile (Hunt, 1991). Disappointment has been expressed about their failure to move beyond the simple social versus task dimensions or autocratic versus participative dimensions that underscored the work of early theorists (Bryman, 1986). As Bass and Avolio (1993) point out, "Initiation and consideration were not sufficient to explain the full range of leadership behaviors commonly associated with the best and also the worst leaders" (p. 50). Many scholars who pursued the modal trends of past leadership research thus seemed to have ignored certain core aspects of leader role activities and behaviors. These core aspects include the leader's role in

1. the critical assessment of the environment and status quo,
2. the formulation and articulation of a future vision or the formulation of goals for the followers, and
3. the building of trust and credibility in the minds of followers, which is crucial to developing commitment to a vision.

The act of leading implies that a future vision or goal for the group or organization must be formulated on the basis of an environmental assessment and that followers have to be led to achieve such a goal. One cannot lead when the status quo is satisfactory and when there is no future goal to pursue. In addition, leading implies fostering changes in followers through the building of trust and credibility. In turn, trust enables and builds enduring commitment in the pursuit of a future goal. Leading does not exist when followers' routine compliance is obtained simply to maintain the group's or the organization's status quo.

The limits of the existing theories and research on leadership also is reflected in the inadequate attention given to the study of followers' behavior—their perceptions and motivations in submitting to their leaders. As Hollander and Offermann (1990) point out, "Although the study of leadership has always presumed the existence of followers, their roles were viewed as essentially passive" (p. 182). There is a great need for follower-centered approaches to leadership research.

The narrowness of the leadership models discussed so far stems from three research strategies employed to understand the phenomena. First, these models are based principally on observations of small groups. When leadership is studied in small groups, whether in a laboratory or in an organization, certain elements of leadership as observed in large corporations or in religious, social, and political organizations are overlooked. For example, studies based on small groups can easily overlook the formulation of a mission or a strategic vision because group goals are often more tactical and mundane.

Second, studies of supervision in organizations have always used follower attitudes and behaviors as dependent variables, rather than as antecedents or explanations for leadership phenomena. Consequently, these studies have neglected to utilize follower-centered approaches. As a result, understanding leadership as an attributional process remains seriously incomplete.

Third, as pointed out in Chapter 1, most leadership studies in organizational contexts have, in fact, been studies of supervision or day-to-day routine maintenance rather than actual leading behaviors observed among leaders. The core element of supervision or managership is the effective maintenance of the status quo, whereas a core element of leadership is to bring about improvements, changes, and transformations in the existing system and in its members.

In view of such differences, it is imperative that the focus of leadership research change from a preoccupation with supervisory or managerial styles (task, people, participative role orientations) to the study of leader role behaviors such as formulating a vision, articulating the vision, and developing strategies to achieve the vision—activities observed in leaders who bring about profound changes in their organizations and in their members (Bass, 1990; Conger & Kanungo, 1988b). Likewise, follower-centered approaches with an emphasis on follower perceptions, attributions, and value transformations in the leader-follower relational dynamics must receive greater attention (Hollander & Offermann, 1990). This paradigm shift already is taking place, as can be seen by the recent emergence of interest in charismatic and transformational leadership (Bass & Avolio, 1993; Conger, 1989a; Conger & Kanungo, 1987; House, 1995; Kanungo & Mendonca, 1996a, 1996b), follower attributions (Meindl et al., 1985), and empowerment (Conger & Kanungo, 1988c; Hollander & Offermann, 1990; Spreitzer, 1995, 1996; Thomas & Velthouse, 1990).

This emerging trend in leadership research to move beyond the task, social, and participative leadership roles to other roles is called the neo-charismatic paradigm (House, 1995). The neo-charismatic paradigm recognizes the limitations of conventional paradigms in the sense that past research has neglected to study two of the most important leadership behaviors as defined by Cartwright and Zander (1968): "setting group goals" and "moving the group toward its goals" (p. 304). Through these activities, leaders bring about changes in groups and organizations and transform their members' beliefs and values. The neo-charismatic paradigm (House, 1995) asserts that leaders are visionary (in the sense that they set future goals for the organization) and induce significant organizational change.

As described in Chapter 1, several behavioral theories have been proposed to explain the charismatic leadership role under this neo-charismatic paradigm (Bass, 1985; Conger & Kanungo, 1987; House, 1977; Sashkin, 1988). In the following section, the behavioral model proposed by Conger and Kanungo (1987, 1988a) will be described.

CHARISMATIC LEADERSHIP: A BEHAVIORAL MODEL

Most of us carry in our heads a naive theory of what constitutes charismatic leadership. What is needed is a more precise and scientific understanding of the phenomenon. It was toward this end, a decade ago, that we proposed a behavioral theory of charismatic leadership (Conger & Kanungo, 1987). In our theory, a leader's charismatic role, like any other type of leadership role (e.g., task, social, participative), is considered an observable behavioral process that can be described and analyzed in terms of a formal model.

Our model builds on the idea that charismatic leadership is an attribution based on followers' perceptions of their leader's behavior. For example, most social psychological theories consider leadership to be a by-product of the interaction between members of a group. As each member works with others to attain group objectives, each begins to realize his or her status in the group as either a leader or a follower. This realization is based on observations of the influence process within a group, which helps members determine their status. The individual who exerts maximum influence over other members is perceived to be filling the leadership role. Leadership is then consensually validated when the membership recognizes and identifies the leader on the basis of their interactions with that person. In other words, leadership qualities are attributed to an individual's influence.

Charismatic leadership is no exception to this process. Thus, charisma must be viewed as an attribution made by followers. This is consistent with the assumption stated earlier that leadership is a relational and attributional phenomenon. The leadership role behaviors displayed by a person make that individual (in the eyes of followers) not only a task leader or a social leader and a participative or directive leader but also a charismatic or noncharismatic leader. The leader's observed behaviors can be interpreted by his or her own followers as expressions of charismatic qualities. Such qualities are seen as part of the leader's inner disposition or personal style of interacting with followers. These dispositional attributes are inferred from the leader's observed behavior in the same way as other styles of leadership that have been identified previously (Blake & Mouton, 1964; Fiedler, 1967; Hersey & Blanchard, 1977). In this sense, charisma can be considered an additional inferred dimension of leadership behavior or an additional leadership role. As such, it can and should be subjected to the same empirical and behavioral analysis as participative, task, or social dimensions of leadership.

THE BEHAVIORAL COMPONENTS
OF CHARISMATIC LEADERSHIP

If a follower's attribution of charisma depends on the observed behavior of the leader, what are the behavioral components responsible for such an attribution? Can these components be identified and operationalized so that we might understand the nature of charisma among organizational leaders? In the following sections, we describe the essential and distinguishable behavioral components of charismatic leadership. These behaviors are interrelated, and the presence and intensity of these characteristics are expressed in varying degrees among different charismatic leaders.

To begin, we can best frame and distinguish these components by examining leadership as a process that involves moving organizational members from an existing present state toward some future state. This dynamic also might be described as a movement away from the status quo toward the achievement of desired longer-term goals.

This process can be conceptualized in a stage model with three specific stages (see Figure 2.1). In the initial stage, the leader must critically evaluate the existing situation or status quo. Deficiencies in the status quo or poorly exploited opportunities in the environment lead to formulations of future goals. Before devising appropriate organizational goals, the leader must assess what resources are available and what constraints stand in the way of realizing future goals. In addition, the leader must assess the inclinations, the abilities, the needs, and the level of satisfaction experienced by followers. This evaluation leads to a second stage: the actual formulation and articulation of goals. Finally, in Stage 3, the leader demonstrates how these goals can be achieved by the organization. It is along these three stages that we can identify behavioral components unique to charismatic leaders.

Before we identify these behaviors, a caveat is in order. In reality, the stages just described do not follow such a simple linear flow. Instead, most organizations face ever-changing environments, and their leadership must constantly revise existing goals and tactics in response to unexpected opportunities or other environmental changes. This model, however, nicely simplifies and approximates this dynamic process and allows us to more effectively contrast the differences between charismatic and noncharismatic leadership. The reader should simply keep in mind that, in reality, a leader is constantly moving back and forth between the stages or engaging in them simultaneously.

Behaviorally, we can distinguish charismatic leaders from noncharismatic leaders in Stage 1 by their sensitivity to environmental constraints and by their ability to identify deficiencies and poorly exploited opportunities in the status quo. In addition, they are sensitive to follower abilities and needs. In Stage 2, it is their formulation of an idealized future vision and their extensive use of articulation and impression management skills that sets them apart from other leaders. Finally, in Stage 3, it is their deployment of innovative and unconventional means to achieve their vision and their use of personal power to influence followers that are distinguishing characteristics. Table 2.1 highlights these essential differences. The behavioral components in each of the three stages are discussed in the sections that follow.

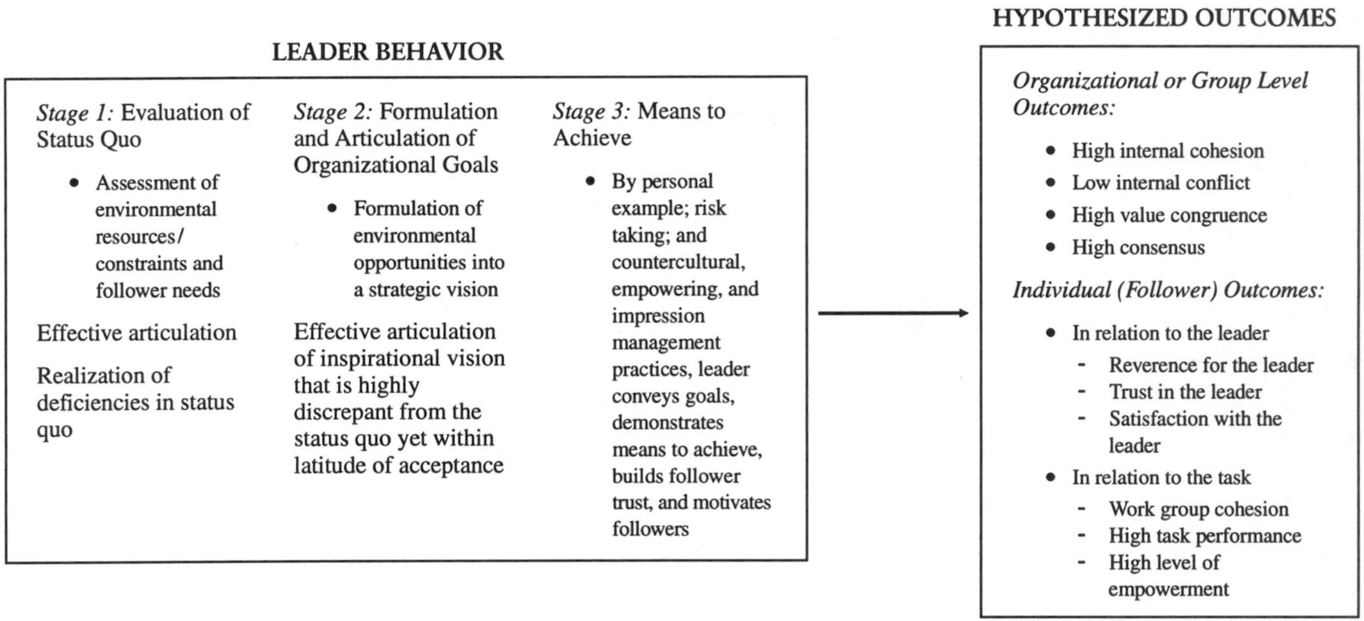

LEADER BEHAVIOR

Stage 1: Evaluation of Status Quo

- Assessment of environmental resources/constraints and follower needs

Effective articulation

Realization of deficiencies in status quo

Stage 2: Formulation and Articulation of Organizational Goals

- Formulation of environmental opportunities into a strategic vision

Effective articulation of inspirational vision that is highly discrepant from the status quo yet within latitude of acceptance

Stage 3: Means to Achieve

- By personal example; risk taking; and countercultural, empowering, and impression management practices, leader conveys goals, demonstrates means to achieve, builds follower trust, and motivates followers

HYPOTHESIZED OUTCOMES

Organizational or Group Level Outcomes:

- High internal cohesion
- Low internal conflict
- High value congruence
- High consensus

Individual (Follower) Outcomes:

- In relation to the leader
  - Reverence for the leader
  - Trust in the leader
  - Satisfaction with the leader
- In relation to the task
  - Work group cohesion
  - High task performance
  - High level of empowerment

Figure 2.1. A Stage Model of Charismatic Leadership

TABLE 2.1 Distinguishing Attributes of Charismatic and Noncharismatic Leaders

	Noncharismatic Leaders	*Charismatic Leaders*
Stage 1		
Environmental sensitivity	Low need for environmental sensitivity to maintain status quo	High need for environmental sensitivity to change the status quo
Relation to status quo	Essentially agrees with status quo and strives to maintain it	Essentially opposes status quo and strives to change it
Stage 2		
Future goals	Goals not too discrepant from status quo	Idealized vision that is highly discrepant from status quo
Likableness	Shared perspective makes him or her likable	Shared perspective and idealized vision make him or her likable and worthy of identification and imitation
Articulation	Weak articulation of goals and motivation to lead	Strong and/or inspirational articulation of future vision and motivation to lead
Stage 3		
Behavior novelty	Conventional, conforming to existing norms	Unconventional or counternormative
Trustworthiness	Disinterested advocacy in persuasion attempts	Passionate advocacy, incurring great personal risk and cost
Expertise	Expert in using available means to achieve goals within the framework of the existing order	Expert in using unconventional means to transcend the existing order
Influence Strategy		
Power base usage	Position power and personal power (based on reward and/or expert power, and liking for a friend who is similar other)	Personal power (based on expert power; respect and admiration for a unique hero)

Stage 1: Sensitivity to the Environmental Context

Charismatic leaders are very critical of the status quo. They tend to be highly sensitive to both the social and physical environments in which they operate. When a leader fails to assess properly either constraints in the environment or the availability of resources, his or her strategies and actions may not achieve organizational objectives. That leader, in turn, will be labeled ineffective. For this reason, it is important that a leader be able to make realistic assessments of the environmental constraints and resources needed to bring about change within the organization. This is where the knowledge, experience, and expertise of the leader become critical. A leader also must be sensitive to both the abilities and the emotional needs of followers—the most important resources for attaining organizational goals. As Kenny and Zacarro (1983) point out, "Persons who are consistently cast in the leadership role possess the ability to perceive and predict variations in group situations and pattern their own approaches accordingly. Such leaders are highly competent in reading the needs of their constituencies and altering their behaviors to more effectively respond to these needs" (p. 683).

Such assessments, although not a distinguishing feature of charismatic leaders, are nevertheless particularly important for these leaders because they often assume high risks by advocating radical change. Their assessment of environmental resources and constraints then becomes extremely important before planning courses of action. A leader's environmental assessment may dictate that instead of launching a course of action as soon as a vision is formulated, he or she prepare the ground and wait for an appropriate time and place, and/or for the availability of resources. It is presumed that many times charisma has faded because of a lack of sensitivity for the environment.

In the assessment stage, what distinguishes charismatic from noncharismatic leaders is the charismatic leaders' ability to recognize deficiencies in the present context. In other words, they actively search out existing or potential shortcomings in the status quo. For example, the failure of firms to exploit new technologies or new markets might be highlighted as a strategic or tactical opportunity by a charismatic leader. Likewise, a charismatic entrepreneur might more readily perceive marketplace needs and transform them into opportunities for new products or services. In addition, internal organizational deficiencies may be perceived by the charismatic leader as platforms for advocating radical change.

Thus, as noted in Chapter 1, any context that triggers a need for a major change and/or presents unexploited market opportunities is relevant for the emergence of a charismatic leader. In some cases, contextual factors so overwhelmingly favor transformation that a leader can take advantage of them by advocating radical changes for the system. For example, when an organization is dysfunctional or when it faces a crisis, leaders may find it to their advantage to advocate radical changes, thereby increasing the probability of fostering a charismatic image for themselves.

During periods of relative tranquillity, charismatic leaders play a major role in fostering the need for change by creating the deficiencies or exaggerating existing minor ones. They also may anticipate future changes and induce supportive conditions for these. In any case, context can be viewed as a precipitating factor, sometimes facilitating the emergence of certain behaviors in a leader that form the basis of his or her charisma.

Because of their emphasis on deficiencies in the system and their high levels of intolerance for them, charismatic leaders are always seen as organizational reformers or entrepreneurs. In other words, they act as agents of innovative and radical change. The attribution of charisma, however, is dependent not on the outcome of change but simply on the actions taken to bring about change or reform.

From the perspective of managing and fostering change, charismatic leaders need to be distinguished from administrators and supervisors. As mentioned earlier, administrators generally act as caretakers who are responsible for the maintenance of the status quo. They influence others through the power of their positions as sanctioned by the organization. As such, they have little interest in significant organizational change. Supervisors, in their task, social, and participative leadership roles, therefore often act as noncharismatic leaders. Sometimes they act as change agents who may direct or nudge their followers toward established and more traditional goals. Although they may advocate change, it usually is incremental and within the bounds of the status quo. Charismatic leaders, however, seek radical reforms for the achievement of their idealized goals and transform their followers (instead of directing or nudging them). Charisma, then, can never be perceived either in an administrator (caretaker) role or in a supervisory role designed only to nudge the system.

Stage 2: The Future Vision

After assessing the environment, a leader will formulate goals for achieving the organization's objectives. Charismatic leaders can be distinguished from others by the nature of their goals and by the manner in which they articulate them. Charismatic leaders are often characterized by a sense of strategic vision (Bass & Avolio, 1993; Berlew, 1974; Conger, 1985; Dow, 1969; House, 1995; Marcus, 1961; Willner, 1984; Zaleznik & Kets de Vries, 1975). Here the word *vision* refers to some *idealized goal* that the leader wants the organization to achieve in the future. The nature, formulation, articulation, and means for achieving this goal as proposed by the charismatic leader can be distinguished from those advocated by other types of leaders.

Formulating the Vision

The more idealized or utopian the future goal advocated by the leader, the more discrepant it becomes in relation to the status quo. The greater the discrepancy of the goal from the status quo, the more likely is the attribution that the leader has extraordinary vision, not just an ordinary goal. Moreover, by presenting a very discrepant and idealized goal to followers, a leader provides a sense of challenge and a motivating force for change. If we turn to the attitude change literature, it is suggested that a maximum discrepant position within the latitude of acceptance puts the greatest amount of pressure on followers to change their attitudes (Hovland & Pritzker, 1957; Petty & Cacioppo, 1981). Because the idealized goal is articulated to represent a perspective shared by the followers and promises to meet their hopes and aspirations, it tends to be within this latitude of acceptance in spite of its extreme discrepancy. Leaders then become charismatic as they succeed in changing their followers' attitudes to accept their advocated vision. We argue that leaders are charismatic when their vision represents an embodiment of a perspective shared by followers in an idealized form.

What are the attributes of charismatic leaders that make them successful advocates of their discrepant vision? Research on persuasive communication suggests that to be a successful advocate, one needs to be a credible communicator and that credibility comes from projecting an image of being a likable, trustworthy, and knowledgeable person (Hovland, Janis, & Kelley, 1953; Sears, Freedman, & Peplau, 1985).

It is the shared perspective of the vision and its potential for satisfying followers' needs that make leaders "likable" persons. Both the perceived similarity and the need satisfaction potential of the leaders form the basis of their attraction (Byrne, 1977; Rubin, 1973). The idealized (and therefore discrepant) vision, however, also makes such leaders admirable persons deserving of respect and worthy of identification and imitation by the followers. It is this idealized aspect of the vision that makes them charismatic. Charismatic leaders are not just similar others who are generally liked (as popular consensus-seeking people) but similar others who are also distinct because of their idealized vision.

Articulating the Vision

To be charismatic, leaders not only need to have visions and plans for achieving them but also must be able to articulate their visions and strategies for action in effective ways so as to influence their followers. Here, articulation involves two separate processes: articulation of the context and articulation of the leader's motivation to lead. First, charismatic leaders must effectively articulate for followers the following four scenarios representing the context:

1. the nature of the status quo and its shortcomings;
2. a future vision;
3. how the future vision, when realized, will remove existing deficiencies and fulfill the hopes of followers; and
4. the leader's plan of action for realizing the vision.

In articulating the context, the charismatic's verbal messages construct reality such that only the positive features of the future vision and only the negative features of the status quo are emphasized. The status quo usually is presented as intolerable, and the vision is presented in clear, specific terms as the most attractive and attainable alternative. In articulating these elements for subordinates, the leader often constructs several scenarios representing the status quo, goals for the future, needed changes, and the ease or difficulty of achieving goals depending on available resources and constraints. In his or her scenarios, the charismatic leader attempts to create among followers a disenchantment or discontentment with the status quo, a strong identification with future goals, and a compelling desire to be led in the direction of the goal despite environmental hurdles. This process of influencing followers is similar to the path-goal approach to leadership behavior advocated by many theorists (for example, see House, 1971).

In addition to verbally describing the status quo, future goals, and the means to achieve them, charismatic leaders also must articulate their own motivation for leading their followers. Using expressive modes of action, both verbal and nonverbal, they manifest their convictions, self-confidence, and dedication to materialize what they advocate. In the use of rhetoric, words are selected to reflect their assertiveness, confidence, expertise, and concern for followers' needs. These same qualities also may be expressed through their dress, their appearance, and their body language. Charismatic leaders' use of rhetoric, high energy, persistence, unconventional and risky behavior, heroic deeds, and personal sacrifices all serve to articulate their high motivation and enthusiasm, which then become contagious among their followers. These behaviors form part of a charismatic leader's impression management.

Stage 3: Achieving the Vision

In the final stage of the leadership process, effective leaders build in followers a sense of trust in their abilities and clearly demonstrate the tactics and behaviors required to achieve the organization's goals. The charismatic leader does this by building trust through personal example and risk taking, as well as through unconventional expertise. It is critical that followers develop a trust in the leader's vision. Generally, leaders are perceived as trustworthy when they advocate their position in a disinterested manner and demonstrate a concern for followers' needs rather than their own self-interest (Walster, Aronson, & Abrahams, 1966). To be charismatic, leaders must make these qualities appear extraordinary. They must transform their concern for followers' needs into a total dedication and commitment to a common cause they share, and they must express this in a disinterested and selfless manner. They must engage in exemplary acts that are perceived by followers as involving great personal risk, cost, and energy (Friedland, 1964). In this case, personal risk might include the possible loss of personal finances, the possibility of being fired or demoted, and the potential loss of formal or informal status, power, authority, and credibility. Examples of such behaviors entailing risk include Lee Iacocca's reduction of his salary to $1 in his first year at Chrysler (Iacocca & Novak, 1984) and John DeLorean's confrontations with the senior management at General Motors (Martin & Siehl, 1983). The higher the manifest personal cost or sacrifice for the common goal, the greater is the trustworthiness of a leader. The more leaders are able to demonstrate that they are indefatigable workers prepared to take on high personal risks or incur high personal costs to achieve their shared vision, the more they reflect charisma in the sense of being worthy of complete trust.

Finally, charismatic leaders must appear to be knowledgeable and experts in their areas of influence. Some degree of demonstrated expertise, such as reflected in successes in the past, may be a necessary condition for the attribution of charisma (Conger, 1989a; Weber, 1947). For example, Steven Jobs's success with the Apple I personal computer and Lee Iacocca's responsibility for the Ford Mustang made each more credible with employees. Research by Puffer (1990) has shown that, under conditions of successful outcomes, leaders are in turn credited with greater charisma and expertise. This positive impression may then be used to foster an illusion that the leader has control over uncontrollable events (Meindl et al., 1985). Furthermore, it is hypothesized that the attribution of charisma generally is influenced by the expertise of leaders in two areas. First, charismatic leaders use their expertise in demonstrating the inadequacy of the traditional technology, rules, and regulations of the status quo as a means of achieving the shared vision (Weber, 1947). Second, charismatic leaders show an expertise in devising effective but unconventional strategies and plans of action (Conger, 1985). We can say that leaders are perceived as charismatic when they reveal expertise in transcending the existing order through the use of unconventional or countercultural means. Iacocca's use of government-backed loans, money back guarantees on cars, union representation on the board, and advertisements featuring himself are examples of unconventional strategic actions in the automobile industry.

The attribution of charisma to leaders also depends on followers' perceptions of their leaders' "revolutionary" and "countercultural" qualities (Berger, 1963; Conger, 1985; Dow, 1969; Friedland, 1964; Marcus, 1961). The countercultural qualities of leaders are manifested partly in their discrepant idealized visions. More important, charismatic leaders must engage in unconventional, countercultural, and therefore innovative behavior while leading their followers toward the realization of their visions. Martin and Siehl (1983) demonstrated this in their analysis of John DeLorean's countercultural behavior at General Motors. Charismatic leaders are not consensual leaders but active innovators and entrepreneurs. Their plans and strategies for achieving desired changes and their exemplary acts of heroism involving personal risks or self-sacrificing behaviors must be novel and unconventional. Their uncommon behavior, when successful, evokes in their followers emotional responses of surprise and admiration. Such uncommon behavior also leads to a dispositional attribution of charisma.

We now turn to the actual influence process under charismatic leadership.

THE INFLUENCE PROCESS
UNDER CHARISMATIC LEADERSHIP

A charismatic leader's behaviors can be viewed as attempts on the part of the leader to influence his or her followers' values, attitudes, and behaviors. The following section describes the psychological underpinnings or explanations of the influence process involved in charismatic leadership. As mentioned earlier, the leader's role behaviors constitute the "content," or what leaders do, whereas the influence process adopted by the leader constitutes the "process," or how and why the leader's behavior is effective in influencing followers. To further elaborate on the "process" explanation of leadership, one can use Burns's (1978) idea that there are basically two influence processes, or ways of influencing followers, available to leaders. These are (1) the transactional influence processes and (2) the transformational influence processes.

Under transactional influence, the leader ensures that the followers perform the required behaviors through the use of rewards and sanctions. The success of the transactional influence model obviously is limited to the effectiveness of the "life span" of the commodities offered in exchange. In other words, in the transactional influence mode, followers' compliance is governed by the value-in-exchange of rewards and sanctions. When the major concern of supervisors and managers is to attend to the day-to-day administrative or the operational demands of their organization—that is, to maintain the status quo—they are more likely to use transactional influence to induce compliance in their subordinates. The transactional mode of exercising leadership influence is implicit in the traditional supervisory roles of consideration (or the social role), initiating structure (or the task role), and participation.

The psychological mechanisms and dynamics of the transactional influence process, described in the section on modal orientations, can be explained briefly in terms of a host of resources, under the control of supervisors and managers, that are valued by followers because these resources are instrumental in satisfying the subordinates' salient needs. These resources generally are limited to contingent or noncontingent rewards and punishment and to the authority of an office or a position of power. In their traditional supervising roles, managers can offer these resources to subordinates in exchange for subordinates' compliance with the managers' demands or directives as well as for the subordinates' commitment and loyalty to managers. As demonstrated by the work of Katz and Kahn (1978), the compliance behaviors can be traced to the reward, coercive, and legal power strategies of the manager. This motivational process may be understood best by expectancy theory (Kanungo & Mendonca, 1997; Lawler, 1973). Subordinates are motivated to perform the behaviors desired by their managers when they can consistently expect certain valued outcomes following their performance behaviors.

On the other hand, the transformational mode of exercising influence is explicit in the charismatic leadership role (see Kanungo and Mendonca [1996b] for an extensive treatment of this issue). When managers no longer accept the status quo of their organizations and instead formulate an idealized vision that is discrepant from the status quo and that is shared by subordinates, then such managers move away from being caretakers or administrators and instead function as transformational leaders. In this case, the leader works to bring about a change in the followers' attitudes and values, as he or she moves the organization toward its future goals. This change in followers' attitudes and values essentially is achieved through empowering techniques that increase the self-efficacy beliefs of the followers and affirm that they are capable of achieving the future goals. Followers' compliance is the result of two important factors: (1) their internalization of the leader's vision and (2) an increase in their self-efficacy beliefs. The effects of transformational influence on followers therefore is more enduring and potentially permanent.

To understand the psychological dynamics underlying transformational influence, we draw on social psychological theories of influence processes (notably French & Raven, 1959; Kelman, 1958) and empowerment (Conger & Kanungo, 1988c; Thomas & Velthouse, 1990). A leader's influence over followers can stem from different bases of power, as suggested by French and Raven (1959). Charismatic influence stems from the leader's personal idiosyncratic power (referent and expert powers) rather than from position power (legal, coercive, and reward powers) determined by organizational rules and regulations. Participative leaders also may use personal power as the basis of their influence. Their personal power, however, is derived from consensus seeking. In addition, some organizational leaders may use personal power through their benevolent but directive behavior. Charismatic leaders, however, are different from both consensual and directive leaders in the use of their personal power. The sources of charismatic leaders' personal power are manifest in their elitist idealized vision, their entrepreneurial advocacy for radical changes, and their depth of knowledge and expertise. In charismatic leaders, all these personal qualities appear extraordinary to followers, and these extraordinary qualities form the basis of both their personal power and their charisma. Although the use of a personal power base (as opposed to a position power base) helps us to understand the charismatics' transformational influence on followers, the leaders' empowerment strategies and the resulting empowering experience of followers are the ingredients critical to the success of the transformational influence process (Kanungo & Mendonca, 1996b). Also critical to the effectiveness of the transformational influence process is the idealized and shared vision. After leaders formulate an idealized vision, they articulate it by demonstrating their identification with the vision and their commitment to achieve the vision. The leader's identification and commitment, and the exertion of efforts to realize the idealized and shared vision, serve as a model to inspire the followers to undergo a self- or inner transformation consistent with the vision.

Another effect of the leader's formulation and articulation of the vision is to engender in followers a trust in the leader. Followers' trust is earned not only through an inspirational articulation of the vision—although this is a necessary element. It is not developed by a statement of the vision, nor by statements of the leader's expertise in glowing and convincing terms—although these also are necessary. The followers begin to trust their leader when they perceive, beyond a shadow of a doubt, that their leader is unflinchingly dedicated to the vision and is willing to work toward it even at the risk of considerable personal cost and sacrifice.

Here it may be pointed out that the empowerment of followers (building follower self-efficacy and having trust in the leader) is greatly enhanced when charismatic leaders exercise the expert and referent power bases, as mentioned earlier (French & Raven, 1959). The leader's expert power is effective in exerting transformational influence because followers perceive their leader to possess the knowledge, abilities, and expertise that followers can draw on and that they see to be necessary for attainment of the vision. The followers' perception that their leader possesses the needed expertise makes the leader credible and trustworthy. Similar to expert power, the leader's referent power also lies in the followers' perception of the leader's commitment to followers' welfare. The leader's transformational influence on followers is derived from the fact that followers perceive their leader's efforts to be selfless and his or her intent to be altruistic. As a result of such perceptions, the followers are attracted to and identify with the leader.

The transformational influence processes in charismatic leadership also can be examined from the viewpoint of attitudinal change processes. According to Kelman (1958), there are three processes of attitude change: compliance, identification, and internalization. We can think of compliance in terms of when "an individual accepts influence . . . [and] adopts the induced behavior—not because he believes in its content—but because he expects to gain specific rewards or approval and avoid specific punishments or disapproval by conforming" (Kelman, 1958, p. 53). The change in the followers is temporary and superficial; it does not extend to self-transformation of the followers. This type of attitude change is typical of the transactional influence process in supervisory roles.

Identification occurs when "an individual accepts influence because he wants to establish or maintain a satisfying self-defining relationship to another person. . . . The individual actually believes in the responses which he adopts through identification, but their specific content is more or less irrelevant" (Kelman, 1958, p. 53). The followers are attracted to the charismatic leader "as a person." That is, the leader's personal qualities and behavior make him or her adorable, like a hero figure or a model to imitate. In the internalization process of attitude change, an individual is willing to accept influence because "the content of the induced behavior—the ideas and actions of which it is composed—is intrinsically rewarding . . . because it is congruent with his value system" (Kelman,

1958, p. 53). In the context of the leader-follower interaction, the charismatic leader's articulation of the vision, values, and goals and his or her empowering and tactics bring about profound change in the followers. This change is the transformation of the followers' innermost values and goals resulting from the internalization of the leader's vision. With very rare exceptions, it is unlikely that the identification and internalization processes will occur simultaneously. More likely, the leader's use of empowerment strategies first results in the followers' identification with the leader, and then, over time, in their internalization of the values and the idealized vision professed by the leader.

CHARISMA AS A CONSTELLATION OF BEHAVIORS

Through the leadership roles and influence process models just discussed, we have identified a number of behavioral components that distinguish charismatic from noncharismatic leaders. Although each component, when manifested in a leader's behavior, can contribute to a follower's attribution of charisma to the leader, we consider all these components interrelated because they often appear in a given leader in the form of a constellation rather than in isolation. It is this constellation of behavior components that distinguishes charismatic leaders from other leaders.

Certain features of the components listed under the three stages in Figure 2.1 are critical for the perception of charisma in a leader. It is quite probable that effective and noncharismatic leaders will sometimes exhibit one or more of the behavioral components we have identified. The likelihood of followers attributing charisma to a leader will depend on three major features of these components: the number of these components manifested in a leader's behavior, the level of intensity of each component as expressed in a leader's behavior, and the level of saliency or importance of individual components as determined by the existing situation or organizational context and the level of follower proximity to the leader.

As the number of behavioral components manifested in a leader's behavior increases, the likelihood of a follower's attribution of charisma to the leader also increases. Thus, a leader who is only skillful at detecting deficiencies in the status quo is less likely to be seen as charismatic than is one who not only detects deficiencies but also formulates future visions, articulates them, and devises unconventional means for achieving them.

In addition to differing in the total number of manifested behavioral components, leaders may differ in the magnitude (and/or frequency) of a given behavioral component they exhibit. The higher the manifest intensity or frequency of a behavior, the more likely it is to reflect charisma. Thus, leaders who engage in advocating highly discrepant and idealized visions and use highly unconventional means to achieve these visions are more likely to be perceived as charismatic. Likewise, leaders who express high personal commitment to an objective, who take high personal risk, and who use intense articulation techniques are more likely to be perceived as charismatic.

Followers are more likely to attribute charisma to a leader when they perceive his or her behavior to be contextually appropriate and/or in congruence with their own values. Thus, in a traditional organizational culture that subscribes to conservative modes of behavior among employees and the use of conventional means to achieve organizational objectives, leaders who engage in excessive unconventional behavior may be viewed more as deviants than as charismatic figures. Similarly, a leader whose vision fails to incorporate important values and lacks relevance for the organizational context is unlikely to be perceived as charismatic. Certain behavioral components are more critical and effective sources of charisma in some organizational or cultural contexts, but not in others. For example, in some contexts, unconventionality may be less valued as an attribute of charisma than articulation skills, and in other contexts it may be more valued. The constellation of behaviors and their relative importance as determinants of charisma will differ from one organization to another or from one cultural (or national) context to another. Thus, to develop a charismatic influence, a leader must have an understanding of the appropriateness or importance of the various behavioral components for a given context.

Finally, proximity to the leader may influence the importance of certain behavioral components in attributions of charisma. For example, the components that influence follower attributions of charisma among a close circle of followers having direct contact with the leader may differ from those that influence attributions among a larger group of followers who have no direct contact with the leader. For example, in a recent study, Shamir (1995) showed that rhetorical skills were more frequently attributed as an important characteristic of distant charismatic leaders, whereas being considerate of others and exhibiting unconventional behavior were more important in attributions to close charismatic leaders. Leaders wishing to promote a charismatic influence therefore need an understanding of the relative importance of various behavioral components given their proximity to or distance from followers.

OUTCOMES OF CHARISMATIC
LEADERSHIP BEHAVIOR

Our discussion of charismatic leadership in three distinct stages points to a number of ways in which leaders serve their organizations. To ensure the survival and growth of their organizations, they act as status evaluators, constantly monitoring the environment for constraints to overcome and opportunities to utilize. On the basis of their environmental assessment, they act as visionaries and set realistic future task goals for the organization, for work groups, and for individuals. Finally, to achieve these goals, they influence organizational members' beliefs, attitudes, values, and behaviors. The outcomes of these leadership behaviors can be observed either in terms of the end results for the organization, such as the objective indexes of return on investment, units produced, cost per unit, or cost savings, or in terms of follower outcomes, such as changes in follower beliefs, attitudes, and behavior. Earlier in this chapter, we argued that the effects on followers are the more appropriate measures of leadership effectiveness, because the objective indexes of end results often depend not only on followers' instrumental behavior but also on other environmental contingencies over which leaders have little control.

Following the above rationale, we postulate that leadership behavior outcomes can be assessed best through followers' attitudes and behaviors and can be identified both at an aggregate (organizational and group level outcomes) and at an individual level. The hypothesized outcomes are presented in Figure 2.1.

At the aggregate level, we hypothesize that charismatic leadership behaviors will result in high internal cohesion, low internal conflict, high value congruence, and high consensus. Under a charismatic leader, there will be a greater degree of sharing of the vision and a greater degree of agreement with respect to the means for achieving the vision.

At the individual level, followers' outcomes can be assessed in two ways: the followers' behaviors and attitudes toward the leader and toward the task. With respect to followers' relations with the charismatic leader, we hypothesize that followers will show a high degree of reverence for the leader, a high degree of trust in the leader, and a high level of satisfaction with the leader. With respect to the followers' relations to the task, we hypothesize that followers will show a high degree of cohesion with the work group, a high level of task performance, and a high level of feeling empowered within the organization to accomplish tasks.

SOME TESTABLE HYPOTHESES ON CHARISMATIC LEADERSHIP

In terms of the charismatic leadership model discussed in the previous sections, it is suggested that the attribution of a charismatic role to people who assume leadership positions is based on a set of leader behaviors. This implies that understanding the phenomenon of charismatic leadership involves an examination of two sides of the same coin: a set of dispositional attributions by followers and a set of leaders' manifest behavior. The two sides are linked in the sense that the leader's behaviors form the basis of followers' attributions. A comprehensive understanding of the charismatic influence process will involve both the identification of the various components of leaders' behavior and assessment of how the components affect the perceptions and attributions of followers.

To validate the behavioral model, we have proposed a set of hypotheses for empirical testing (Conger & Kanungo, 1987). This set of testable hypotheses is reproduced in Table 2.2. Evidence in the literature supports the general framework we have suggested here, but the specific predictions listed in Table 2.2 also provide directions for future research.

RELATING TO OTHER BEHAVIORAL APPROACHES TO CHARISMA

The formalized model of charismatic leadership presented in the previous section is often identified as "the attributional theory of charisma" (House, 1995, p. 414). This is because the model considers followers' attribution of leadership status to a person as the main reason for the existence of the leadership phenomenon in organizational contexts. As we have asserted, without the followers' attribution of "leadership" to a given person based on their perception of that person's role behaviors, the leadership phenomenon simply would cease to exist.

How can this attributional approach be integrated with other approaches to charismatic leadership? In what ways is the approach similar to or different from other existing charismatic leadership roles? Our review of literature to answer these questions suggests that there are more similarities than differences between the attributional model and other approaches to charismatic leadership. See Table 2.3 for a comparison of the various models.

The attributional model may be compared with three other behavioral approaches that are currently in vogue:

1. the transformational leadership theory advanced by Bass and his associates (Bass, 1985; Bass & Avolio, 1993),
2. the charismatic leadership theory advanced by House and his associates (House, 1995; House & Shamir, 1993), and
3. the visionary leadership theory advocated by Sashkin (1988).

These theories can be compared with respect to both the behavioral components identified in charismatic leadership and the nature of the influence process. House and Shamir (1993) compared the behavioral components of charismatic leadership identified in each of these theories and found that there is considerable overlap among the theories, such that differences are marginal. Table 2.3 presents a modified version of the comparison made by House and Shamir. The table shows that both the Bass and House-Shamir models fail to recognize the importance of Stage 1 leader behaviors (evaluation of status quo) in charismatic leadership. As House and Shamir (1993) assert, "While these behaviors have pragmatic value in such circumstances, we see no self-implicating or motive-arousing effects on followers. . . . Thus we do not believe these attributes to be unique to charismatic leaders" (p. 101). This difference between the Conger-Kanungo and the House-Shamir and Bass models stems from two sources. First, the Conger-Kanungo approach provides a stage model analysis of charismatic leadership, where Stage 1 behaviors (status quo evaluation) are necessary for the emergence of Stage 2 behaviors (visioning and articulation). Perhaps this is the reason why House and Shamir consider Stage 1 behaviors to have only pragmatic value. Second, House and Shamir suggest that Stage 1 behavior may not have direct motive-arousing effects on followers. In a stage model of analyses, however, status quo evaluation forms the basis of vision formulation and articulation; hence, Stage 1 behaviors affect followers in an indirect manner. Beyond this, the articulation of status quo deficiencies that results from the status quo evaluation does indeed affect followers' attitudes and values toward change in a direct fashion. It may be noted that only through an evaluation of the status quo can the leader present the current situation as either a crisis to overcome or as an opportunity to avail if the vision is pursued.

TABLE 2.2 Some Testable Hypotheses on Charismatic Leadership

Hypotheses on Charisma and Context

1. Charismatic leaders, to foster or retain their charisma, engage in realistic assessments of the environmental resources and constraints involving their visions. They put their innovative strategies into action when they find the environmental resource constraint is favorable to them.
2. Contextual factors that cause potential followers to be disenchanted with the prevailing social order, or that cause followers to experience psychological distress, although not a necessary condition for the emergence of charismatic leaders, facilitate such emergence.
3. Under conditions of relative social tranquillity and lack of potential follower psychological distress, the induction of an organizational context by a leader that fosters or supports an attribution of charisma will facilitate the emergence of that leader as a charismatic leader.
4. Charismatic leaders act as reformers or agents of radical changes, and their charisma fades when they act as administrators (caretaker role) or managers (nudging role).

Hypotheses on Charisma and Vision Formulation and Articulation

1. Leaders are charismatic when their vision represents an embodiment of a perspective shared by followers in an idealized form that is highly discrepant from the status quo yet within a latitude of acceptance.
2. Charismatic leaders articulate the status quo as negative or intolerable and the future vision as the most attractive and attainable alternative.
3. Charismatic leaders articulate their motivation to lead through assertive behavior and expression of self-confidence, expertise, unconventionality, and concern for followers' needs.

Hypotheses on Charisma and Achieving the Vision

1. Charismatic leaders take on high personal risks (or incur high costs) and engage in self-sacrificing activities to achieve a shared vision.
2. Charismatic leaders demonstrate expertise in transcending the existing order through the use of unconventional or extraordinary means.
3. Charismatic leaders engage in behaviors that are novel, unconventional, and counternormative, and as such involve high personal risk or high probability of harming their own self-interest.

Furthermore, while comparing the models, House and Shamir (1993) in their analysis failed to notice the presence of frame alignment and the intellectually stimulating articulation of the vision in Stage 2 of the Conger-Kanungo model. Frame alignment implies that communication by the leader should be aligned with followers' attitudes, values, and perspectives. In the Conger-Kanungo model, a leader's vision must represent a perspective shared by followers. In other words, the vision, although discrepant from the status quo, must be within the followers' latitude of acceptance. The Conger-Kanungo model also implicitly recognizes the fact that charismatic leaders engage in intellectually stimulating articulation. When leaders challenge the status quo and formulate their

TABLE 2.2 *Continued*

Hypotheses on Charisma and Personal Power

1. Charismatic leaders' influence on their followers stems from the use of their personal idiosyncratic power (expert and referent) rather than the use of their position power (legal, coercive, and reward) within the organization.
2. Charismatic leaders exert personal influence over their followers through elitist, entrepreneurial, and exemplary behavior rather than through consensus-seeking and directive behavior.

Hypotheses on Outcomes of Charisma

1. Charismatic leaders' influence on their followers will result in high levels of "we-feelings," or internal cohesion and a high level of value congruence in work groups.
2. Charismatic leaders' influence on their followers will result in high levels of agreement with respect to the organizational and task goals and with respect to the means for achieving them.
3. Charismatic leaders' influence on their followers will result in low levels of internal conflicts in work groups.
4. Under charismatic leaders' influence, followers show a high degree of reverence for the leader, a high degree of trust in the leader, and a high degree of satisfaction with the leader.
5. Under charismatic leaders' influence, followers show a feeling of cohesion with the work group, a feeling of being empowered within the organization, and a high level of task performance.

vision in a discrepant and idealized manner, the followers are intellectually challenged to examine their behavior supporting the status quo and to reflect on the idealized vision.

As can be seen in Table 2.3, the greatest overlap is between the Conger-Kanungo, House-Shamir, and Sashkin models. These three models focus more on the behaviors of the leader, whereas the Bass model is more descriptive of the nature of the leadership effects on followers.

The transformational leadership model proposed by Bass and his associates (e.g., Bass & Avolio, 1993) claims that charismatic and transformational forms of leadership are distinguishable in organizational contexts. Charismatic leadership is seen as one of the four components in transformational leadership. The four components in transformational leadership are

1. charisma or idealized influence on followers (sample item measuring the component: "Has my trust in his or her ability to overcome any obstacle"),

2. inspirationally motivating followers (sample item measuring the component: "Uses symbols and images to focus our efforts"),

3. intellectually stimulating followers (sample item measuring the component: "Enables me to think about old problems in new ways"), and

TABLE 2.3 Comparison of Behavioral Attributes in Charismatic Leadership
Theories

	Conger-Kanungo	Bass	House-Shamir	Sashkin
Stage 1: Evaluation of Status Quo				
Environmental sensitivity to resources and constraints	X			X
Concern for follower needs	X	X		X
Stage 2: Formulation and Articulation of Goals				
Vision:				
Formulation of goals	X	X	X	X
Setting challenging expectations	X		X	
Articulation:				
Inspirational	X	X		
Frame alignment	X		X	
Intellectually stimulating	X	X	X	
Stage 3: Means to Achieve Goals				
Empowering:				
Showing confidence in followers	X	X	X	X
Setting personal examples (role modeling)	X	X	X	X
Displaying competence (role modeling)	X		X	X
Showing self-confidence (role modeling)		X	X	X
Taking risks (establishing trust)	X		X	X
Showing selfless effort (role modeling)	X		X	X
Unconventional tactics to transcend existing order	X		X	X

4. individualized consideration of followers (sample item to measure component:
   "Coaches me if I need it").

The distinction made by Bass between charismatic and transformational leadership is based on a narrow specification of charismatic influence (i.e., limited to formulation of vision or challenging goals). The other three models of charismatic leadership have used the term to include all four components specified in the Bass model. In addition, as we noted in Chapter 1, empirical research on the Bass model consistently shows that the charisma component is the most prominent factor explaining transformational leadership. Research literature on both charismatic and transformational leadership models itself portrays the leader's strategic vision as playing a central role in animating and empowering followers (Bryman, 1992).

From our vantage point, what distinguishes transformational from charismatic leadership has little to do with any fundamental differences in leader behavior or tactics but rather with the perspective from which the leadership phenomenon is viewed. The charismatic theories and research have measured leadership from the standpoint of *perceived leader behavior*, whereas the transformational theories to date have concerned themselves primarily with *follower outcomes*. In the case of the transformational forms, this was the natural outcome of Burns's (1978) original conceptualization focusing on elevating *follower* needs and motives to the forefront of the leadership experience. On the other hand, the earlier formulations of charismatic leadership emerging from the fields of sociology and political science were concerned primarily with which *leader behaviors* and *contexts* induced follower responses. In essence, the two formulations of charismatic and transformational in the organizational literature are highly complementary and study the same phenomenon, only from different vantage points.

In addition to the overlap of specific behavior components of charismatic leadership identified in various models, there also is an overlap with respect to the nature of the leadership influence process in these models. All four models of charismatic leadership discussed above suggest that leaders use empowerment rather than control strategies to achieve transformational influence over their followers. Conger and Kanungo (1988c) have proposed a model of the empowerment process that explains a leader's empowerment strategies (see also Kanungo & Mendonca, 1996b). During the evaluation of the status quo, the leader identifies organizational and environmental conditions that are alienating followers and hence need to be changed. Such a diagnosis prepares the leader in empowerment strategies such as the idealization of the vision, inspirational articulation, and modeling behavior (personal risk taking and sacrifice) that provide self-efficacy information to the followers. As a result of receiving self-efficacy information from the leader's behaviors, followers strengthen their self-determination belief and feel empowered and self-assured. Such feelings in turn make them more productive and committed to the leader and to the vision.

House and Shamir (1993, p. 88) also suggest that the charismatic leader's behavior influences the self-concept of followers by creating high self-esteem, self-worth, and self-efficacy. This, in turn, results in heightened commitment in followers to a leader and his or her vision.

Bass and Avolio's (1993, p. 56) behavioral indication of transformational leadership clearly has empowering effects on followers. For example, behavioral indicators such as (1) promoting self-development among followers (individualized consideration), (2) convincing followers that they have the ability to achieve high performance levels (inspirational motivation), (3) fostering a readiness for changes in thinking (intellectual stimulation), and (4) modeling through self-sacrifice (idealized influence) do provide self-efficacy information to followers and consequently have empowering effects on them. Recently, Bass (1977) himself has pointed out that "envisioning, enabling, and empowering leadership . . . are central to transformational leadership" (p. 131). In addition, Sashkin (1988) suggests that visionary leaders "boost the sense of self-worth of those around them by expressing unconditional positive regard, paying attention, showing trust, sharing ideas, and making clear how important and valued organization members are" (p. 145).

All these charismatic leadership models advocate the transformational influence of leaders, where the main goal is to change followers' core attitudes, beliefs, and values rather than only to induce compliance behavior in them. Again, all the models agree that charismatic leadership leads to attitude changes among followers, characterized by identification with the leader and the internalization of values embedded in the leader's vision.

Because all the charismatic leadership models discussed above are behavioral models, they agree that the leadership behavior components and their effects on followers can be observed at all levels of the organizations. As Bass and Avolio (1993) point out, however, "Even though transformational leadership behavior has been observed at lower organizational levels, it is likely to occur more frequently at the highest organizational levels" (p. 54) because organizations provide greater scope for visioning (or mission formulation and implementation) behavior at the higher rather than the lower levels.

In conclusion, the Conger-Kanungo model of charismatic leadership is the most comprehensive (across all three leadership stages) of the proposed leadership theories on charismatic and transformational leadership. We now turn our attention to reviewing what we have learned from empirical tests of the Conger-Kanungo model. In the next chapter, we explore the results of six empirical studies undertaken to operationalize the model, which in turn have led to the development of a charismatic leadership measure.

NOTE

1. The "romance of leadership" refers to a school of thought arguing that followers and others exaggerate the importance of a leader in their need to explain events and attribute causality to an individual in a position of authority.

3

Charismatic Leadership

Measurement and Empirical Validity

There are two steps to developing our understanding of charismatic leadership in organizations. The first step, which we accomplished in the last chapter, involves the development of a formal conceptual framework. The framework identifies the construct of charismatic leadership by defining it, describing its contents or its various components, and linking it to its antecedent and consequence conditions in a way that explains the entire process underlying the phenomenon. This step was taken in the previous chapter, where we presented a behavioral model of charismatic leadership, the Conger-Kanungo model.

A conceptual model—with all its theoretical constructs explaining the phenomenon and its hypothesized relationships regarding antecedents and consequences of the phenomenon—is meaningless, however, without operationalization of the constructs and tests of the empirical validity of hypothesized relationships. Thus, measuring charismatic leadership and empirically verifying predictions as stipulated in the model constitute the necessary next steps for our understanding of the phenomenon. This chapter describes our efforts in this direction.

The Conger-Kanungo model suggests that charisma is attributed to a manager in a leadership position by organizational members. A manager will be perceived as having charisma when organizational members perceive the manager behaving in certain ways. The manager's observed behaviors are interpreted by organizational members as expressions of charisma in the same sense as a manager's behaviors reflect his or her participative, people, and task orientations. The model provides a three-stage framework to identify the various components of the perceived behavior of a manager that contribute to the perception of charisma. In addition, the model predicts that such perceived behavior affects attitudes, beliefs, and behaviors of organizational members. These were described in Figure 2.1 and Table 2.2 in the previous chapter.

The remaining section of this chapter reports six different empirical studies that were conducted to develop a reliable and valid measure of charismatic leadership and to test a number of predictions derived from the Conger-Kanungo model.

STUDY 1[1]

The purpose of the first study was to examine a number of theorized relationships proposed in the model. Using subordinates occupying mid-level management positions in a number of organizations, the following hypotheses were subjected to empirical test.

Under Stage 1 of our model (sensitivity to the environment), it was hypothesized that *managers would be viewed as charismatic when*

> *Hypothesis 1:* Managers are perceived to be acting as reformers or agents of radical change.
> *Hypothesis 2:* Managers are perceived to be striving to change the status quo.
> *Hypothesis 3:* Managers are perceived to be sensitive to their environments by engaging in realistic assessments of environmental opportunities and barriers.
> *Hypothesis 4:* Managers are perceived to be exhibiting sensitivity to follower needs.

Hypotheses 2, 3, and 4 may not be distinguishing attributes of charisma per se, but rather are necessary for the perception of any form of leadership to emerge. They are all the more important for the perception of charisma, however, because of the demands for realizing an idealized vision or a difficult goal.

Stage 2 (vision formulation and articulation) of our model suggests the following hypotheses. Managers will be perceived to be charismatic when

Hypothesis 5: Managers are perceived to be advocating future visions representing an embodiment of a perspective shared by followers in an idealized form.

Hypothesis 6: Managers are perceived to be effectively articulating their vision in a strong and inspirational manner.

Finally, under Stage 3 of the model (building trust through personal example, risk taking, and unconventional expertise), it is hypothesized that managers would be seen as charismatic when

Hypothesis 7: Managers are perceived to be taking on personal risks and engaging in self-sacrificing behavior.

Hypothesis 8: Managers are perceived to be demonstrating innovative and unconventional behavior.

Method

A questionnaire was constructed in two parts. The first part contained a total of 41 items designed to measure subordinate perceptions of six managerial leadership roles and several behavioral attributes exhibited by the manager. All these items appeared in a randomized order in the questionnaire. The second part of the questionnaire elicited demographic information. The following is a description of the leadership roles and behavioral attribute measures.

Measures of Managerial Roles

Items were constructed to measure the following six perceived roles of managers: charismatic, participative, people-oriented, task-oriented, caretaker, and resource coordinator. For measuring the perceived charismatic leadership role of a manager, six items were chosen from a questionnaire developed by Bass (1985) to measure transformational leadership. These six items had the highest loading on a "charismatic leadership" factor in previous studies (Bass, 1985). Each of the remaining five roles was measured by single item with considerable face validity. The single-item leadership role measures were used to avoid a very lengthy questionnaire and to provide an indication of the discriminant and convergent validities of the measures of the charismatic role and the behavioral attributes. Furthermore, use of the single-item measure was considered adequate in view of the fact that the primary purpose of the study was not to develop rigorous test instruments to measure various forms of managerial roles, but rather to identify the perceived behavioral attributes of the charismatic roles distinguished from other commonly ascribed roles of managers. In studies of the global assessment of perceptions, beliefs, and attitudes, use of overall single-item measures is not an uncommon practice (e.g., Pierce, Gardner, Cummings, & Dunham, 1989). Questionnaire items for each of the six role measures are presented in Table 3.1.

Measures of Behavioral Attributes

Eight different behavioral attributes derived from the Conger-Kanungo model were chosen to be included in the questionnaire. These components were "acts as an agent of radical change" (three items), "strives to change the status quo" (three items), "makes realistic assessment of environmental opportunities and constraints" (four items), "sensitive to follower needs and expectations" (three items), "formulates idealized future vision" (four items), "provides strong articulation" (three items), "incurs personal risk" (four items), and "engages in unconventional behavior" (six items). The items measuring the above behavioral components are presented in Table 3.1.

Sample and Procedure

A total of 121 employees belonging to a number of organizations participated in the study. The respondents were asked to think of a familiar manager in their organization with leadership abilities whom they had followed in the past and assess this person in terms of each item presented in the questionnaire. They were requested to indicate on a 6-point scale the degree to which each item is a characteristic of the person (6 = *very characteristic* and 1 = *very uncharacteristic*).

The respondents were all university graduates with a mean age of 27.25 years ($SD = 5.29$). There were 70% male and 30% female respondents, and 69% of the respondents were married. The annual income level of the respondents ranged from $20,000 to $50,000, with 37% earning between $30,000 and $40,000. The majority of the respondents (72%) came from the private sector.

Results

Table 3.1 presents the means, standard deviations, and internal reliability coefficients of the multi-item measures of perceived charismatic leadership role and the eight behavior components. For the remaining five single-item managerial role measures, only means and standard deviations are presented. The reliability coefficients range from .60 to .85 for the multi-item measures.

TABLE 3.1 Mean, *SD*, and Reliability Indexes of Perceived Managerial Roles and Behavior Components Measures

	Item Description	*Mean*	SD	*Reliability Coefficient*
a. Managerial Roles				
Caretaker role	Often acts as a caretaker for the day-to-day maintenance of the organization	3.64	1.45	—
Resource coordinator role	Often acts as a traditional manager of the physical and human resources of the organization	4.11	1.18	—
Task-oriented role	Overall, he/she is a task-oriented leader	−4.52	0.96	—
People-oriented role	Overall, he/she is a people-oriented leader	−4.72	1.20	—
Participative role	Overall, he/she is a participatory leader	4.83	1.25	—
Characteristic role:		28.66	4.62	.85
Items from Bass scale	Is a model for me to follow			
	Makes me proud to be associated with him/her			
	Has a special gift of seeing what is really important for me to consider			
	I have complete faith in him/her			
	Encourages understanding of points of view of other members			
	Has a sense of mission which he/she transmits to me			
b. Behavior Components				
Radical change agent	Creates significant organizational change	12.68	2.81	.73
	Often acts as a reformer to change the values and goals of the organization			
	Introduces needed change even in the face of opposition			
Strives to change status quo	Tries to change status quo by creating a new order	11.04	3.02	.60
	Tries to maintain the status quo or the existing order (way of doing things)			
	Advocates future goals that are not very different from present goals of the organization			

(continued)

TABLE 3.1 *Continued*

	Item Description	*Mean*	SD	*Reliability Coefficient*
Realistic assessment of environment	Readily recognizes new environmental opportunities (favorable physical and social conditions) that may facilitate achievement of organizational objectives	18.32	3.08	.69
	Readily recognizes barriers/ forces within the organization or the larger environment that may block or hinder achievement of his/her goals			
	Readily recognizes constraints in the organization's social and cultural environment (cultural norms, lack of grassroots support, etc.) that may stand in the way of achieving organizational objectives			
	Readily recognizes constraints in the physical environment (technological limitations, lack of resources, etc.) that may stand in the way of achieving organizational objectives			
Sensitivity to follower needs	Perceptive of the abilities and skills of other organizational members	13.59	2.89	.75
	Often expresses personal concern for the needs and feelings of other organizational members			
	Shows sensitivity for the needs and feelings of the organizational members			
Idealized future vision	Has vision, often brings up ideas about potentials and possibilities for the future	18.61	3.37	.80
	Provides inspirational strategic and organizational goals			
	Often generates new ideas for the future of the organization			
	Advocates idealized future goals for the organization			

TABLE 3.1 *Continued*

	Item Description	Mean	SD	Reliability Coefficient
Strong articulation	Inspirational, exciting public speaker	13.62	2.84	.61
	Inspirational, able to articulate effectively the importance of what organizational members are doing			
	Skilled at performing, being on stage			
Personal risk	In pursuing organizational objectives, engages in activities involving considerable self-sacrifice and personal risk	15.19	4.44	.82
	Takes high personal risks for the sake of the organization			
	From time to time engages in acts of exemplary heroism			
	Often incurs high personal costs for the good of the organization			
Unconventional behavior	Advocates following entrepreneurial and risky paths and courses of action to achieve organizational goals	22.33	5.85	.83
	Uses nontraditional or countercultural means to achieve organizational goals			
	Engages in unconventional behavior in order to achieve organizational objectives			
	Often exhibits very novel behavior that surprises other members of the organization			
	Demonstrates expertise in the use of unconventional tactics for achieving organizational goals			
	Advocates following non-risky, well-established paths and courses of actions to achieve organizational goals			

SOURCE: Adapted from "Perceived Behavioral Attributes of Charismatic Leadership" (pp. 92-95), Conger and Kanungo. © 1992 by the Canadian Psychological Association. Reprinted with permission.

TABLE 3.2 Intercorrelations Among Managerial Role Perceptions

	1	*2*	*3*	*4*	*5*	*6*
1. Caretaker	—					
2. Resource manager	.38**	—				
3. Task-oriented leadership	.28**	.18	—			
4. People-oriented leadership	−.02	−.09	.24**	—		
5. Participative leadership	.08	−.04	−.13	.60***	—	
6. Charismatic leadership	.04	−.09	.14	.41***	.39***	

SOURCE: Adapted from "Perceived Behavioral Attributes of Charismatic Leadership" (p. 96), Conger and Kanungo. © 1992 by the Canadian Psychological Association. Reprinted with permission.
*p < .05. **p < .01. ***p < .001.

Intercorrelations Among
Perceived Managerial Roles

Table 3.2 presents the correlations among the six managerial role measures. These correlations reveal two distinct clusters. One cluster represented administrative roles of managers with a primary emphasis on day-to-day task accomplishment, and the other represented leadership roles that primarily emphasize the manager's influence on followers' attitudes and behavior. Caretaker and resource manager roles are the administrative roles of a manager, and although they are positively related to each other, they are not related to the other three leadership roles directed toward influencing followers (people-oriented, participative, and charismatic). These three leadership roles show significant positive correlations with one another. The charismatic leadership role is perceived by followers to be distinct from administrative, task-related roles; however, the charismatic role is positively related to both participative and people-oriented leadership roles. This was expected because exhibiting sensitivity to followers' needs (Hypothesis 4) was hypothesized to be related to charisma.

Relationship of the Charismatic Leadership
Role to Behavioral Components

Table 3.3 presents correlations between the six perceived roles of a manager and the eight behavioral attributes hypothesized to be the characteristics of charismatic leadership. These correlations clearly reveal that the charismatic leadership role is perceived to be positively associated with each of the eight behavioral components. Such significant positive associations are not found in

TABLE 3.3 Correlations Between Perceived Roles of Managers and Their Predicted Behavioral Components as Perceived by Subordinates

Perceived Roles of Managers	Agent of Radical Change	Striving to Change Status Quo	Realistic Assessment of Environment	Sensitivity to Follower Needs	Idealized Future Vision	Strong Articulation	Personal Risk	Unconventional Behavior
Caretaker role	-.22*	-.37**	.01	.06	-.04	-.04	.22*	-.22*
Resource management role	-.12	-.21*	.10	.01	-.05	-.04	-.03	-.28**
Task-oriented role	-.02	-.06	.14	-.13	.00	-.14	.12	-.14
People-oriented leadership role	.24**	.06	.27**	.58***	.30***	.30***	.24**	.19*
Participative leadership role	.07	-.03	.30***	.52***	.24***	.22*	.18*	.11
Charismatic leadership role (Bass scale)	.34***	.23*	.36***	.50***	.45***	.37***	.37**	.27***

SOURCE: Adapted from "Perceived Behavioral Attributes of Charismatic Leadership" (p. 97), Conger and Kanungo. © 1992 by the Canadian Psychological Association. Reprinted with permission.
*p < .05. **p < .01. ***p < .001.

TABLE 3.4 Percentages of Variance Explained by Two Blocks of Independent Variables in Regression Analysis

Dependent Variables	Block 1		Block 2		F Value for
	R_2	F	R^2	F	R^2 Change
Agent of radical change	.07	4.20*	.13	5.83**	8.54**
Strive to change status quo	.01	.53	.06	2.68*	6.70*
Assessment of environment	.10	6.69**	.16	7.25**	7.59**
Sensitivity to follower needs	.39	37.42**	.45	31.49**	12.41**
Idealized future vision	.09	5.79**	.21	10.55**	18.37**
Strong articulation	.10	6.31**	.16	7.45**	8.88**
Personal risk	.05	3.25*	.14	6.25**	11.65**
Unconventional behavior	.03	2.15	.07	3.02*	4.63*

SOURCE: Adapted from "Perceived Behavioral Attributes of Charismatic Leadership" (p. 98), Conger and Kanungo. © 1992 by the Canadian Psychological Association. Reprinted with permission.
NOTE: Block 1 included participative and people-oriented roles as independent variables, and Block 2 included charismatic role as the third independent variable.
$*p < .05. **p < .01$.

the cases of the three administrative roles (task, caretaker, and resource management roles). Out of a total of 24 correlations, only 1 (between caretaker role and personal risk) positive association is significant. In fact, behavioral components such as "striving to change status quo" and "unconventional behavior" have significant negative correlations with both the caretaker and resource management roles.

Although the charismatic leadership role is positively related to each of the eight behavioral attributes as predicted in Hypotheses 1 to 8, both the people-oriented and participative leadership roles also have significant positive correlations with several of the behavioral components. Because all three perceived leadership roles (charismatic, participative, and people-oriented) are significantly related to each other and are also related to several perceived behavioral components, it is necessary to ascertain whether the perceived charismatic leadership role independently explains a significant amount of variance in each of the eight behavioral attributes. Eight separate regression analyses were performed, one for each behavior component as a dependent variable, to determine the independent contribution of the charismatic role. Each analysis was performed in two blocks. In Block 1, people-oriented and participative roles were included as independent variables, and in Block 2, the charismatic role was introduced as the third independent variable. Changes in R^2s were then tested for significance. These results are presented in Table 3.4. In each case, the charismatic role significantly explained the variance, providing support for all eight hypotheses.

Discussion

Several elements of the Conger-Kanungo model that identify the behavioral basis of perceived charisma among managers find strong support in this study. First, subordinates do perceive charismatic leadership of managers to be distinct from administrative task-related roles. Perceived behavioral attributes in this managerial role are different from those responsible for perceived day-to-day administrative task roles.

Second, the study clearly suggests that charismatic leadership can be studied as a dimension of leadership much like other leadership dimensions such as participative, task, or people orientations.

Third, the results provide both predictive convergent and discriminant validity tests of the construct. By demonstrating that scores on the Bass scale for charisma are positively related to each of the eight behavioral attributes (as predicted by the Conger-Kanungo model), predictive convergent validity is established. On the other hand, discriminant validity of the construct is established through a lack of relationship (and in some cases a negative relationship) between measures of behavioral attributes and other administrative task roles.

Fourth, a close examination of R^2 changes in Table 3.4 suggests some of the differentiating behavioral features that the charismatic role shares with people-oriented and participative roles in explaining variance in several of the behavior components. Although the charismatic leadership role independently explains a significant amount of variance with respect to all eight behavioral attributes, R^2 changes in the cases of the "idealized future vision" and "personal risk" particularly stand out. With the addition of the charismatic role as an independent variable, the variance explained jumps from 9% to 21% and from 5% to 14% in the two cases, respectively. In the case of the two other behavioral attributes, "striving to change status quo" and "unconventional behavior," only the addition of the charismatic role as an independent variable made the R^2 and R^2 change significant.

STUDY 2[2]

The test of a number of hypotheses derived from the Conger-Kanungo model in Study 1 provided the necessary impetus for conducting Study 2. This study was directed mainly at operationalizing the charismatic leadership construct in a more rigorous manner, as developed in the Conger-Kanungo model. The objective of this study was to develop a reliable and valid questionnaire measure of the perceived behavioral attributes of charismatic leadership. Such a measure would be different from the Bass (1985) charisma scale because the Bass scale items reflected follower outcomes more than behavioral attributes.

Method

Design of Questionnaire and Procedure

To operationalize the behavior components through a questionnaire measure of charismatic leadership, the following method was employed. Drawing from previous studies and a review of the literature, 49 items were constructed. These items described 49 different behaviors of a manager perceived by subordinates to be charismatic. On the basis of the results of a pilot study, 24 items were eliminated on grounds of ambiguity, redundancy, and lack of discriminatory power. The remaining 25 items were selected for the present study to represent the Conger-Kanungo scale of charismatic leadership. A 6-point *very characteristic* to *very uncharacteristic* response format was used for the respondents. The three stages of the Conger-Kanungo model described in Chapter 2 are linked to the items representing various perceived behavioral components in the following manner. As shown in Table 3.6, the items under "Environmental sensitivity," "Sensitivity to member needs," and "Does not maintain status quo" are directly related to Stage 1—the environmental assessment. These items seek to reveal a leader's ability to see opportunities and constraints in the environment, in members' abilities and needs, and in challenges to the status quo. The second stage—vision formulation—is captured in the items labeled "Vision and articulation." These items describe the leader's ability to devise an inspirational vision and to be an effective communicator. Finally, Stage 3—implementation—is measured in the "Personal risk" and "Unconventional behavior" items. Here the aim of the items is to demonstrate the degree to which a leader is seen to be assuming personal risk and engaging in unconventional behavior, which in turn reveals extraordinary commitment and uniqueness.

A questionnaire containing three parts was designed for the purpose of testing the reliability and validity of the Conger-Kanungo scale. One part contained the 25 items describing the behavioral components, and a second part contained the Bass charisma scale (1985) and three other measures of leader/manager

behavior (task orientation, people orientation, and participative orientation—
adapted from standardized measures). The Bass charisma scale contained the
six items, as shown in Table 3.1. To measure other behavioral orientations, items
were constructed from a pool of items taken from standard scales such as the
Ohio State leadership behavior scales (see Halpin & Winer, 1957). Five items
were selected to measure each of the task ("schedules the work to be done,"
"assigns subordinates to particular tasks," "maintains definite standards of
performance," "encourages use of uniform procedures," and "overall, he/she is
a task oriented leader"), people ("looks out for the personal welfare of subordinates," "finds time to listen to his/her subordinates," "shows personal favors for
his/her subordinates," "tends to be friendly and approachable," and "overall,
he/she is a people-oriented leader"), and participative ("acts after consulting
subordinates," "seeks consensus among subordinates to create a pleasant working atmosphere," "gets group approval," "gets approval of subordinates in
important matters before going ahead," and "overall, he/she is a participatory
leader") orientations. The Bass scale (1985) and the three other behavior
orientation scales were used for purposes of testing the convergent and discriminant validities of the proposed Conger-Kanungo measure. To reduce the effects
of method bias, the two parts of the questionnaire were administered with a 1-day
separation between them. In addition, the order of presentation of the two parts
was reversed for half of the total sample. The third part of the questionnaire was
designed to determine the demographic characteristics of the respondents and
was administered at the end of the testing.

Sample Description

The questionnaire was written in both English and French following the
translation-retranslation procedure (Brislin, Lonner, & Thorndike, 1973) and
was administered to 750 full-time English- and French-speaking managers in
four corporations in the United States and Canada. Distribution of the questionnaires was performed by the human resources departments of the participating
companies. Each respondent received an envelope containing the first part of the
questionnaire with a postage-paid mailer addressed to the researchers. Part 2,
with the demographic questionnaire attached, was distributed 1 day later with
instructions to answer it no sooner than 24 hours after completing Part 1. This
second part also was accompanied by a postage-paid mailer to the researchers.
Parts 1 and 2 of the questionnaires from individual respondents were identified
through matching identical serial numbers given to the parts of each question-

naire pair. At no point did the questionnaires pass back through the human resources or other organizational departments. The final count revealed that 488 completed questionnaires were returned.

Results

In terms of demographics, respondents were managers belonging to four corporations. Eighty percent of the sample came from large organizations (more than 1,000 employees). Of the respondents, 89% were male and 11% were female, with a mean age of 41.5 for the total sample. Eighty-six percent were married, and 14% were single. Their education levels ranged from high school to advanced graduate degrees, and their income levels ranged from under $25,000 to more than $105,000. Sixty-two percent spoke English as their mother tongue, and 25% spoke French as their mother tongue. Half of the sample had organizational tenure of 12 years or more.

Psychometric Properties of the Measures

The means, standard deviations, and reliability coefficients (Cronbach alpha) for each of the scales and for each of the four organizations from where samples were drawn are presented in Table 3.5. The reliabilities for the Conger-Kanungo scale varied from 0.88 to 0.91 across samples. For the total sample ($N = 488$), the reliability index was 0.88. The item-total correlations for the 25 items in the Conger-Kanungo scale ranged from 0.25 to 0.66, with an average correlation of 0.44.

Dimensions of Charismatic Leadership

Principal components analysis with varimax rotation was performed on the 25 items of the Conger-Kanungo scale to determine if the various behavioral dimensions proposed by the Conger-Kanungo model could be verified empirically. The total sample was broken into two groups (Ns = 241 and 244), and separate analyses were performed on each to determine the stability of the factor structures across the samples. Separate factor analyses of the two samples reported here yielded essentially similar factor structures. Analysis of the total sample yielded six clear interpretable factors of charismatic leadership (see Table 3.6).

The first factor contained six items that reflected *strategic vision and articulation behavior* (Stage 2 of our model) components (item loadings ranged from 0.50 to 0.82). The second factor contained seven items reflecting *sensitivity to*

TABLE 3.5 Internal Consistency Index, Mean, and Standard Deviation for All Measures

	Org 1 (N = 241)			Org 2 (N = 71)			Org 3 (N = 63)			Org 4 (N = 113)			Total (N = 488)		
	Alpha	Mean	S.D.	Alpha	Mean	S.D.	Alpha	Mean	S.D.	Alpha	Mean	S.D.	Alpha	Mean	S.D.
Bass scale for charisma (six items)	0.88	27.13	5.22	0.92	29.01	4.92	0.85	28.38	4.15	0.78	30.31	3.57	0.88	28.29	4.87
Task orientation (five items)	0.72	23.40	3.53	0.69	23.22	3.48	0.72	22.98	3.40	0.71	22.07	3.92	0.71	23.01	3.63
Participation orientation (five items)	0.86	21.11	4.66	0.82	22.68	3.55	0.76	22.25	3.62	0.78	21.72	3.90	0.83	21.63	4.25
People orientation (five items)	0.85	21.89	4.77	0.87	23.49	4.10	0.72	22.63	3.40	0.76	23.63	3.65	0.83	22.62	4.33
Conger-Kanungo scale for charisma (25 items)	0.88	104.32	14.98	0.91	107.57	13.73	0.87	108.82	13.03	0.88	114.66	12.43	0.88	107.78	14.52

SOURCE: Adapted from "Charismatic Leadership in Organizations: Perceived Behavioral Attributes and Their Measurement" (p. 446), Conger and Kanungo, *Journal of Organizational Behavior.* © 1994 by John Wiley & Sons Limited. Reproduced with permission.

TABLE 3.6 Exploratory Factor Analysis

Factor Names and Items	Factor 1	Factor 2	Factor 3	Factor 4	Factor 5	Factor 6
Vision and articulation						
Exciting public speaker	**0.82**	0.06	0.06	0.07	0.21	–0.01
Appears to be a skillful performer when presenting to a group	0.80	0.11	–0.06	0.04	–0.02	–0.02
Inspirational, able to motivate by articulating effectively the importance of what organizational members are doing	**0.55**	0.31	–0.04	0.25	0.40	0.05
Has vision, often brings up ideas about possibilities for the future	0.61	0.31	0.19	0.22	0.06	0.26
Provides inspiring strategic and organizational goals	**0.53**	0.31	0.14	0.19	0.24	0.19
Consistently generates new ideas for the future of the organization	0.50	0.21	0.22	0.31	0.06	0.31
Environmental sensitivity						
Readily recognizes constraints in the organization's social and cultural environment (cultural norms, lack of grassroots support, etc.) that may stand in the way of achieving organizational objectives	0.22	**0.69**	0.03	0.07	0.22	0.02
Readily recognizes constraints in the physical environment (technological limitations, lack of resources, etc.) that may stand in the way of achieving organizational objectives	0.11	**0.68**	0.05	0.03	0.19	–0.15
Readily recognizes barriers/forces within the organization that may block or hinder achievement of his/her goals	0.07	**0.68**	0.14	0.04	0.00	–0.02
Recognizes the abilities and skills of other members in the organization	0.25	**0.67**	–0.06	0.12	0.27	0.05
Recognizes the limitations of other members in the organization	0.11	**0.75**	–0.14	0.03	0.15	–0.06
Readily recognizes new environmental opportunities (favorable physical and social conditions) that may facilitate achievement or organizational objectives	0.53	**0.45**	0.16	0.15	0.18	0.19
Entrepreneurial; seizes new opportunities in order to achieve goals	0.35	**0.37**	0.35	0.16	0.02	0.27

the environment (Stage 1 of our model) with item loadings ranging from 0.37 to 0.75. The third (three items) and fourth (four items) factors reflected *unconven-*

TABLE 3.6 *Continued*

Factor Names and Items	Factor 1	Factor 2	Factor 3	Factor 4	Factor 5	Factor 6
Unconventional behavior						
Engages in unconventional behavior in order to achieve organizational goals	0.00	0.06	**0.79**	0.09	–0.12	0.13
Uses nontraditional means to achieve organizational goals	0.05	0.09	**0.71**	0.13	0.09	0.32
Often exhibits very unique behavior that surprises other members of the organization	0.03	0.04	**0.68**	0.15	–0.09	–0.06
Personal risk						
In pursuing organizational objectives, engages in activities involving considerable personal risk	0.13	0.08	0.24	**0.81**	0.04	0.18
In pursuing organizational objectives, engages in activities involving considerable self-sacrifice	0.12	0.04	0.08	**0.73**	0.00	0.01
Takes high personal risk for the sake of the organization	0.12	0.07	0.18	**0.78**	0.14	0.18
Often incurs high personal costs for the good of the organization	0.13	0.09	0.11	**0.78**	0.12	0.02
Sensitivity to member needs						
Shows sensitivity for the needs and feelings of other members in the organization	0.06	0.25	–0.08	0.04	**0.86**	–0.02
Influences others by developing mutual liking and respect	0.15	0.20	–0.06	0.04	**0.79**	–0.02
Often expresses personal concern for the needs and feelings of other members of the organization	0.15	0.20	0.00	0.18	**0.80**	–0.07
Does not maintain status quo						
Tries to maintain the status quo or the normal way of doing things	0.12	0.10	0.16	0.09	–0.06	**0.75**
Advocates following nonrisky, well-established courses of action to achieve organizational goals	–0.03	–0.07	0.22	0.13	0.11	**0.73**

SOURCE: Adapted from "Charismatic Leadership in Organizations: Perceived Behavioral Attributes and Their Measurement" (pp. 448-449), Conger and Kanungo, *Journal of Organizational Behavior.* © 1994 by John Wiley & Sons Limited. Reproduced with permission.
NOTE: $N = 488$.

tional behavior (item loadings 0.68 to 0.79) and *personal risk* (Stage 3 of our model; item loadings 0.73 to 0.81), respectively. The fifth (three items) and sixth (two items) factors were respectively *sensitivity to organizational members'*

TABLE 3.7 Reliability Indexes, Means, and Standard Deviations for the Six
Subscales

	Alpha	Mean	S.D.	Test-Retest Reliability
Vision and articulation (six items)	0.84	27.14	4.89	0.80
Environmental sensitivity (seven items)	0.81	33.24	4.71	0.70
Unconventional behavior (three items)	0.74	10.95	3.36	0.73
Personal risk (four items)	0.83	15.74	4.12	0.72
Sensitivity to member needs (three items)	0.83	13.53	3.05	0.84
Does not maintain status quo (two items)	0.62	7.24	2.16	0.69

SOURCE: Adapted from "Charismatic Leadership in Organizations: Perceived Behavioral Attributes and
Their Measurement" (p. 449), Conger and Kanungo, *Journal of Organizational Behavior*. © 1994 by John
Wiley & Sons Limited. Reproduced with permission.

needs (item loadings from 0.79 to 0.86) and *action orientation away from the
maintenance of the status quo* (item loadings 0.73 and 0.75; Stage 1 of our
model). The eigenvalues were 7.54 (factor 1), 3.73 (factor 2), 1.81 (factor 3),
1.59 (factor 4), 1.41 (factor 5), and 1.25 (factor 6), explaining 60% of the total
variance. Each of the six orthogonal factors represented a subscale measuring a
distinct dimension of the composite Conger-Kanungo scale. The means, standard deviations, and reliability coefficients for these subscales are presented in
Table 3.7.

In a separate study using 75 respondents, the scales were administered twice
with a 2-week interval. The test-retest reliability coefficients were calculated for
each of the subscales, and these results are also presented in Table 3.7. For the
composite Conger-Kanungo scale, the test-retest reliability was 0.69.

Confirmatory Factor Analyses

A confirmatory factor analysis of the items measuring the six dimensions of
the Conger-Kanungo scale was conducted using the maximum likelihood method
of LISREL 7 (Jöreskog & Sörbom, 1988). Using this analysis, two hypothesized
models, one with six factors and the other with a single factor, were compared
for the best fit to the data.

Following a suggestion (Bentler & Chou, 1987) that the total number of
variables preferably should be less than 20 in structural modeling analysis, the
total number of indicators for the six latent variables was reduced from 25 to 13.
For each of the following four latent variables—vision and articulation, envi-

ronmental sensitivity, personal risk, and sensitivity to member needs—two indicators were created by combining items on the basis of content similarity and intercorrelations (Harris, 1991). For the other two latent variables, unconventional behavior and does not maintain status quo, each of the respective individual items (three and two items respectively, as in Table 3.6) served as indicators. Thus, there was a total of 19 variables (13 indicators and 6 latent). The covariance matrix recommended for large samples was used in the analysis (Harris & Schaubroeck, 1990).

The model that hypothesized six factors to underlie the Conger-Kanungo scale of charismatic leadership yielded a $\chi^2(52, N = 488) = 200.30, p < .001$, for a chi-square/degrees of freedom ratio of 3.85, and a goodness-of-fit index of 0.942. Because chi-square is very sensitive to sample size and number of variables, it is not surprising that trivial differences between the present sample and reproduced covariance matrices would result in a significant chi-square value in the present study, which used a sample size of 488 with 19 variables (Bentler, 1980; Brooke, Russell, & Price, 1988). Consequently, the goodness-of-fit index and ratio of chi-square to degrees of freedom can be used to assess the goodness of model fit. Because the goodness-of-fit index is above 0.90 (Jöreskog & Sörbom, 1989) and the ratio is less than 5 (Marsh & Hocevar, 1985), the six-factor model provides a good and acceptable fit to the data. By comparison, the second model, which hypothesized a single factor, provides a very poor fit, with $\chi^2(65, N = 488) = 641.23, p < 0.001$, for a chi-square/degrees of freedom ratio of 9.86, and a goodness-of-fit index of 0.813. The difference between the two models is significant, $\chi^2(13, N = 488) = 440.93, p < .001$, and suggests that the six-factor model provides a significantly better fit to the data.

Convergent and Discriminant Validity of the Conger-Kanungo Scale of Charismatic Leadership

Table 3.8 presents intercorrelations among the five leadership role behavior measures for the total sample. These correlations reveal two distinct clusters, one representing the task-directed role of managers, which primarily emphasizes day-to-day administration and task accomplishment, and the other representing follower-directed roles, which primarily emphasize influencing followers' attitudes and behavior. The relationship of the task-oriented role to the four other follower-directed roles (participative, people-orientated, Bass charisma, and Conger-Kanungo charismatic) are of a lower magnitude (*r*s range from 0.25 to 0.35). The follower-directed roles show significant positive correlation with each other (*r*s range from 0.53 to 0.75). Although perceived as distinct from the task-oriented

TABLE 3.8 Intercorrelations Among Leadership Measures

	1	*2*	*3*	*4*
1. Task-oriented leadership	—			
2. Participative leadership	0.35**	—		
3. People-oriented leadership	0.25**	0.75**	—	
4. Bass charisma	0.34**	0.73**	0.70**	—
5. Conger-Kanungo charismatic leadership	0.26**	0.53**	0.57**	0.69**
Subscales				
Vision and articulation (six items)	0.27**	0.47**	0.44**	0.62**
Environmental sensitivity (seven items)	0.39**	0.54**	0.52**	0.63**
Unconventional behavior (three items)	−0.03	−0.05	0.05	0.06
Personal risk (four items)	0.16**	0.24**	0.31**	0.42**
Sensitivity to member needs (three items)	0.15**	0.71**	0.75**	0.60**
Does not maintain status quo (two items)	−0.18**	−0.08	0.02	0.14**

SOURCE: Adapted from "Charismatic Leadership in Organizations: Perceived Behavioral Attributes and Their Measurement" (p. 450), Conger and Kanungo, *Journal of Organizational Behavior.* © 1994 by John Wiley & Sons Limited. Reproduced with permission.
**$p < 0.01$.

role, the Conger-Kanungo scale measuring charismatic leadership is positively related to the other leadership measures such as Bass charisma, participation, and people orientation. The Conger-Kanungo scale has its highest correlation with the Bass scale ($r = 0.69$) and its lowest correlation with task orientation measures ($r = 0.26$), suggesting convergent and discriminant validities of the scale, respectively.

The Unique Features of the Conger-Kanungo Scale

The correlations of each of the Conger-Kanungo charismatic leadership subscales with other perceived leadership behavior measures are also presented in Table 3.8. These correlations further illustrate the distinctive nature of the charismatic leadership construct in the Conger-Kanungo model and the Conger-Kanungo scale as its operational measure. For example, although the charismatic leadership role as measured by Bass scale is moderately associated with articu-

TABLE 3.9 Stepwise Regression Analysis With Conger-Kanungo Dimensions as Independent and Other Leadership Scales as Dependent Variables

	Task		*Participative*		*People*		*Bass*	
	Partial R^2	F	*Partial* R^2	F	*Partial* R^2	F	*Partial* R^2	F
Vision and articulation	—	—	0.01	10.85	—	—	0.06	72.40
Environmental sensitivity	0.15	85.18	0.06	62.53	0.03	41.46	0.40	319.33
Unconventional behavior	—	—	—	—	—	—	—	—
Personal risk	—	—	—	—	0.02	22.68	0.02	28.59
Sensitivity to member needs	—	—	0.50	488.58	0.56	618.31	0.12	122.40
Does not maintain status quo	0.05	28.51	0.01	16.01	—	—	—	—

SOURCE: Adapted from "Charismatic Leadership in Organizations: Perceived Behavioral Attributes and Their Measurement" (p. 450), Conger and Kanungo, *Journal of Organizational Behavior*. © 1994 by John Wiley & Sons Limited. Reproduced with permission.
NOTE: All *F* values significant below 0.001 level.

lation and vision ($r = 0.62$), personal risk ($r = 0.42$), and environmental sensitivity factors ($r = 0.63$), all other types of leadership roles are associated with these factors to a lesser extent (*r*s = 0.27 to 0.47 in the case of articulation and vision, *r*s = 0.16 to 0.31 in the case of personal risk, and *r*s = 0.39 to 0.54 in the case of environmental sensitivity). In the charismatic role, there is some emphasis on changing the status quo ($r = 0.14$), whereas in the task role, the emphasis is on maintaining the status quo ($r = -0.18$).

To avoid the problems of multicollinearity in interpreting the correlations of the Conger-Kanungo subscales with the other four leadership role measures in Table 3.8, four separate stepwise regression analyses were performed—one for each leadership role measure as the dependent variable. The partial R^2 and F ratios are presented in Table 3.9. Clearly, in the task-oriented role, environmental sensitivity is an important factor. Sensitivity to member needs explains a large amount of variance in the participative and people-oriented roles. In the Bass scale of charismatic leadership, sensitivity to the environment and member needs explain a significant portion of the variance. Vision and articulation and the personal risk factors are of lesser importance. The dimensions of unconventional behavior and negative orientation toward the status quo do not account for variance in the Bass scale.

TABLE 3.10 LISREL Estimates of Relations Between Conger-Kanungo
Dimensions and Other Leadership Measures

	Task	Participative	People	Bass
Vision and articulation	0.087	0.155***	0.060	0.255***
Environmental sensitivity	0.408***	0.252***	0.183***	0.322***
Unconventional behavior	−0.056	−0.047	0.029	−0.61**
Personal risk	0.088**	0.065*	0.106**	0.147***
Sensitivity to member needs	−0.076*	0.445***	0.542***	0.270***
Does not maintain status quo	−0.167***	−0.095***	−0.034	0.028

SOURCE: Adapted from "Charismatic Leadership in Organizations: Perceived Behavioral Attributes and
Their Measurement" (p. 451), Conger and Kanungo, *Journal of Organizational Behavior*. © 1994 by John
Wiley & Sons Limited. Reproduced with permission.
*$p < .05$. **$p < .01$. ***$p < 0.001$.

The LISREL estimates of the relationships between the Conger-Kanungo
subscales and other leadership measures corresponding to the stepwise regression analysis are presented in Table 3.10. The results from the LISREL analysis
provide unbiased estimates and are consistent with the regression analysis. They
support the following conclusions. First, four of the Conger-Kanungo dimensions (vision and articulation, environmental sensitivity, personal risk, and
sensitivity to member needs) have positive relations with the Bass scale, but the
other two dimensions (unconventional behavior and does not maintain status
quo) constitute unique features of the Conger-Kanungo scale that make it a more
comprehensive measure of charismatic leadership. This observation is consistent
with what we described earlier as some of the overlap between the charismatic
and transformational formulations, especially on the vision and member/
follower sensitivity dimensions. The absence of additional leader behavior
dimensions in Bass's scale points to the restrictive nature of the formulation of
the transformational forms. Second, sensitivity to environment seems to have
positive relations with all the other leadership measures. Third, sensitivity to
member needs is an important feature in the participative, people, and Bass
scales. Finally, vision and articulation, unconventional behavior, personal risk,
and striving to change the status quo seem to constitute the major features that
distinguish charismatic leadership as measured by the Conger-Kanungo scale
from the other forms of leadership measures.

Refinement of the Conger-Kanungo Scale

Although the analysis described above revealed sound psychometric properties of the measure, with adequate reliability, convergent and discriminant validity coefficients, and a stable six-factor structure, an attempt was made to refine and shorten the Conger-Kanungo scale. In this attempt, a number of concerns were addressed. The first set of concerns dealt with the issues of dimensionality, parsimony, and scale brevity. In the principal components analysis described earlier, the six factors were selected on the basis of the "eigenvalue > 1" rule. An examination of the wording of individual items and associated factor loadings, however, suggested possible item redundancy and fewer factors. Analysis of the factor loadings (Table 3.6) revealed several items with significant loadings on more than one factor. For example, the item "readily recognizes new environmental opportunities" was classified under Factor 2 (environmental sensitivity) based on a factor loading of .45; however, this item has a loading of .53 on Factor 1 (vision and articulation). In addition, both items constituting Factor 6 (does not maintain status quo) were reverse coded, raising the possibility that the emergence of this factor may be an artifact. Finally, in the interest of scale brevity, it was worthwhile to examine the 25 scale items for undue redundancy.

The 25 items in Table 3.6 were subjected to scrutiny for possible redundancies. Based on the wording of items and the factor loadings in the original principal components analysis, it was decided to drop the two reverse-coded items forming the factor "does not maintain status quo." This eliminated the possibility that the emergence of these two items as a separate factor was an artifact. Moreover, the import of the two items is captured to some extent by other items. For example, the significance of the reverse-coded item "tries to maintain the status quo or the normal way of doing things" is reflected to an extent in the item "uses nontraditional means to achieve organizational goals." Three more items were dropped using this latter logic. For example, the item "appears to be a skillful performer when presenting to a group" was dropped because this notion is largely captured by the item "exciting public speaker." The above exercise resulted in a shortened scale of 20 items.

Based on their wording, these 20 items were then reclassified into five subscales (see Table 3.11) based largely on the behavioral subdimensions suggested by the Conger-Kanungo model described earlier. Seven items were hypothesized to constitute the first factor, strategic vision and articulation (SVA; Stage 2 of the Conger-Kanungo model). The first five of these items were earlier classified under the original factor "vision and articulation," whereas the latter two items were earlier classified under "environmental sensitivity." This group-

TABLE 3.11 The Refined Conger-Kanungo Scale of Charismatic Leadership

Strategic Vision and Articulation (SVA)

1. Provides inspiring strategic and organizational goals.
2. Inspirational; able to motivate by articulating effectively the importance of what organizational members are doing.
3. Consistently generates new ideas for the future of the organization.
4. Exciting public speaker.
5. Has vision; often brings up ideas about possibilities for the future.
6. Entrepreneurial; seizes new opportunities in order to achieve goals.
7. Readily recognizes new environmental opportunities (favorable physical and social conditions) that may facilitate achievement of organizational objectives.

Sensitivity to the Environment (SE)

8. Readily recognizes constraints in the physical environment (technological limitations, lack of resources, etc.) that may stand in the way of achieving organizational objectives.
9. Readily recognizes constraints in the organization's social and cultural environment (cultural norms, lack of grassroots support, etc.) that may stand in the way of achieving organizational objectives.
10. Recognizes the abilities and skills of other members of the organization.
11. Recognizes the limitations of other members of the organization.

Sensitivity to Member Needs (SMN)

12. Influences others by developing mutual liking and respect.
13. Shows sensitivity for the needs and feelings of the other members in the organization.
14. Often expresses personal concern for the needs and feelings of other members in the organization.

Personal Risk (PR)

15. Takes high personal risks for the sake of the organization.
16. Often incurs high personal cost for the good of the organization.
17. In pursuing organizational objectives, engages in activities involving considerable personal risk.

Unconventional Behavior (UB)

18. Engages in unconventional behavior in order to achieve organizational goals.
19. Uses nontraditional means to achieve organizational goals.
20. Often exhibits very unique behavior that surprises other members of the organization.

ing reflects the fact that environmental assessment and the formulation of a strategic vision are intimately related. The leader's vision arises from an assessment of environmental opportunities that either have yet to be exploited or have been only partially explored. The vision is in essence a strategic targeting of these opportunities.

Four items were hypothesized to constitute the second factor, sensitivity to the environment (SE; Stage 1 of the Conger-Kanungo model). These items were originally classified under the factor "environmental sensitivity." Three items each were hypothesized to constitute the factors sensitivity to member needs (SMN; Stage 1 of the model), personal risk (PR; Stage 3 of the model), and unconventional behavior (UB; Stage 3 of the model). These classifications are in line with the original classification of these items under the original factors sensitivity to member needs, personal risk, and unconventional behavior, respectively.

The five-factor model proposed above was then tested through a confirmatory factor analysis using LISREL 7. Convergent and discriminant validities of the subscales were assessed by testing a structural model using LISREL 7, with the subscales as exogenous latent constructs and the four other leadership scales (task-oriented, participative, people-oriented, and Bass charisma) as endogenous latent variables.

Results of the Refinement

Confirmatory factor analysis of the 20-item five-factor model yielded a $\chi^2(160) = 458.06$, $p = .000$. Comparison to an absolute null model with $\chi^2(190) = 4118.54$, $p = .000$, yielded a Normed Fit Index (NFI) of .89 and a Non-Normed Fit Index (NNFI) of .91 (see Medsker, Williams, & Holahan [1994] for the method of calculation of these indexes). This was considered a very good fit considering the large sample size of more than 400. The Cronbach's alpha reliabilities of the individual subscales were .87 (SVA), .77 (SE), .84 (SMN), .85 (PR), and .74 (UB).

Convergent and Discriminant Validity

Because the five subscales of the Conger-Kanungo scale are hypothesized to be tapping different behavioral dimensions, they can be expected to have differing relationships with the four other leadership scales included in Study 2. For example, given the nature of the two constructs, the subscale "strategic vision and articulation" (SVA) should be positively related to the Bass charisma scale (BASS). By the same token, given the context and scope of leader behaviors associated with formulation and articulation of a strategic vision, SVA should not be strongly related to leadership scales such as "task-oriented," "people-oriented," and "participative," which are more concerned with day-to-day, routine organizational matters. Similarly, the assessment of the internal environment of the organization is a component of successful task leadership; therefore, the subscale "sensitivity to the environment" should be strongly and

TABLE 3.12 LISREL (Gamma) Estimates of Relationships Between the Refined
Conger-Kanungo Subscales and Other Leadership Scales

Leadership Scales	SVA	SE	SMN	PR	UB
BASS	.381***	.209**	.248***	.214***	−.099***
TASK	.044	.580***	−.204***	.133	−.113**
PPL	.043	.070	.682***	.143**	.033
PART	.139	.209*	.485***	.035	−.065

SOURCE: Adapted from "Measuring Charisma: Dimensionality and Validity of the Conger-Kanungo Scale
of Charismatic Leadership" (p. 295), Conger, Kanungo, Menon, and Mathur. © 1997 by the *Canadian
Journal of Administrative Sciences*. Reprinted with permission.
NOTE: See Table 3.11 for definitions of subscales.
$*p < .05. **p < .01. ***p < .001.$

positively related to the task-oriented leadership scale (TASK). On the other
hand, the subscale "sensitivity to member needs" (SMN) should be strongly and
positively related to the people-oriented leadership scale (PPL) and the participative leadership scale (PART). Given the oft-suggested dichotomy between
task and relationship orientations, one can then expect a negative relationship
between SMN and TASK leadership. There is no a priori reason to expect
relationships between the subscales "personal risk" (PR) or "unconventional
behavior" (UB) and each of the other leadership scales.

The above hypotheses were tested by a structural latent variable model, with
the five subscales treated as independent exogenous variables and the four other
leadership scales (BASS, TASK, PPL, and PART) treated as dependent, endogenous variables. The alpha reliabilities for these latter scales are .87 (BASS),
.72 (TASK), .81 (PPL), and .81 (PART). Table 3.12 shows the LISREL (gamma)
estimates.

As hypothesized, the subscale "strategic vision and articulation" (SVA) is
positively and significantly related to the Bass charisma scale (BASS). Furthermore, it is not significantly related to any of the other leadership scales. As
expected, the subscale "sensitivity to the environment" (SE) is strongly related
to the task leadership scale (TASK). The hypotheses involving the subscale
"sensitivity to member needs" (SMN) also are substantiated. As hypothesized,
SMN is strongly related to "people-oriented" (PPL) and "participative" (PART)
leadership scales. It also is negatively related to the TASK leadership scale. The
subscales "personal risk" (PR) and "unconventional behavior" (UB) were not
expected to be strongly related to any of the leadership scales. Table 3.12 reveals
that, in general, this expectation is supported. PR is significantly related to the
BASS scale, and UB does not have strong positive relationships with any of the

leadership scales. These results provide evidence of convergent and discriminant validity for the Conger-Kanungo subscales.

This refinement of the Conger-Kanungo scale resulted in a revised 20-item measure of charismatic leadership with five behavioral dimensions measured by five distinct subscales. The alpha reliability of the total scale is .88, justifying its use as an overall measure of charismatic leadership as proposed in the Conger-Kanungo model.

Although the data in Table 3.12 provide evidence of the convergent and discriminant validity of the subscales, there is some evidence of the convergent and discriminant validity of the overall scale. The overall Conger-Kanungo scale has a correlation of .69 with the Bass charisma scale. Table 3.12 reveals that this degree of convergence is attributable to the positive relationship between four of the Conger-Kanungo subscales and the BASS scale. On the other hand, the dimension of "unconventional behavior" differentiates the Conger-Kanungo scale from the Bass scale, as is revealed by the slight but significant negative relationship between the subscale UB and the BASS scale.

Although the confirmatory factor analysis (CFA) supported a five-factor solution with adequate fit, it must be borne in mind that the CFA was performed on the same data collected in Study 2 as was the original principal components analysis. It is necessary, therefore, to replicate this result using other independent samples. This was done in Study 3.

STUDY 3[3]

To reconfirm the five-factor structure and gather additional evidence of the convergent and discriminant validity of the Conger-Kanungo scale, it was decided to conduct another independent study to correlate the Conger-Kanungo scale and its five behavior dimensions to another more recently developed and widely used leadership measure, namely Yukl's (1988) Managerial Practices Survey (MPS).

The MPS assesses managerial behavior on 14 dimensions representing various managerial functions. For the purposes of this study, the dimensions chosen were supporting (5 items), recognizing (6 items), rewarding (3 items), delegating (3 items), consulting (5 items), problem solving (first 4 items from MPS), planning (first 4 items from MPS), monitoring (6 items), inspiring (6 items), and mentoring (4 items). The original 4-point response format was retained.

Method

The study involved administering a questionnaire containing the Conger-Kanungo scale and the above leadership measure to a sample of organizational employees. To minimize possible method bias, the questionnaire was divided into two parts. Part 1 contained the 20-item Conger-Kanungo scale and demographic variables. Part 2 included select items from the MPS. With the cooperation of the human resources department of a large multinational corporation based in the United States, the questionnaire was administered to employees attending a company training program. Participants were asked to describe their superior in terms of the questionnaire items. Participation was voluntary, and respondents were instructed to allow a minimum of 24 hours between the completion of the two parts.

The mean age of the total sample of 103 respondents (66% male) was 39.6 years. Ninety-seven percent had at least a college degree, and 87% were married. The respondents were predominantly from the middle (69%) and senior (30%) levels and were drawn from all functional departments in the organization. Salary levels ranged from $45,000 to $60,000 to more than $85,000. The average number of years worked was 10.8, and the mean job tenure was 2.8 years.

The Conger-Kanungo scale was first subjected to a confirmatory factor analysis (CFA) to reconfirm the five-factor structure. The subscales were then related to the MPS dimensions through a structural latent variable model to test specific convergent and discriminant validity hypotheses.

Analysis and Results

The confirmatory factor analysis (CFA) on the 20-item Conger-Kanungo scale was conducted using the LISREL 7 program. Given the somewhat small sample size (103) and the relatively large number of items (20), there is a possibility that the number of estimated parameters in the model might be too large for the available sample size. The effects of a poor sample size-to-estimator ratio can be minimized by using testlets of composite items. It may be recalled that the subscale "strategic vision and articulation" has seven items. In line with Anderson and Gerbing's (1988) suggestion, three indicators were constructed to represent this subscale by combining items through random assignment (see Shore, Barksdale, and Shore [1995] for an example of this technique). For the subscale "sensitivity to the environment" with four items, one composite indicator was constructed by combining two randomly selected items. The remaining two items were retained as indicators, unaltered. The three other subscales have three items each, and these were retained as the respective indicators. Thus, all five subscales were represented by three indicators apiece.

The CFA resulted in a model with $\chi^2(80) = 103.27$, $p = .041$. Comparison to an absolute null model with $\chi^2(105) = 698.77$ yielded a Normed Fit Index (NFI) of .85 and a Non-Normed Fit Index (NNFI) of .95. These results lend support for the five-factor structure discussed earlier. The alpha reliabilities of the five subscales were .86 (strategic vision and articulation), .72 (sensitivity to the environment), .75 (sensitivity to member needs), .85 (personal risk), and .81 (unconventional behavior). The alpha reliability of the overall 20-item Conger-Kanungo scale was .87.

Convergent and Discriminant Validity

Evidence of convergent and discriminant validity can be assessed by relating the Conger-Kanungo subscales to the various MPS subscales. It is expected that the Conger-Kanungo subscales should be differentially related to the MPS subscales. For example, the subscale "strategic vision and articulation" (SVA) should correlate highly with the MPS subscale "inspiring" (INS) while having a low correlation with the MPS subscale "monitoring" (MON). This hypothesis is based on the expectation that the intent of leader behaviors classified as "strategic vision and articulation" is to inspire employees, whereas monitoring is a more mundane managerial function. On the other hand, the Conger-Kanungo subscale "sensitivity to the environment" (SE) should correlate highly with MPS subscales associated with activities involving the assessment of the internal environment of the organization such as "monitoring" (MON), "problem-solving" (PRB), and "recognizing" (RCG). With regard to the other Conger-Kanungo subscales, one can expect the subscale "sensitivity to member needs" (SMN) to correlate highly with the MPS subscale "supporting" (SUP). There is no a priori reason to expect significant relationships between the subscales "personal risk" (PR) or "unconventional behavior" (UB) and any of the MPS subscales. These two Conger-Kanungo subscales constitute the distinguishing features of the Conger-Kanungo scale.

The above hypotheses were tested by a structural latent variable model using LISREL 7, with the five subscales treated as independent exogenous variables and the MPS subscales (INS, MON, PRB, RCG, and SUP) treated as dependent, endogenous variables. The alpha reliabilities for these latter scales are .87 (INS), .75 (MON), .81 (PRB), .87 (RCG), and .87 (SUP). Table 3.13 shows the LISREL (gamma) estimates.

TABLE 3.13 LISREL (Gamma) Estimates of the Relationships Between Conger-Kanungo Subscales and MPS Subscales

MPS Subscales	SVA	SE	SMN	PR	UB
INS	.400***	.167	−.041	.063	.067
MON	−.064	.503***	−.112	−.045	.033
PRB	.111	.515**	−.175	−.058	.083
RCG	.132	.477**	−.079	.001	.016
SUP	−.143	−.080	.706***	−.100	.171*

SOURCE: Adapted from "Measuring Charisma: Dimensionality and Validity of the Conger-Kanungo Scale of Charismatic Leadership" (p. 297), Conger, Kanungo, Menon, and Mathur. © 1997 by the *Canadian Journal of Administrative Sciences*. Reprinted with permission.
NOTE: See Table 3.11 for definitions of subscales.
*p < .05. **p < .01. ***p < .001.

As hypothesized, the Conger-Kanungo subscale "strategic vision and articulation" (SVA) is significantly and strongly related to the MPS subscale "inspiring" (INS). Furthermore, it is not significantly related to MPS subscales such as "monitoring" (MON) or "problem solving" (PRB). On the other hand, the Conger-Kanungo subscale "sensitivity to the environment" (SE) is strongly related to the MPS subscales "monitoring" (MON), "problem solving" (PRB), and "recognizing" (RCG), as hypothesized. In line with expectations, the Conger-Kanungo subscale "sensitivity to member needs" (SMN) is strongly and significantly related to the MPS subscale "supporting" (SUP). Finally, as hypothesized, the Conger-Kanungo subscales "personal risk" (PR) and "unconventional behavior" (UB) are not significantly related to any of the MPS subscales, with the exception of "supporting" (SUP), which shows a mild positive relationship with "unconventional behavior" (UB).

Overall, the results provide support for the five-factor structure of the Conger-Kanungo scale using an independent sample. The subscales as well as the overall Conger-Kanungo scale have good to excellent alpha reliabilities that range from .72 to .87. Convergent and discriminant validity were demonstrated by the distinct pattern of relationships between the Conger-Kanungo subscales and the subscales of the MPS.

STUDY 4: A TEST OF DISCRIMINATORY POWER OF THE CONGER-KANUNGO SCALE[4]

Once the Conger-Kanungo scale's dimensionality, reliability, and validity were established in two independent studies (Studies 2 and 3), it was thought appropriate to further test the discriminatory power of the scale as a diagnostic measure of charismatic leadership. Study 4 was conducted to serve this purpose.

The purpose of Study 4 was to assess if the Conger-Kanungo scale of charismatic leadership is able to discriminate between charismatic and non-charismatic leaders. The general hypothesis being tested is that if the Conger-Kanungo scale does measure charismatic leadership, then it should be able to differentiate between leaders who have been identified as charismatic or non-charismatic by an independent source or assessment.

The study was conducted in situ at the leadership convention of a major political party in Canada. The convention was held to elect one of five leadership candidates as the leader of the party. The outcome of the leadership contest was highly significant to party members because the new leader would lead the party campaign in the general elections that were forthcoming. Given the then low popularity ratings of the party, members were expected to elect a charismatic leader who could reverse the fortunes of the party and lead it to victory in the elections. Thus, charisma of the leader was a salient attribute in the minds of party members, making the convention an ideal setting for a test using perceived charisma as a criterion variable.

Method

The study was carried out in two stages. Participants in the study were party members who were attending a leadership convention. Ten members (4 women and 6 men) were included in Stage 1 of the study. They formed the initial panel. Their average age was 51 years, and they had been in the party for an average of 19 years. All of them had followed, in person or on TV, at least one of the four nationally televised leadership debates that were held before the convention. These 10 panel members were asked to rate each of the five leadership candidates as being charismatic on a 6-point scale ranging from 1 = *least charismatic* to 6 = *most charismatic*. These data were used to identify the most and least charismatic of the five leadership candidates.

In Stage 2, respondents chosen at random from among party members attending the convention were administered a questionnaire asking them to compare any one of two leaders identified as charismatic in Stage 1, with any one of two leaders identified as noncharismatic. Respondents were not aware of the classification of "charismatic" versus "noncharismatic" established in Stage 1. The questionnaire contained the Conger-Kanungo scale as well as a global single-item measure of charismatic leadership—"overall, he/she is a charismatic leader." The hypothesis being tested was whether the Conger-Kanungo scale could find significant differences in the charismatic behaviors attributed to the two leaders, with the candidate identified by the panel as the most charismatic receiving higher scores on the Conger-Kanungo scale than the candidate identified as the least charismatic by the panel.

The second stage of the study included 71 party members (22 women and 49 men) with an average age of 42 years. They had been in the political party for an average of 17 years, and 92% of them had followed at least one of the leadership debates.

Analysis and Results

In Stage 1, the panel data yielded mean scores for each of the five candidates, serialized 1 to 5. Their respective means were 3.0, 5.5, 5.1, 3.9, and 2.5. A one-way analysis of variance resulted in a significant $F(4, 45) = 406.45$, $p < .001$, indicating that there are significant differences among the means. Post hoc comparisons revealed that the scores of candidates 2 and 3 were not significantly different. These candidates were classified as charismatic leaders. Likewise, the scores of candidates 1 and 5 were not significantly different, and these leaders were classified as noncharismatic. The score for candidate 2 was significantly different from that of candidate 5, $t = 9.091$, $p < .005$, and from that of candidate 1, $t = 6.757$, $p < .005$. Similarly, the score for candidate 3 was significantly different from that of candidate 5, $t = 5.833$, $p < .005$, and from that of candidate 1, $t = 7.580$, $p < .005$.

On the basis of the above results, in Stage 2, respondents were asked to choose either candidate 2 or 3 and compare him or her with either one of candidates 1 or 5. As a manipulation check, the single-item global measure of charisma included in the questionnaire was first examined to see if the classification in Stage 1 was replicated. Comparison of scores on the single-item global measure revealed that the mean score of charismatic leaders (candidates 2 and 3, mean = 5.09) was indeed significantly higher, $t = 8.42$, $p < .001$, than the mean score for noncharismatic leaders (candidates 1 and 5, mean = 3.19).

The data obtained through the questionnaire were then subjected to a multivariate analysis of variance (MANOVA) with the five subscales of the Conger-Kanungo scale as dependent variables, the classifying variable being charismatic versus noncharismatic. The resulting significant F ratio, $F(5, 136) = 8.42$, $p < .001$, indicates that the Conger-Kanungo subscales as a whole can differentiate between charismatic and noncharismatic leaders. Table 3.14 shows the results of the univariate F tests.

TABLE 3.14   MANOVA Results: Univariate *F* Tests With Conger-Kanungo
Subscales as Dependent Variables and Charisma of Leader as the
Classifying Variable

Conger-Kanungo Subscale	Mean Charismatic	Mean Noncharismatic	F(1, 140)
SVA	4.85	3.93	37.68***
SE	4.57	3.94	15.88***
SMN	4.69	3.94	18.74***
PR	4.41	3.97	4.94*
UB	3.78	3.75	0.03

SOURCE: Adapted from "Measuring Charisma: Dimensionality and Validity of the Conger-Kanungo Scale
of Charismatic Leadership" (p. 298), Conger, Kanungo, Menon, and Mathur. © 1997 by the *Canadian
Journal of Administrative Sciences*. Reprinted with permission.
*$p < .05$. ***$p < .001$.

As can be seen in Table 3.14, the *F* ratio is significant for all the subscales
except "unconventional behavior," indicating that each of these subscales can
differentiate between charismatic and noncharismatic leaders. With regard to the
dimension of "unconventional behavior," the absence of significant differences
between charismatic leaders (mean = 3.78) and noncharismatic leaders (mean =
3.75) could result from the fact that this study was conducted in the context of
a political leadership race in which all candidates campaigned on the motto of
changing the status quo and exhibited unconventional behavior.

The above results indicate that the Conger-Kanungo scale can successfully
distinguish between charismatic and noncharismatic leaders in accordance with
designations of charisma by an independent measure. This result also can be
interpreted as evidence of convergent validity, because there is convergence
between charisma as measured by two independent measures, one being the
Conger-Kanungo scale in Stage 2 and the other being the assessment of the panel
of "judges" in Stage 1.

STUDY 5: FURTHER EVIDENCE OF CONVERGENT AND DISCRIMINANT VALIDITY[5]

The robustness of the Conger-Kanungo scale as a measurement device was
further tested in Study 5. The purpose of this study was to gather further evidence

of convergent and discriminant validity of the Conger-Kanungo scale using an alternative research method. This study used independent assessments by two subordinates of the same manager using the Conger-Kanungo scale and the Bass scale. In this sense, the present study is patterned on the classical multitrait, multimethod approach to convergent and discriminant validity advocated by Campbell and Fiske (1959).

Method

This study was conducted in India using independent assessments by subordinates working for the same manager. The design of the study required that the charismatic leadership roles of a given manager be assessed by two randomly selected subordinates directly working under his or her supervision. A total of 49 pairs of male subordinates (each pair reporting to a different manager) participated in the study. These respondents belonged to a large national corporation. The questionnaire containing both the Conger-Kanungo and the Bass scale items was administered to the respondents in their workplace. The respondents were asked to assess their immediate supervisor by filling in the questionnaire.

Analysis and Results

Convergent and discriminant validity hypotheses were tested by constructing the multitrait, multimethod (MTMM) matrix. The two independent assessments were treated as two separate methods, and the Bass scale and the Conger-Kanungo scale (and subscales) were treated as different traits measured by the two methods. The relevant part of the MTMM matrix is shown in Table 3.15.

For convergent validity, correlations of the different measures of the same trait should be statistically significant and sufficiently large (Campbell & Fiske, 1959). As can be seen from Table 13.5, the coefficients along the convergent validity diagonal (in bold) are very large and statistically significant. The correlation between independent measures of the Conger-Kanungo scale is .84, and the correlation between independent measures of the BASS scale is .80. The convergent validity coefficients for the Conger-Kanungo subscales also are large and significant.

Discriminant validity can be established through two separate comparisons, as outlined in Campbell and Fiske (1959). First, the convergent validity coefficients should be greater than the correlations between one variable and any other variable with which it shares neither method nor trait. In the upper left-hand

TABLE 3.15 Convergent and Discriminant Validity: Multitrait, Multimethod Analysis

	Subordinate 1		Subordinate 2					
	C-K	BASS	C-K	SVA	SE	SMN	PR	UB
Subordinate 2								
C-K	**.84**	(.59)	1.00	.91	.86	.80	.76	.70
BASS	(.51)	**.80**	.72	.69	.65	.67	.56	.40**
Subordinate 1								
BASS	.60	1.00	.59	.53	.64	.48**	.42**	.33*
SVA	.89	.57	.75	**.81**	.70	.48	.37*	.60
SE	.87	.57	.70	.65	**.82**	.48	.37**	.46**
SMN	.77	.68	.69	.63	.67	**.59**	.42**	.52
PR	.71	.37**	.62	.41**	.41**	.44**	**.79**	.53
UB	.73	$.21^{ns}$	.64	.54	.49	.35*	.50	**.71**

SOURCE: Adapted from "Measuring Charisma: Dimensionality and Validity of the Conger-Kanungo Scale of Charismatic Leadership" (p. 299), Conger, Kanungo, Menon, and Mathur. © 1997 by the *Canadian Journal of Administrative Sciences*. Reprinted with permission.
ns = nonsignificant. *$p < .05$. **$p < .01$. All other correlations significant at $p < .001$.

corner of Table 3.15, one can see that the convergent validity coefficients of .84 and .80 are greater than both the correlations (circled) between the Conger-Kanungo scale (Subordinate 1) and Bass scale (Subordinate 2), which is .51, and the correlation between the Conger-Kanungo scale (Subordinate 2) and Bass scale (Subordinate 1), which is .59. The second comparison requires that the convergent validity coefficients should be greater than correlations of different traits measured with the same method. From Table 3.15, one can see that the correlation (boxed) between the Conger-Kanungo and Bass scales is .60 as assessed by Subordinate 1 and .72 as assessed by Subordinate 2. Both these correlations are less than the convergent validity coefficients of .84 and .80, thus satisfying the second criterion for discriminant validity.

The above MTMM approach provides conclusive evidence of the convergent and discriminant validity of the 20-item Conger-Kanungo scale. Table 3.15 also shows the correlations between the Bass scale and the Conger-Kanungo subscales. As can be seen, the largest points of divergence between the scales are the two subscales of "personal risk" (PR) and "unconventional behavior" (UB), which have lower correlations with the Bass scale than do the three other Conger-Kanungo subscales, "strategic vision and articulation" (SVA), "sensitivity to the environment" (SE), and "sensitivity to member needs" (SMN). As suggested in previous sections, the subscales of "personal risk" and "unconventional behavior" constitute the unique features of the Conger-Kanungo scale of charismatic leadership.

STUDY 6: CHARISMATIC LEADERSHIP
EFFECTS ON FOLLOWERS

When subordinates perceive leadership behaviors (as specified in the Conger-Kanungo model) exhibited by their manager, they not only attribute charisma to him or her (follower attribution effect) but also change their attitudes, values, and behavior consistent with what the manager wants from them. Such a leadership influence of a manager on subordinates is referred to as a follower outcomes effect. These outcomes are noticed in subordinates' beliefs, attitudes, and behaviors on two fronts. A manager's leadership behaviors can influence subordinates' reactions toward both the manager as a leader and the task that needs to be accomplished. Several hypotheses with respect to follower outcomes are listed in Chapter 2, Table 2.2. Study 6 was designed to test some of these hypotheses, as presented below. The first three hypotheses relate to subordinates' beliefs and attitudes toward the manager as a leader, and the next three hypotheses relate to their beliefs and attitudes concerning the task. It is hypothesized that charismatic leadership behaviors of a manager will increase the subordinates' (H1) sense of reverence for the manager, (H2) trust in the manager, and (H3) satisfaction with the manager. Furthermore, it is hypothesized that the charismatic behavior of a manager will increase subordinates' (H4) sense of work group solidarity or cohesion, (H5) sense of task efficacy or task achievement, and (H6) feeling of personal empowerment in work contexts.

Method

The study was conducted using 252 managers of a large manufacturing conglomerate attending training sessions in the United States (unrelated to the sample in Study 3). Most of the respondents were male (94%), were married (86%), and had a college degree (80%). The mean age of the respondents was 42.5 years ($SD = 6.89$). The mean organizational tenure was 13.62 years ($SD = 8.86$), and the mean job tenure was 2.9 years ($SD = 2.74$). The respondents were asked to answer a questionnaire in two parts. Part 1 contained the charismatic leadership scale and demographic items, and Part 2 contained measures to assess six other variables: reverence, trust, satisfaction with leader, group cohesion, task efficacy, and empowerment. Part 2 of the questionnaire was administered 24 hours after the administration of Part 1 to minimize method variance.

In Part 1 of the questionnaire, the respondents assessed the charismatic leadership (CHRSMA) of their superior (or leader) by responding to the 20-item Conger-Kanungo scale of charismatic leadership (see Table 3.11). In this case, a 6-point "very characteristic" to "very uncharacteristic" response format was used.

In Part 2 of the questionnaire, reverence for the leader (REV) was measured by the following three items: "I hold him/her in high respect," "I have great esteem for him/her," and "I admire him/her as a leader." Trust in the leader (TRU) was measured by items taken from Bass (1985) and Butler (1991). The items were "I have complete faith in him/her" (Bass, 1985), "Sometimes I cannot trust him/her" (reverse scored; Butler, 1991), and "I can count on him/her to be trustworthy" (Butler, 1991). Satisfaction with the leader (LSAT) was measured by three items based on Bass (1985). The items were "I feel good to be around him/her," I am satisfied that his/her type of leadership is the right one for getting our group's job done," and "I am pleased (or satisfied) with his/her leadership." The above three variables had a focus on the attitude toward the leader (leader focus variables). Among the three other variables that had a task focus, task group solidarity or cohesion (COH) was measured by the following five items: "We see ourselves in the work group as a cohesive team," "In our work group, our conflict is out in the open and is constructively handled," "Members of our organizational unit share the same values about our task and purpose," "Among our work group, we are remarkably similar in our values about what has to be done," and "There is widely shared consensus about our goals and the approaches needed to achieve them." Task efficacy (TSK) also was measured by five items. The items were "We have high work performance," "Most of our tasks are accomplished quickly and efficiently," "We always set a high standard of task accomplishment," "We always achieve a high standard of task accomplishment," and "We almost always beat our targets." Empowerment (EMP) was measured by Menon's 15-item subjective empowerment scale (Menon & Borg, 1995). A 6-point "strongly agree" to "strongly disagree" response format was used for all items in Part 2 of the questionnaire.

Results

Table 3.16 shows the means, standard deviations, scale reliabilities, and bivariate correlations of all the variables. As can be seen, all measures have acceptable reliabilities. Structural equation modeling using the LISREL 7 program was used to test the two sets of hypotheses with respect to subordinates' attitudes toward leader and task. Because the number of items in some of the scales was relatively large (e.g., 20 items in the charisma scale, 15 items in the empowerment scale), it is possible that the number of estimated parameters in a given model might be too large for the available sample size. To minimize this possibility, composite indicators were used to represent scales with more than three items (see Anderson and Gerbing [1988] for a discussion of this technique). For example, charisma was represented by three indicators, formed by combining the 20 items through random assignment. First, the 20 items were randomly assigned into three groups, two groups of seven items and one group of six items. Individual items in each group were then combined to obtain the three composite indicators (see Shore et al., 1995, for a recent illustration of this technique).

Hypotheses Testing

To test the hypotheses involving charisma and the leader focus variables, a saturated structural model with uncorrelated errors and disturbances (Medsker, Williams, & Holahan, 1994) was set up with charisma (CHRSMA) as the exogenous latent variable. This model, which allows for all possible unidirectional relationships between the variables charisma (CHRSMA), reverence (REV), trust (TRU), and satisfaction with the leader (LSAT), had a $\chi^2(48)$ of 128.22, with a goodness-of-fit index (GFI) of .914 and a root mean square residual (rmsr) of .039.

To test the various hypotheses, the following strategy was adopted. First, the coefficient corresponding to the hypothesis in question was set to zero. The resulting model was then compared with the saturated model using a single degree of freedom chi-square difference test to see if the two models were significantly different. For example, to test hypothesis H1, the coefficient γ_{11} representing the direct relationship between charisma and reverence (see Figure 3.1) was set to zero. The resulting model had a $\chi^2(49)$ of 197.38, with a goodness-of-fit index (GFI) of .885 and a root mean square residual (rmsr) of .109. Compared with the saturated model, the chi-square difference ($df = 1$) is 69.16, which is highly significant. This indicates that the coefficient γ_{11} is significantly different from zero. From the sign and magnitude of this coefficient in the saturated model, we can then conclude that hypothesis H1, which predicts a positive relationship between charismatic behavior and reverence, is strongly supported. The complete results of the hypothesis testing are available in Table 3.17.

As can be seen from Table 3.17, hypotheses H2 and H3 are not supported because the reduced models obtained by setting the appropriate coefficients to zero are not significantly different from the saturated model. Thus, in the present

TABLE 3.16 Descriptive Statistics and Intercorrelations

Variable	Mean	S.D.	Alpha	1	2	3	4	5	6
1. Charisma (CHRSMA)	4.50	.50	.82						
2. Reverence (REV)	5.13	.74	.85	.50					
3. Trust (TRU)	3.94	.48	.72	.20**	.39				
4. Satisfaction (LSAT)	5.02	.75	.81	.45	.75	.28			
5. Cohesion (COH)	4.71	.61	.78	.34	.41	.19**	.50		
6. Task efficacy (TSK)	4.83	.61	.85	.35	.42	.16*	.45	.59	
7. Empowerment (EMP)	5.29	.46	.91	.31	.43	.15*	.50	.60	.64

$*p < .05.$ $**p < .01.$ All other correlations significant at $p < .001$.

data set, there is no direct relationship between charismatic behavior and trust or satisfaction. Rather, in this four-variable model, the relationships between charismatic behavior and these two variables respectively seem to be completely mediated by reverence. The relationship between trust and satisfaction is non-significant in the saturated model. As can be seen from Table 3.17, setting the corresponding coefficient to zero does not result in any significant chi-square

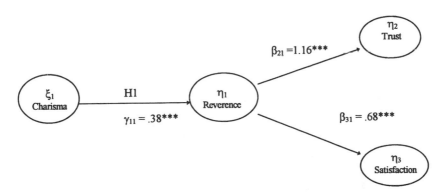

Figure 3.1. Structural Model: Charisma and Leader Focus Variables

NOTE: The coefficients correspond to the model with γ_{21}, γ_{31}, and β_{32} constrained to zero.
$***p < .001.$

TABLE 3.17 Results of Hypothesis Testing: Leader Focus Variables[a]

Model/ Constraints	γ_{11}	γ_{21}	γ_{31}	β_{21}	β_{31}	β_{32}	χ^2	df	Goodness-of-Fit Index	Mean Square Residual	χ^2_{diff}
1. Saturated structural model	.39***	-.00	-.04	.69***	1.30***	-.12	128.22	48	.914	.039	—
2. $\gamma_{11} = 0$	—	.05	.06	.63***	1.16***	-.06	197.38	49	.885	.109	69.16
3. $\gamma_{21} = 0$	.39***	—	-.04	.68***	1.29***	-.11	128.23	49	.914	.039	0.01^{ns}
4. $\gamma_{31} = 0$	.38***	.00	—	.68***	1.23***	-.09	128.68	49	.914	.038	$.046^{ns}$
5. "True Model" $\gamma_{21}, \gamma_{31}, \beta_{32} = 0$	.38***	—	—	.68***	1.16***	—	128.88	51	.913	.038	$.66^{ns}$

a. The corresponding model is depicted in Figure 3.1.
ns = nonsignificant. ***$p < .001$.

difference compared with the saturated model. Thus, the "true model" or the model that best represents this particular data set is as shown in Figure 3.1.

A similar procedure was used to test hypotheses H4 to H6 involving the task focus variables. First, a saturated structural model with all possible unidirectional relationships between charisma (CHRSMA) and the variables task group solidarity or cohesion (COH), task efficacy (TSK), and empowerment (EMP) was set up. This model had a $\chi^2(48)$ of 127.63, with a goodness-of-fit index (GFI) of .920 and a root mean square residual (rmsr) of .021. Hypotheses H4 to H6 were then individually tested by setting the appropriate coefficient of the direct path from CHRSMA to each of the other variables to zero, one variable at a time. The results of this analysis are shown in Table 3.18.

The chi-square difference test reveals that the coefficients γ_{11} and γ_{12}, corresponding to hypotheses H4 and H5 respectively, are significantly different from zero. Hypotheses H4 and H5 therefore are supported. On the other hand, because coefficient γ_{31} is not significantly different from zero, hypothesis H6 is not supported. Given that all the other coefficients are significant in the saturated model, the "true model" or the model that best represents this data set is depicted in Figure 3.2. Charismatic leader behavior is directly related to task group cohesion and task efficacy. These two variables in turn completely mediate the relationship between charismatic behavior and subjective empowerment in this four-variable model.

Thus, charismatic leader behavior seems to directly generate in followers a feeling of reverence, a sense of task group solidarity or cohesion, and a sense of task efficacy. In the following section, we shall investigate which particular aspect of charismatic behavior leads to the above three outcomes.

Subscale Analysis

The Conger-Kanungo scale of charismatic leadership has five subscales: strategic vision and articulation (SVA), sensitivity to the environment (SE), sensitivity to member needs (SMN), personal risk (PR), and unconventional behavior (UB) (see Table 3.11). To confirm the existence of these five subscales in the present data set, the 20-item Conger-Kanungo scale was subjected to a principal components factor analysis using varimax rotation with a five-factor solution. Table 3.19 shows the results of the factor analysis. The pattern of factor loadings in Table 3.19 replicates the pattern of factor loadings observed in Study 2 and Study 3.

Table 3.20 shows the means, standard deviations, scale reliabilities, and intercorrelations among the subscales. Bivariate correlations between the subscales

TABLE 3.18 Results of Hypothesis Testing: Follower Focus Variables[a]

Model/Constraints	γ_{11}	γ_{21}	γ_{31}	β_{21}	β_{31}	β_{32}	χ^2	df	Goodness-of-Fit Index	Root Mean Square Residual	χ^2_{diff}
1. Saturated structural model	.23***	.10*	.01	.64***	.29***	.35***	127.63	48	.920	.021	—
2. $\gamma_{11} = 0$	—	.13***	.02	.64***	.28***	.35***	155.74	49	.906	.049	28.11***
3. $\gamma_{21} = 0$	.25***	—	.01	.74***	.30***	.33***	133.60	49	.917	.024	5.97*
4. $\gamma_{31} = 0$	.23***	.10*	—	.64***	.29***	.36***	127.85	49	.919	.021	0.22^{ns}

a. The corresponding model is depicted in Figure 3.2.
All χ^2 values are significant at $p < .001$. Unmarked gamma and beta coefficients are not significant. For other statistics, ns = nonsignificant. *$p < .05$. ***$p < .001$.

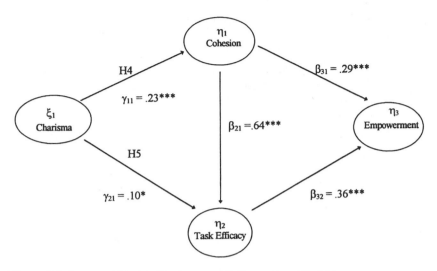

Figure 3.2. Structural Model: Charisma and Follower Focus Variables
NOTE: The coefficients correspond to the model with γ_{31} constrained to zero.
$*p < .05.$ $***p < .001.$

and the three outcome variables—reverence, task group cohesion, and task efficacy—also are presented in Table 3.20. To examine the relative strength of the relationships between the subscales and each of the above three outcome variables, three separate multiple regression analyses were conducted. In each, one of the outcome variables, respectively, was the dependent variable and the five subscales were independent variables. The results of the regression analysis are presented in Table 3.21.

As can be seen from Table 3.21, the outcome variable reverence is most strongly related to the subscale SE (sensitivity to the environment). Three other subscales—SVA (strategic vision and articulation), SMN (sensitivity to member needs), and PR (personal risk)—also contribute to feelings of reverence. Task group cohesion is related strongly both to strategic vision and articulation and to sensitivity to member needs. Task efficacy, on the other hand, is related to the leader's vision but is more strongly related to the leader's sensitivity to the environment. These dependent variables were not related to the leader's unconventional behavior (UB). The effects of the unconventional behavior of superiors on subordinates therefore needs further exploration in future studies. Perhaps the main effect of unconventional behavior lies in drawing followers' attention to the leader's vision and implementation strategies.

TABLE 3.19 Factor Loadings for Conger-Kanungo Scale Items

Item	Factor 1	Factor 2	Factor 3	Factor 4	Factor 5
Strategic Vision and Articulation (SVA)					
Has vision; often brings up ideas about possibilities for the future	**.79**	.19	.15	−.08	.08
Provides inspiring strategic and organizational goals	**.74**	−.01	.26	−.04	−.05
Consistently generates new ideas for the future of the organization	**.66**	.35	.05	.02	.07
Entrepreneurial; seizes new opportunities in order to achieve goals	**.65**	.10	.04	.00	.20
Readily recognizes new environmental opportunities (favorable physical and social conditions) that may facilitate achievement of organizational objectives	**.58**	.12	.37	.09	.12
Inspirational; able to motivate by articulating effectively the importance of what organizational members are doing	**.58**	.16	.26	.20	.01
Exciting public speaker	**.54**	.02	−.16	.28	.13
Personal Risk (PR)					
In pursuing organizational objectives, engages in activities involving considerable personal risk	.10	**.86**	.05	.07	.20
Takes high personal risks for the sake of the organization	.23	**.81**	.04	.10	.18
Often incurs high personal cost for the good of the organization	.19	**.78**	.08	.12	.09
Sensitivity to the Environment (SE)					
Readily recognizes constraints in the physical environment (technological limitations, lack of resources, etc.) that may stand in the way of achieving organizational objectives	.09	.09	**.74**	.00	−.08
Readily recognizes constraints in the organization's social and cultural environment (cultural norms, lack of grassroots support, etc.) that may stand in the way of achieving organizational objectives	.07	.14	**.71**	.14	−.03
Recognizes the limitations of other members of the organization	.18	−.11	**.60**	.24	.08
Recognizes the abilities and skills of other members of the organization	.35	.01	**.50**	.22	−.01

TABLE 3.19 *Continued*

Item	Factor 1	Factor 2	Factor 3	Factor 4	Factor 5
Sensitivity to Member Needs (SMN)					
Shows sensitivity for the needs and feelings of the other members in the organization	.06	.11	.25	**.78**	−.17
Influences others by developing mutual liking and respect	.09	−.08	.04	**.78**	−.05
Often expresses personal concern for the needs and feelings of other members in the organization	.02	.19	.26	**.76**	−.09
Unconventional Behavior (UB)					
Engages in unconventional behavior in order to achieve organizational goals	.02	.06	−.11	−.04	**.86**
Use nontraditional means to achieve organizational goals	.25	.17	.05	−.10	**.79**
Often exhibits very unique behavior that surprises other members of the organization	.12	.30	.03	−.16	**.61**

CONCLUSION

The studies reported in this chapter used diverse samples from different companies and from different organizational contexts. The studies aimed at establishing the perceived behavioral dimension; the reliability and validity of a measuring instrument, the Conger-Kanungo scale of charismatic leadership; and the effects of charismatic leadership on the follower. Analysis of the 20-item Conger-Kanungo scale as reported in Study 2, the results of Study 3 using the Yukl (1988) MPS scales, and the results of Study 6 support a stable five-factor structure of charismatic leadership in organizations. These studies, conducted in three different countries—Canada, India, and the United States—also provide evidence of the convergent and discriminant validity of the Conger-Kanungo scale for measuring charisma in both political and organizational contexts.

It may be noted that the five-factor solution representing the dimensions of sensitivity to the environment (Stage 1 of the Conger-Kanungo model), sensitivity to member needs (Stage 1), strategic vision and articulation (Stage 2), personal risk (Stage 3), and unconventional behavior (Stage 3) closely parallels Max Weber's (1968) conceptualization of the charismatic leader. To Weber, the charismatic's power was vested in the exceptional nature of the individual's

TABLE 3.20 Conger-Kanungo Subscales: Descriptive Statistics and Intercorrelations

Variable	Mean	S.D.	Alpha	1	2	3	4	5
Conger-Kanungo Subscales								
1. SVA	4.80	.63	.81					
2. SE	4.76	.64	.64	.43				
3. SMN	4.51	.91	.77	.21**	.40			
4. PR	4.15	1.08	.84	.39	.18**	.16*		
5. UB	3.83	1.00	.71	.28	$-.02^{ns}$	$-.20**$	.38	
Outcome Variables								
6. REV	5.13	.74	.85	.41	.49	.35	.30	$.04^{ns}$
7. COH	4.71	.61	.78	.32	.32	.32	$.10^{ns}$	—
8. TSK	4.83	.61	.85	.31	.37	.22**	$.11^{ns}$	$.09^{ns}$

ns = nonsignificant. $*p < .05$. $**p < .01$. All other correlations significant at $p < .001$.

personal gifts and abilities. In the five-factor formulation of the Conger-Kanungo model, followers perceive the exceptional nature of the leader through the leader's behavior corresponding to the dimensions of unconventional behavior and personal risk. Second, according to Weber, charismatic leaders are individuals with a prophetic vision or vision of the future. In the five-factor formulation, this would correspond to the dimension of strategic vision and articulation. Finally, Weber described the charismatic leader as an individual who would "minister" to the needs of the followers. This would require charismatic leaders to be aware of their environments as well as the needs of the followers. This aspect is captured by the dimensions of sensitivity to the environment and sensitivity to member needs in the Conger-Kanungo model.

TABLE 3.21 Regression (Beta) Coefficients

Independent Variables	REV	Dependent COH	Variables TSK
SVA	.17**	.23**	.17*
SE	.33**	.13	.28***
SMN	.16**	.23***	.08
PR	.13*	−.04	−.04
UB	−.02	.01	.09

$*p < .05$. $**p < .01$. $***p < .001$.

The results of the above studies suggest that a five-factor model provides a significantly better fit to both the empirical data reported in this chapter and the theoretical notions advanced by Weber on charismatic leadership.[6] The results reported in this chapter also provide evidence of the construct validity of the Conger-Kanungo scale for measuring charisma. In future studies, the scale can be used not only as a diagnostic tool but also to reveal specific effects of the perceived behavioral components of charismatic leaders on followers' attitudes and behaviors.

In the three chapters that follow, we will illustrate in greater depth the dimensions of charismatic leadership described by the Conger-Kanungo model through more elaborate description and with examples of noted charismatic leaders. We will also expand on our own theory and suggest additional dimensions and nuances not captured by our earlier work. We have organized each chapter around a specific activity corresponding to several of our five factors. For example, Chapter 4 explores the leader's sensitivity to the environment and to member needs, from which the leader then formulates visions and goals for the organization (illustrating sensitivity to the environment, sensitivity to member needs, and a portion of strategic vision and articulation). Chapter 5 analyzes the role of the charismatic leader's vision and how it is articulated and communicated (strategic vision and articulation). Finally, Chapter 6 examines how the leader employs personal risk, unconventional behavior, and other activities to ensure that his or her vision is implemented (personal risk and unconventional behavior). As such, the chapters follow a flow of leadership activities: (1) the search for opportunities in the larger environment and among followers (Chapter 4); (2) the formulation of these opportunities into a strategic vision (Chapter 4); (3) the use of vision to set direction, build commitment, and align the activities of the organization (Chapter 5); and (4) the realization of the vision through leader and follower activities that empower, foster cooperative relations, and encourage unconventional marketplace approaches (Chapter 6).

NOTES

1. This study was reported in Conger and Kanungo (1992). Copyright 1992 Canadian Psychological Association. Reprinted with permission.

2. This study was reported in Conger and Kanungo (1994).

3. This study was reported in Conger and colleagues (1997). Used with permission.

4. This study was reported in Conger and colleagues (1997). Used with permission.

5. This study was reported in Conger and colleagues (1997). Used with permission.

6. We tested six-factor and one-factor models in an earlier study (Conger & Kanungo, 1994, pp. 445-447), and neither proved to be good fits in contrast to the five-factor model.

PART II

COMPONENTS OF CHARISMATIC LEADERSHIP

4

The Leader's Search for Opportunity

Setting direction is one of the primary roles of leadership. To be effective at this activity, the leader must be adept at perceiving not only environmental opportunities but also obstacles that stand in the way. Failure to do so will result in failed ventures and follies that discredit the leader. The leader must then be able to translate these opportunities into organizational goals and enlist organizational members in their achievement. In the enlistment process, the leader must be capable of realistic assessments of followers' needs and abilities and must ensure that targeted opportunities offer rewards meaningful enough to garner follower commitment and task efforts. Charismatic leadership is no exception to these fundamental requirements of leading others.

In the first stage of our leadership model, we described the charismatic leader's heightened sensitivity to environmental opportunities, constraints, and follower abilities. In our empirical research, this sensitivity to the environment was corroborated. We also found that this characteristic was shared with other forms of leadership. In addition, the leader's sensitivity to member needs proved to be a common feature of both participative and people-oriented forms of leadership. As such, these two dimensions of sensitivity are not unique to charismatic leadership but instead are baseline attributes of leading in general. What we did find in the assessment stage that was unique to charismatic leaders was their desire to challenge the status quo and to act as reformers or agents of radical reform. It would appear that they are significantly more sensitive than other leaders both to the constraints inherent in the status quo and to opportunities that run counter to current conventions.

This chapter is devoted to understanding how charismatic leaders assess the state of their environments and from this activity then formulate environmental opportunities into visions and goals. We will first examine what we know about leadership and environmental assessments and the related process of seeking opportunities beyond the status quo. We will follow this discussion with a look at follower assessments by the leader. Although there is widespread agreement about leaders' sensitivity to their environment, there are two schools of thought concerning sensitivity to followers. One line of thinking believes that leaders gain follower commitment to a vision through finding a common denominator between themselves and follower motives (Avolio & Bass, 1988). The other sees visions as shaped largely by external opportunities detected by the leader with little or no influence from follower needs (Locke et al., 1991). We will explore both sides of this debate and provide our own perspective. We will follow this discussion with an examination of how charismatic leaders challenge the status quo around them and the implications of such actions for enhancing follower perceptions of leadership. Finally, we will turn to the complex process of formulating the leader's vision. This is the first step that the leader undertakes in Stage 2 of our model. We include it in this chapter, which is devoted largely to Stage 1 of the model, because it is a natural by-product of the environmental assessment. The formulation process is another area of considerable debate. Popular notions believe it to be largely leader-based. Others feel that vision is shaped by many individuals and by contextual events often far beyond the leader. Some argue that it is a largely rational, planned process. Others see it as a more intuitive, opportunistic process. We will provide some resolution to the debate. In the next chapter, we explore the actual content, articulation, and communication of the vision—the rest of our model's Stage 2.

SENSING OPPORTUNITIES AND CONSTRAINTS
IN THE LARGER ENVIRONMENT

To be effective, a leader must be capable of making realistic assessments of the environment. These assessments will in turn dictate the shape of initiatives and their timing as well as the resources the leader must seek out and where they will be deployed. In Mintzberg's (1973) taxonomy of the 10 roles that managers play, two roles—the monitor and the liaison—describe the activities of leaders in the assessment stage. As Yukl (1994) explains, the monitor role concerns itself with information processing:

> Managers [in this role] continually seek information from a variety of sources, such as reading reports and memos, attending meetings and briefings, and conducting observational tours. . . . Most of the information is analyzed to discover problems and opportunities, and to develop an understanding of outside events and internal processes within the manager's organizational subunit. (pp. 29-30)

Monitoring or assessing is a vital activity for the leader. It ensures that the leader is able to identify not only opportunities but also emerging problems and obstacles to the achievement of goals. Ultimately, the purpose of much of this information gathering is to formulate more effective visions and marketplace strategies and to devise organizational initiatives that will realize these aims. The leader uses this information to set goals and strategies rather than the reverse order of setting goals followed by a later assessment of the environment (Kotter, 1982). Although this would seem like rational behavior, it appears in reality to be infrequently practiced. Instead, as noted by Jan Carlzon, the charismatic former CEO of Scandinavian Airlines,

> Remarkably, many business executives begin by devising goals and strategies, and only later back into an examination of the business climate and the customers' needs. Obviously, this is proceeding in the wrong order. How can you know what your goals or strategies should be if you don't have a clear picture of the environment you're working in or of what your customers want? (Carlzon, 1987, p. 42)

The liaison role concerns itself with the manager's ability to establish relationships with individuals outside the manager's immediate work group. Although this network is crucial for implementing initiatives, it also serves as a rich source of information for the monitoring or assessment role. It is in essence a set of important pipelines bringing information to the leader on markets, customers, competition, the economy, regulation, the organization, and so on (Kotter, 1982).

With a few exceptions, charismatic leaders are more concerned with boundary spanning and adaptation activities (Thompson, 1967) than with activities related to technical efficiency of day-to-day operations. (Those who are not tend to create maladaptive visions at some point in their careers. Examples include Steven Jobs and his NeXT computer and Edwin Land and his SX-70 instant camera.) Their interest lies in constantly maintaining an interface with the larger environment and devising appropriate adaptations or change strategies for organizational survival and growth. For this reason, Pawar and Eastman (1997) propose that transformational leadership will be more accepted in organizations where boundary spanning and adaptive functions are dominant than in organizations where technical and efficiency functions are dominant.

We know from the research literature that active information gathering is directly correlated with organizational effectiveness (Komaki, 1986). For example, in a sample of 128 manufacturing companies, Jenster (1987) discovered that the successful firms were those that both identified and monitored more closely the activities and conditions essential for implementing the firm's strategy. Similarly, Bourgeois (1985), in an examination of 20 nondiversified companies, found that profitability was greater for the organizations whose executives had realistic perceptions of market and technology volatility in their industry. In a comparison of 28 companies that experienced rapid performance improvements with a matched sample of companies with only average performance, Grinyer, Mayes, and McKiernan (1990) discovered that a key difference was that company executives of the high-performing firms conducted more external monitoring and were faster at spotting and acting on opportunities. From these examples, it is clear that active assessment of the environment by a leader is a crucial activity (Yukl, 1994, pp. 103-104).

Although it would seem evident that organizational leaders must be effective at scanning their environments, research shows that many executives in formal leadership positions are not. They are instead strongly influenced by the existing beliefs and assumptions underlying current organizational strategies, and these impede their assessment efforts. As Miller (1990) has shown, the more successful and established an organization's strategy, the more its managers rely on ingrained habits and routines that prevent them from seeing and actively reflecting on new challenges: "Yesterday's programs will shape today's perceptions and give rise to tomorrow's actions" (p. 17). In addition, managers are often risk averse—unwilling to "see" the potential implications of market changes (Miller, 1990). For example, we know that a major shift in strategy generally produces a temporary decline in performance as employees learn new routines and as resources are diverted to invest in new activities (Lord & Maher, 1991). Knowing this, managers are reluctant to deploy new strategies even though long-term environmental conditions may demand them. Pressures for short-term performance simply are too high. Moreover, there are no guarantees of success with any new strategy—short-term declines may become long-term declines because of inappropriate strategic choices. Such concerns then heighten the perceived riskiness of acting on perceptions of environmental changes and can lead to narrow or biased assessments. As a result, what tends to occur is that executives make less risky improvements or incremental changes to the existing strategy rather than questioning it (Staw, Sandelands, & Dutton, 1981). These responses may produce short-term successes that further reinforce perceptions that the executives are effective (Johnson, 1992) despite impending crises. For example, Cooper and Schendel (1976) demonstrated that established firms facing competitive threats of radically new technologies simply increased their efforts at perfecting the existing technology rather than adapting to the new one.

In addition, the extent of growth opportunities in an organization's particular domain may be so high that managers resist considering or acting on market information that suggests that this domain may one day be supplanted (Burgelman, 1991). As a result of these forces, it would appear that visionary leaders who are willing to see and undertake bold initiatives to reinvent their firms are quite rare. In a study of 40 companies in environments undergoing major change, Tushman and Anderson (1986) found that in only 15% of the cases was the current CEO willing to initiate a major reorientation. (We have no way of knowing how many of the six CEOs were charismatic leaders, because the executives' charisma was not measured in the study.) In these six cases, the CEOs often were outsiders hired to implement change, and in all cases several members of the executive team were replaced with new individuals.

Finally, managers can be blindsided by their prior experiences and training, which can constrain their ability to conduct broad assessments of their environments or choose appropriate responses. For example, Gabarro (1985) found that managers placed in change situations tended to make initial changes principally in their area of functional expertise. Thus, a marketing executive will more likely focus on changes in marketing rather than on changes in manufacturing or sales. Similarly, early initiatives are likely to mirror lessons from the CEO's prior experiences in executive positions. This is even more likely if the individual believes that prior programs and strategies were the reason for his or her selection to the position (Yukl, 1994). Recent research on senior executives by Waller, Huber, and Glick (1995) suggests that although they may be open to a broad range of information, their sense of the sources of organizational effectiveness is shaped by their functional backgrounds. The problem, they suggest, may be more accentuated for non-executives.

> We found that in at least one area (organizational effectiveness), executives' functional backgrounds were related to what they perceived. It seems reasonable to conclude that the results would have been even stronger for functional

managers than for the CEOs, COOs, and general managers whom we studied. That is, function-related selective perception resulting from conditioning or schema development processes is probably greater for managers currently working in functional areas than for top executives. Thus, whichever is the more valid explanation, had the participants in our study been functional managers rather than top executives, it is very likely that the effect of either current functional position or previous functional background (these would be highly correlated) on perception across effectiveness categories would have been stronger. (Waller et al., 1995, p. 968)

In summary, the majority of managers will tend to focus their assessments in the areas of their functional expertise and career experiences and in turn fail to conduct broader assessments. An illustrative counterexample of this tendency would be Jan Carlzon, the charismatic former CEO of Scandinavian Airlines (SAS), whose behavior supports the notion that effective leaders are capable of more profound assessments. Carlzon had successfully managed Linjeflyg, the domestic airline of Sweden, for a number of years when he was invited to serve as the chief operating officer of SAS in 1980. Accepting the position, he faced the task of revitalizing a bureaucracy-riddled organization that was in the midst of its second year of losses. We can see in his comments below that he quickly realized essential differences in markets, comparing those of SAS and his former companies, rather than slipping into the trap of employing his earlier strategies. His broad-based assessment led him to a different conclusion about how to approach the problem:

Many people at SAS assumed that I would cut fares dramatically, as I had done at Linjeflyg, and squeeze costs as much as possible, as I had done at Vingresor (a vacation tour company). But it wasn't that simple. At Vingresor we were faced with a slumping market, so we had to cut costs. . . . At Linjeflyg we had fixed costs, so we had to increase revenues. . . . But at SAS the situation was different—and required a different approach. . . . We realized that SAS had already cut costs to the bone. Continuing to cut would have been like hitting the brakes of a car already standing still. . . . SAS's top management at the time used the standard weapon: the cheese slicer, which disregards market demands and instead cuts costs equally from all activities and departments. . . . [It] eliminated many services that customers wanted and were prepared to pay for while retaining others of little interest to the customer. In cutting costs, the company was, in effect, slicing away its own competitive strengths . . . the only solution for SAS's predicament was to increase revenue . . . we had to create a new strategy. . . . We wanted SAS to be profitable in its airline operations even in a zero-growth market such as we were then experiencing. . . . We had pegged the businessmen as the only stable part of the market. Unlike tourists, businessmen must travel in good times and bad. Perhaps most important, the business market has special requirements, and developing services to meet those requirements would enable us to attract their full-fare business. (Carlzon, 1987, pp. 21-22)

Adept at recognizing that SAS's principal market from a profitability stand-point would be the business traveler, Carlzon avoided employing the cost-cutting strategy that would have undermined the business traveler strategy. This market segment is not as cost sensitive as it is service sensitive. In addition, SAS is an international carrier, in contrast to Linjeflyg, Scandinavia's domestic airline. This means that SAS has a significantly greater number of competitors, and the business traveler has more air carrier choices. To compete in this segment, SAS must offer a higher level of service to differentiate itself from other airlines. As Carlzon rightly notes, SAS needed investments that are not cost-cutting. This is in sharp contrast to his prior strategies of cost cutting at Vingresor and fare cutting at Linjeflyg.

To be effective at such broad-based assessments, leaders generally must be acutely sensitive to their environments, possess a breadth of focus beyond their functional expertise and prior experiences, and be active learners. For example, Hambrick and Fukutomi (1991) have found that CEOs who generally remain flexible and vigilant in the face of environmental shifts are those who are able to continually learn from experiences, who possess a high tolerance for ambiguity, and who have an orientation toward achievement. We suspect that a disposition toward curiosity also plays a role, especially as it relates to one's own industry. For example, a *Fortune* magazine journalist recently accompanied Bill Gates, the CEO of Microsoft, on an international business trip. What he discovered was that Gates was like "a college student cramming for a final" (Schlender, 1997, p. 81). While on airplanes, Gates would read magazines and books on each upcoming destination to understand its historical and current context. At each destination, he questioned those whom he met in each country or city. As the journalist explained,

Once on the ground, he peppers his escorts with endless questions about everything from architecture to local politics to, yes, even the weather. [For example] In India he pumped U.S. ambassador Frank Wisner to explain that country's complex linguistic and religious heritage. (Schlender, May 26, 1997, p. 81)

These conversations or environmental assessments inevitably led to tactical actions on the part of Microsoft. On returning from his trip to India, Gates decided to make some important product revisions and to expand operations there. As Gates stated in an interview,

> I never realized that there are 14 distinct written and spoken languages in India. Now that I understand that, we're going to invest a whole lot more in localizing our products. And the raw software talent you see there really grabs you. A billion people is a lot of people, and even though the country is really poor, there are a lot of talented people with world-class educations, and companies that are as forward-looking and capable as anywhere. I came back quite enthused about taking some of our software development overload here and moving it over there. (Schlender, 1997, p. 81)

Given the critical importance of environmental monitoring not only for charismatic leadership but also for leadership in general, what do we know about the process itself? The existing research tells us that leaders use multiple vehicles to make their assessments. For example, to ascertain the capabilities of their subordinates, they rely on their own observations and those of trusted others. They also may assign challenging responsibilities or unusual projects to test the competence of subordinates. We know of several turnaround leaders who as company outsiders assigned projects outside the functional expertise of their subordinates to assess individuals' ability to think broadly. In other cases, assignments may be used to determine a subordinate's openness to radical change or to unconventional approaches.

To assess the resources and capabilities of the organization itself, performance measurement systems are a common resource for the leader. As Yukl (1994) notes, the more effective of these measures employ multiple indicators (e.g., sales trends, quality, costs, productivity, customer satisfaction) and measure process variables as well as outcomes. They also include independent sources of information wherever possible to provide comparisons for accuracy. For example, Tichy and Devanna (1986) found that change-agent leaders typically benchmark company performance measures against those of their competition. This tends to mitigate against the insularity and complacency that often arises when benchmarks are all generated internally. Recently, a number of companies such as General Electric have been benchmarking internal competencies against "best in class" organizations outside their own industry. Lew Platt, the CEO of Hewlett Packard, recently insisted that the company's personal computers group benchmark its distribution system not against industry competitors but against L. L. Bean, the high-volume catalogue retailer in Maine. As it turns out, L. L. Bean is a world leader in this competency.

It is critical, however, that performance measures match marketplace realities or future realities or else they will provide misleading information. For example, Xerox in the 1970s employed as one principal measure of quality a gauge titled "mean time to repair." This measure assessed how much time was required for a repairperson to arrive at a customer site and to repair a machine. The measurement was built around the assumption that machines would fail on a recurrent basis (which they did). Quality then was interpreted as the *speed* of repair rather than the *failure frequency* of the machine itself. Although this measure was adequate for an earlier phase of the industry, Japanese manufacturers had instead adopted quality measures built around minimizing machine failure rates. In hindsight, Xerox's measure proved deceptive. Although the company met its quality targets based on speedy repair work, its clients were migrating to Japanese copiers that had far fewer service demands. Relying on an outdated measure, senior management at Xerox were ineffectively monitoring their environment.

A second set of assessment vehicles is the leader's involvement in industry associations, organizational task forces, meetings and personal contacts with managers and individuals from all levels of the firm, meetings with customers and suppliers, and direct observation of operations. Internal contact, especially with middle-level managers, may provide rich sources of ideas (Burgelman, 1991) for the organization's future strategic direction—particularly in large firms. As Bennis and Nanus (1985) note, the majority of leaders expend

a substantial portion of their time interacting with advisers, consultants, other leaders, scholars, planners, and a wide variety of other people both inside and outside their own organizations in this search [for ideas]. Successful leaders, we have found, are great askers, and they do pay attention. (p. 96)

One illustrative example is Ryoichi Kawai, the former chairman of the Japanese heavy equipment manufacturer Komatsu. Although he was the senior leader of a multibillion dollar company, he kept himself informed through two means. First, he ensured that he had constant personal contact with managers throughout all levels of the organization. Second, he participated in an organization-wide program of auditing quality control. This program consisted of monthly meetings held between a Tokyo University professor and different groups of company managers. In these sessions, the managers would be queried by the professor concerning the quality of the company's products, especially from the angle of customers' perceptions and needs. From these interactions,

Kawai was able to discern the attitudes of employees toward quality and the state of quality initiatives within the company. In addition, Kawai led a task force of executives that performed quality control audits annually on operations at the head office, the research center, and certain functional units. This provided him with a broad view of one of the corporation's most important initiatives and showcased his commitment to quality (Bartlett, 1989).

Beyond task forces, formal meetings, and one-on-one contacts, organizational leaders can use informal public settings and opportunistic moments to ensure contact and a flow of information within their organizations. In a study of effective general managers, Kotter (1982) observed that information gathering was an ongoing, opportunistic event:

> In gathering information for agenda-setting purposes, these GMs relied largely on discussions with other people. . . . These people tended to be individuals with whom they had relationships, not necessarily people in the "appropriate" job or function (such as a person in the planning function). They obtained information in this way by continuously asking questions, day after day, not just during planning meetings. (p. 63)

Similarly, Peters and Austin (1985) describe executives who hold informal coffee breaks in company reception areas or have breakfast twice a week in the company cafeteria so employees can join them to discuss issues.

In change efforts or organizational turnarounds where there are time and political pressures, leaders also may need to target their assessments. One example is the CEO of a Canadian bank, interviewed by the authors, who was widely described as a charismatic leader. Appointed from the outside to head this particular bank, he soon realized that the bank was in jeopardy because of its excessive overhead. Bank employees, however, did not perceive the problem as a serious one given the organization's prior history of financial success. The leader's own background was in financial investments rather than retail banking, so his credibility and ability to persuade based on expertise alone were limited in the eyes of company managers. To enhance his knowledge rapidly, he undertook two activities. First, he hired an external consultant to benchmark the bank against its competition: "That would force everyone to confront the fact that they were by no means the low-cost producer they thought they were. I needed an objective reality they could not deny." Next, he targeted carefully his fact-finding or assessment visits to the operations that he considered most essential to the organization:

I asked myself "Where is the true power in this organization?" The true power is in the distribution system—the branches. So I got out and spent three months walking the branches, talking to people. I've seen every branch we have.

This step allowed him to obtain very rich information on the issues facing the bank in its most vital areas. Just as important, it served to build his credibility in the eyes of the organization by demonstrating a deep commitment to learning about the organization:

If I have the distribution system saying that I'm their man, that I'm the first guy who actually understands what is going on, then I've got their trust. What happened was that I built up credibility with this group in a relatively short time. . . . The real test, however, came when I had to answer questions back at headquarters. They were testing to see if I really understood issues in the field. Pretty soon people were saying to each other, "Wow, we can ask Tom about the retail branches, and he actually understands them."

When it comes to assessments of their external world, leaders must generally consider a broad range of environments. We know from researchers who study environmental scanning that the following areas tend to be relevant to most organizations (Ginter & Duncan, 1990; Narchal, Kittappa, & Bhattacharya, 1987; Terry, 1977): (1) societal demographics, (2) technology, (3) political-regulatory events, (4) social and cultural trends, (5) the economy, and (6) international affairs. We would imagine that effective leaders consider the impact of events in all these arenas as they potentially affect their organization's future direction. For example, the leader of a regional bank will necessarily consider the ramifications of laws deregulating interstate banking in the United States. The leader of a manufacturer of paperboard containers in Georgia may weigh business opportunities in Poland given deregulation of that country's markets and a friendly foreign investment environment. The sources for such information tend to be many—both contacts and published sources.

Strong networks external to the leader's organization also are essential. For example, by spending considerable time with their clients and with the products or services of their competition, effective leaders learn about market opportunities and the shortcomings of their own organizations (Peters & Austin, 1985; Yukl, 1994). Peters and Austin (1985) describe how Stew Leonard, the charismatic founder of a small chain of dairy and food stores, would regularly conduct visits to competing operations. He typically took along several managerial and hourly employees on these intelligence-gathering trips. Each individual was challenged to identify one effective practice at the competition that they could implement back in their own operations soon thereafter.

External networks may provide more objective evaluations of the company and its environment (Tichy & Devanna, 1986). They also ensure that the leader has multiple and outside sources of information rather than single or only internal sources on any one issue (Yukl, 1994). This is crucial for making accurate assessments given that any one individual alone has biases in how he or she perceives and interprets information, which in turn leads to discounting or exaggerating his or her perceptions of events (Milliken & Vollrath, 1991). In the aggregate, the assessments of multiple individuals both inside and outside the organization ensure a more accurate portrayal of reality.

To ensure reliable information, most of the activities we have been describing depend on the leader's ability to establish a climate of trust, candid rapport, objective critiques, and open debate (Tichy & Devanna, 1986). To do so, the leader must often "protect" individuals who bring problems to their attention (Peters & Austin, 1985). For example, subordinates may fear retaliation from their bosses or the organization if they share negative information. It is essential that the leader himself or herself role-model nonpunitive, constructive behavior when dealing with sensitive information from employees. This might include responding quickly to identified problems, helping staff learn from errors rather than punishing them, and demonstrating appreciation for reliable information even if it is negative (Yukl, 1994).

CHALLENGES TO THE STATUS QUO

In the assessment phase, the one characteristic that distinguishes charismatic leaders from others is their greater sensitivity to recognizing deficiencies within the present context. They actively search out shortcomings in the status quo. They may, for example, exploit overlooked market opportunities or launch initiatives that successfully undermine the standard practices or conventions of an industry. Moreover, they may challenge internal organizational deficiencies. As such, any environment that offers unexploited market opportunities or requires major change is relevant to the emergence of a charismatic leader.

Because of this emphasis on the shortcomings of an environment, these leaders always will be perceived as entrepreneurs or agents of change. In contrast, we can think of managers as the maintainers of the status quo. As we noted in an earlier chapter, they, at best, advocate incremental changes to organizational systems—making the existing approach more efficient often is their primary aim. The changes that traditional managers propose will usually be within the bounds of the status quo.

There are perhaps a variety of reasons why charismatic leaders are by nature entrepreneurial and change-oriented. Some may have to do with dispositional characteristics. For example, many appear to have high achievement needs and power motivation. They also seem to enjoy a high degree of visibility and attention. Their needs are fulfilled by challenging conventions and convincing others to accept their views. In addition, the environments in which charismatic leaders appear to be most frequently found are themselves contexts that would encourage if not demand challenges to the status quo. For example, entrepreneurial ventures often compete by offering new products for which no comparable product exists—so, by their nature, they are outside existing conventions (Balakrishnan, Gopakumar, & Kanungo, in press; McClelland, 1987). In both entrepreneurial and major change situations, shortages of resources may require innovative behavior that challenges industry conventions. In other words, necessity is indeed the mother of invention. For example, Southwest Airlines is today known for its remarkable productivity, which consistently breaks industry standards (and for its charismatic leader, Herb Kelleher). Many of the company's approaches are considered unconventional relative to the airline industry. For example, while turnaround time at airport gates typically ranges from 30 to 50 minutes, Southwest is able to turn its planes around in under 15 minutes. This competence was borne out of necessity (Petzinger, 1995). In mid-1972, when Southwest was in serious financial straits, the company was forced to sell one of its four 737 jets, which meant a 25% reduction in capacity. Employees realized that layoffs would soon have to follow. Rather than face a layoff, the workforce proposed to company president Kelleher (a charismatic leader) and senior management that Southwest maintain its existing schedule built around four planes even though it would have only three aircraft. To succeed, they would turn planes around in 10 minutes—an unheard-of feat for the airline industry. Greater teamwork and job redesigns were the solutions. Soon supervisors and pilots were assisting with baggage. Planes were stocked through the rear of the craft while passengers were disembarking at the front. Flight service crews worked their way up to the front of each plane collecting trash and crossing seat belts as passengers deplaned ahead of them. Tickets were collected on the plane instead of at the gate. No seat assignments meant that passengers could be moved quickly into the plane at a rapid but orderly pace. With these initiatives that broke industry rules, Southwest achieved its target of the 10-minute turnaround, much to the shock of its competitors. Out of sheer necessity, Southwest successfully challenged the status quo of an industry (Petzinger, 1995, pp. 31-32).

FOLLOWER ASSESSMENTS
BY THE LEADER

The most important resources for attaining the leader's vision are the human ones. To engage these effectively, the charismatic leader must be a keen observer, skillful in reading the abilities of followers. Typical of what we have heard in interviews with subordinates of charismatic leaders would be the comments below describing such capabilities in Orit Gadiesh, the charismatic vice chairman of the consulting firm Bain & Company (Rothbard & Conger, 1993):

> She has extremely good antennae. She knows exactly what is going on [with staff and clients].

> The risks she chooses are carefully calculated and balanced with an uncanny knack for reading people and situations exactly right.

> In most cases you begin to see executives gradually get a certain detachment from the day-to-day operations of the business. It's a natural progression . . . but you never see that with Orit. She can articulate a vision for the company, for the work, for the client, and in the next sentence be completely conversant in the details of what you are working on.

People sensitivity allows the leader to assess realistically the talent and resources followers possess and in turn where best to deploy them and where critical gaps exist. There also are other advantages to this form of sensitivity. Because followers perceive that the leader's actions are meant to serve them rather than serve solely the leader, a people-oriented sensitivity may help the leader to garner "idiosyncrasy credits" (Hollander, 1958, 1979). These in turn permit him or her to deviate from certain norms of the organization. These also can lead to greater tolerance of whatever personality quirks the leader may have. In addition, subordinates may be more willing to suspend their judgment of innovative or risky proposals advocated by the leader. Failures are not likely to be evaluated as harshly. A sensitivity to followers also helps to build credibility for the leader. Credibility is essential for garnering follower commitment to the leader's goals and to the high performance standards that will be necessary to achieve the organization's vision.

To illustrate this point, we will draw on the example of one charismatic leader whom we studied quite extensively—Jim Dawson, president of Zebco. Zebco is the world's largest fishing tackle company, based in Tulsa, Oklahoma. Zebco had developed in 1949 what was called "balanced tackle," with the rod, reel, and line functioning as a single, integrated unit. The next year, this innovation appeared in the Zebco 202 model, which would become the largest selling reel worldwide, with more than 62 million sold. Products like the 202 and the growing popularity of sport fishing would propel Zebco to grow almost 10 times in size through the early 1980s.

By the 1980s, however, fishing equipment from Japan and Taiwan began to flood the market. Not only were Asian products less costly, but they also had important improvements in operating features and technology. Given the company's historically strong market position, Zebco's senior management was relatively unconcerned about the inroads being made by these new competitors. They, in essence, chose to ignore them. Typical was their reaction to the inflationary pressures of the 1980s, which had been driving up production costs at the company. Instead of the problem being addressed head-on, the added costs simply were passed on to the consumer in the form of higher retail prices. The issue of product quality also was largely ignored. Moreover, management-labor relations at Zebco had disintegrated. A unionization movement had succeeded in unionizing the plant, and the company had its first strike.

During this time, Zebco would be acquired by the sporting equipment company Brunswick, which immediately sensed there were serious problems to be addressed. In 1976, it appointed the company's marketing vice president as president. To bring critical issues to the surface, the new president held forums with employees and laid the foundation for the company's first quality control initiative. In 1981, he would bring Jim Dawson on board as senior vice president of technical operations. Dawson quickly realized the magnitude of Zebco's problems, but he faced a thorny dilemma. He was an outsider and a member of "management." Trust would be a major concern for his workforce—the very group he needed to enlist in fundamentally changing the operations. Sensitive to employee feelings about prior management, Dawson undertook a series of personal initiatives to demonstrate not only his understanding of worker concerns but also his desire to build a strong relationship with his workforce. As he explained to us in interviews,

Very few people understand the damage it does when you set up different classes of people, and you encourage them. I wanted to eliminate all the barriers between people and things that create classes of people. Once you break these down, you start this chain reaction. People start to feel a little more comfortable in facing issues, in bringing issues up. We were really working on trust factors in the beginning, building a new trust in the company especially at the bottom of the organization. . . . It is so important to understand that the people at the bottom see the needs for change. . . . The people at the top are protected from it. Very few people understand workforces and what turns them on and what turns them off, how you can create openness, and the fact that generally people are afraid to talk to people about unpleasant things. They also want total honesty and clarity from people at the top.[1]

To demonstrate this sensitivity in his actions, Dawson undertook a series of initiatives that would symbolically end the class differences between the workforce and management. He choose three highly visible actions to send a clear message. First, he removed all parking spaces reserved for senior managers, explaining that these types of perks simply reaffirmed the attitude that "We [management] are better than you are." Reserved parking instead became a reward program called the President's Club. Now anyone who had a 100% attendance record—line employee or manager—would receive a space. Dawson then removed the time clocks in the manufacturing department. These were another visible barrier between the workers and managers and a stark symbol of a lack of trust on management's behalf. The manner in which he did it was as important as their actual removal. He arrived at check-in time one morning with a crowbar and began to rip the clocks off the walls. As the broken time clocks crashed to the floor one by one, workers appeared from all over the company to witness the event. He used the drama of the event to send a very clear and emotional message that he was on the workers' side. For his third action, he asked his management team to be role models in their own arrival times at work. One executive explained Dawson's thinking on the issue:

What we realized was that it wasn't just Jim but we managers who had to make sure that people could see there were no double standards. As a manager, I often work long hours. It's not unusual to work 10 hours a day. I often go home at 7:00 p.m. Now the clerical and line staff don't see that we are here until 7 because they are here only until 4:45 p.m. As managers, we don't allow ourselves to use that as an excuse: "Well, I am going to come in a little late tomorrow because I stayed in the office until eight o'clock last night." Then it appears to the workforce that you have a double standard. An hourly person out on the line cannot come in at 7:05 a.m. He has got to be in here at 7:00 a.m. So we have to be here at the same time.

By showing great sensitivity to employees, these actions allowed Dawson to very quickly establish credibility with his workforce. He had demonstrated that he intended for equality to be the norm in the plant and was willing to forgo his own perks for it. Later initiatives would further reinforce these intentions. In return, the workforce provided him with important concessions that soon dramatically improved both productivity and quality. The outcome was such that within 15 years, Dawson and his team had increased the size of Zebco sevenfold despite continued competition from Asia. Production efficiencies increased threefold. The Zebco model 33 that sold for $19.95 in 1954 can be found for prices as low as $9.95 today. In 1991, the company won the Wal-Mart vendor-of-the-year award—distinguishing itself from among 8,000 suppliers. It was also the first sporting goods company to receive such an honor. The next year, it won the same award from Wal-Mart.

A final area that some believe involves the leader's sensitivity to followers is the actual formulation of the organizational vision. Here we find some debate. One group of researchers argues that the vision is to a significant degree shaped around the followers' own needs, values, and aspirations. Representative of this viewpoint would be the positions of Bass and Avolio (1993) and Shamir and colleagues (1993), who argue that leaders acquire commitment to their visions by addressing follower motives while formulating the vision. For example, Shamir and colleagues posit that the visions of charismatic leaders are built primarily around the self-concepts of followers. In other words, the vision must be formulated in a way that incorporates values and an ideology that have intrinsic meaning for followers—"Doing so makes action oriented towards the accomplishment of these goals more meaningful to the follower in the sense of being consistent with his or her self-concept" (p. 583). A vision cannot be implemented if it is not compatible with followers' needs and values.

There are others, however, such as Locke and colleagues (1991), who argue that the vision is shaped almost entirely by the external environment. They believe that the leader looks to the larger business environment and envisions future possibilities. Such possibilities come not from the leader's analysis of followers' values but rather from the leader's analysis of the business environment. Vision formulation therefore is a form of creative genius on the part of the leader based on environmental scanning. As Locke (in press) points out, Bill Gates, John D. Rockefeller, and Sam Walton did not formulate their visions by first testing whether they were meaningful to their employees. Rather, these individuals detected opportunities in their industries that held great future promise. Their visions then evolved with successes and failures, marketplace changes, competitor moves, and technological breakthroughs. To the extent that subordinates were involved, it was related to business ideas, not their own needs. Enlisting subordinate commitment by taking into account their needs and values actually comes *after* the vision has been formulated, not beforehand.

We believe that reality is closer to the position of Locke and colleagues, at least for charismatic leaders in the business world. We say this because a business organization must first and foremost address its marketplaces if it wishes to succeed. Its goals cannot be aimed primarily at satisfying the needs of organizational members but rather must address those of clients who purchase its goods and services. For example, in the next chapter, we will examine the strategic vision and actions of Charlotte Beers, the charismatic leader of the New York advertising agency Ogilvy & Mather. What is apparent in her case is that the new vision she devised for the firm initially had far more appeal to clients than it did to members of the organization (Sackley & Ibarra, 1995). The firm's vision spoke directly to client needs to build stronger brands for their products during a time when high-end, private label (generic) products were stealing market share away from brand names. As a result, it allowed Beer to regain past clients of the firm such as American Express and to add new clients such as Jaguar and IBM. In doing so, she successfully turned around the firm's fortunes. Only after these successes and several other initiatives would her vision become widely accepted by organizational members and ultimately be seen as meaningful to them. In a review of the more effective visions of charismatic leaders, Bryman (1992) notes:

> It is noticeable that the more striking visions that have been examined often entail a strong market orientation, combining a concern for customers with an acute awareness of competitors, or the inculcation of an entrepreneurial spirit through the creation of relatively autonomous business lines within the organization. . . . Thus, much more significant in many instances than the mere possession of a vision is the question of whether that vision points the company in a particular direction that is in tune with the times [marketplace dynamics]. (p. 150)

Effective visions then are far more likely to be shaped by markets than by follower needs. This is not to say that followers are uninvolved in the formulation of the vision. Quite to the contrary, they may actively assist the leader in both developing and articulating elements of the vision—but it is largely around their insights into marketplace opportunities, internal product and service developments, and organizational developments that support and implement the vision and strategy. In these areas, the leader actively involves followers to develop the strategies and tactics that shape and help to realize goals.

At the same time, when the vision is being formulated, the charismatic leader often will thoughtfully frame and interpret it in a manner that is inspirational for organizational members. (This capacity at framing follows from the leader's ability to assess followers.) These leaders in essence persuade followers of its meaningfulness. As Locke (in press) argues, however, they assume that their goals will be motivational for most members without actively tailoring goals to individual needs:

> It is true that leaders have to draw upon some common motivational core among subordinates, but usually this core is assumed rather than assessed. For example, almost any employee who is carefully selected will buy into a vision that stresses such aspirations as wanting to be a high growth, high quality, innovative, pro-customer service, cutting edge of technology, etc., company, because all will share the desire to work for a competent, successful organization.

Leaders also acquire commitment to goals simply by hiring individuals who agree with their vision (Locke, in press). Considering both the positions discussed above, one might conclude that environmental scanning is more crucial for *vision formulation*, but follower sensitivity is more important for *vision acceptance* and *implementation*.

THE PROCESS OF VISION FORMULATION

As previously pointed out, vision formulation is intimately linked to environmental assessment. There are essentially two areas of debate in the field concerning the actual formulation process of vision after the status quo is challenged. One has to do with whether the leader is the principal source of creating a vision, and the other is concerned with whether the process is a rational one or more intuitive and opportunistic. We will examine the two sides of these debates.

We begin with the debate about whether the actual visioning process resides largely *within the leader* (Kouzes & Posner, 1987; Sashkin, 1988) or is a by-product of multiple decision makers and influences (Bennis & Nanus, 1985; Conger, 1989a). The popular notion that vision is the product of a single individual most likely is derived from ancient notions of a "visionary leader"—a individual who seemingly has greater foresight than others. This myth continues to this day as a belief in a genius-like quality possessed only by a certain few, such as Bill Gates or Rupert Murdoch. It is presumed that such talents are innate gifts. Two interrelated forces have shaped this perception (Locke, in press). One is the perception throughout history that extraordinary talent is the product of an innate ability or divine gifts. The second involves romantic notions about leadership itself.

Popular legend has long held that certain individuals such as prophets were given gifts from the gods. Interestingly, even the term *charisma* comes from a Greek word meaning "gift." Its oldest known literary references are those found in the Bible describing divine gifts, one of which includes prophecy:

> Now there are varieties of gifts [charismata]. . . . But to each one [individual] is given the manifestation of the Spirit for the common good. For to one is given the word of wisdom through the Spirit, and to another the word of knowledge, to another faith, and to another gifts of healing, and to another the effecting of miracles, and to another prophecy. . . . But one and the same Spirit [God] works all these things, distributing to each one individually as He wills. (1 Corinthians 12:4-11)

The notion that such unusual talents were of a divine origin has had a resilient and long history. Since Biblical times, a widespread bias toward attributing special abilities to "gifts" rather than to experience has persisted. As Ericsson and Charness (1994) have shown, this mythology of the gift has continued to this day, especially in domains of expertise where only a small number of individuals reach the highest performance levels such as music, sports, and chess.

In recent years, however, this mythology of the "gift" has been challenged in a parallel field by a body of researchers investigating how individuals achieve expert status. Although individual characteristics and intelligence do mediate the process of acquiring expertise (Johnson & Mervis, 1994), expertise is now understood to be the product of a very extended period of active learning, with the expert constantly refining and improving skills and learning from others (Ericsson & Charness, 1994). For example, the vast majority of adult experts were never child prodigies. Despite these facts, popular mythology continues to this day that talents simply flower without enormous efforts at cultivation. They are either innate or God-given to a select few.

The second force shaping notions of a visionary leader concerns romanticized beliefs about leaders and their powers. This too has ancient roots—after all, leaders such as the pharaohs were assumed to be divine representatives of the gods on earth. Before the French Revolution, practically all kings and nobles claimed their privileged status and the birthrights of their children based on divine legitimization (Ericsson & Charness, 1994). With the rise of democracy, increased social mobility, and modern science, these beliefs gradually have been eroded; nevertheless, a legacy—that leaders possess unusual powers—remains widespread.

Culturally, humans appear to have a need to imagine that a singular individual can play a heroic role in shaping the destiny of their organizations. As Meindl and colleagues (1985) point out, this is in part due to the fact that organizational events typically involve multiple determinants and are therefore complex and difficult to comprehend fully. Organizational members seek to make sense out of their environment to gain a sense of control. An essential element of this sense-making process is to create causal attributions for events. Because organizational leaders are often visible and have a formal position of authority, organizational members have a tendency to attribute causality to them (Calder, 1977; Pfeffer, 1977). As Yukl (1994) points out, this process of attribution also reflects societal biases toward explaining experiences in terms of the rational actions of human beings in contrast to natural forces or random events. Underpinning this belief is the assumption that organizations themselves are largely rational, goal-oriented systems that aim to meet the needs of their members and society. Individuals in senior leadership positions of organizations therefore come to symbolize the controlling or guiding forces behind this promise of the organization (Meindl et al., 1985). This in turn leads organizational members to overemphasize the personal characteristics of their leader and to minimize the situational factors when seeking explanations for outcomes (Meindl et al., 1985). As such, they may make errors of attribution (Ross, 1977), overlooking contributing factors beyond the leader. The leadership field, with its strong emphasis on the leader's behavior rather than on followers and contextual forces, coincidentally has reinforced this perspective.

Since the turn of the century, scholars of leadership have challenged the notion of the "larger than life" leader. For example, earlier students of religious and social movements (e.g., Weber, 1947) found that leaders' ideas and sense of direction were shaped by a larger social context, including not only their followers but society at the time (Westley, 1992). Today, we know that social interactions and other processes that surround those perceived as visionary leaders are as important as the characteristics of the leader (Westley & Mintzberg, 1988, 1989). For example, based on their research on innovative or visionary companies, Hamel and Prahalad (1994) conclude that industry foresight is the product of many people's visions. Often, a point of view about the future, which is in fact an amalgam of many individual perspectives, is represented by journalists or sycophantic employees as the "vision" of one person. So while Mr. Kobayashi may have taken much of the credit for NEC's visionary concept of "computers and communication," the idea of exploiting the convergence between the two industries wove together the thoughts of many minds in NEC, not just one. Senior executives aren't the only ones with industry foresight. In fact, . . . their primary role is to capture and exploit the foresight that exists throughout the organization. (pp. 76-77)

We share a similar belief that the "visionary leader" is more mythology than reality. From our own research, the formulation of a vision most often involves many others and is shaped as much by environmental forces as by the leader and the organization. We suspect that the process may vary a bit depending on several variables. For example, we hypothesize that for leaders who are entrepreneurial founders, the probability is higher that they are principal assemblers of the vision. On the other hand, a leader who is a professional manager in a large corporation is more likely to enlist to a greater extent the assistance of multiple individuals in the formulation of a vision. In addition, the more rapid the pace of change within an industry, the more likely it is that the leader will rely on others for ideas. This is confirmed by research in the strategy literature (e.g., Bower & Doz, 1979). If an industry is undergoing very rapid technological and market changes, it is far less likely that leaders will themselves possess sufficient, up-to-date knowledge to formulate an effective vision. They will require greater assistance from multiple organizational levels.

For example, Intel is today one of the world's leading semiconductor companies, having survived and prospered in a very dynamic environment for more than 25 years. Intel built its initial success around memory chips called DRAMs. In 1985, the company made a remarkable decision to exit the very business on which the firm was built and craft a new vision for itself (Burgelman, 1991).

Andy Grove, the company's CEO, who was in charge of engineering and manufacturing in the company's early days, had understood that silicon rather than metal was the crucial material for memory storage and that process technology would be the driver of the business. Intel's product strategy was to get more and more transistors on the same size silicon chip, creating denser devices with greater memory. These DRAMs shaped the company's future. In the 1980s, however, the Japanese introduced intense price competition into this business. This and a significant cyclical downturn in semiconductor demand in 1985 caused Intel to face a loss of more than $100 million while simultaneously needing to invest several hundred million dollars in plant and equipment for the next generation of DRAMs. The company stood at a crossroads. It would choose to adopt a new vision for itself by abandoning its DRAM or memory business and becoming a "microprocessor" or microcomputer company in 1985. How Andy Grove and others formulated this new vision is a story of both corporate culture and entrepreneurial activity at mid-levels of the corporation.

The company's early initiatives in microprocessors were largely the by-product of unplanned initiatives begun in the 1970s that were outside the scope of Intel's strategy at the time. These were championed mostly by middle-level managers. While setting a strong strategic tone, Grove and the other company founders had nevertheless crafted an organizational culture that allowed for facts and knowledge to win out over position at Intel (Burgelman, 1991). Young engineers could directly interact with Grove on important technological issues. Grove described his own role in this process:

> You need to be able to be ambiguous in some circumstances. You dance around it a bit, until a wider and wider group in the company becomes clear about it. That's why continued argument is important. Intel is a very open system. No one is ever told to shut up, but you are asked to come up with better arguments. People are allowed to be persistent. (Grove, quoted in Burgelman, 1991, p. 252)

Through these interactions, Grove and other members of the senior management team realized the necessity of a new vision built around microprocessors. As Burgelman (1988, 1991) has shown, new strategic visions at Intel and other large companies often are shaped by middle-level managers who essentially educate senior managers about what is feasible.

We will further illustrate our point that vision formulation is a complex process stretching beyond the leader with two well-documented examples— Donald Burr, the founder of People Express Airlines, and Dr. Balfort Mount of the Royal Victoria Hospital. Both are regarded as visionary individuals who have been involved with major transformations within both their organizations and their fields.

DONALD BURR AND PEOPLE EXPRESS

Donald Burr founded People Express, an airline that essentially altered the national landscape of air travel in the United States. By ushering in an era of the "supersaver" or excursion fare, People Express made airline travel far more accessible. The airline's strategy was unique—offer very low fares and a high frequency of flights on any one route in markets that were overpriced and underserved by existing competition. In a drive to keep costs down, services were minimal or carried additional charges—for example, snacks and baggage handling carried extra charges. Essentially, the objective was to create passenger traffic by transforming airline travel into a substitute for automobile and bus travel.

In addition, People Express was conceived of as an experiment in human resources practices. Burr was deeply interested in creating a humane organization and was guided by a fundamental belief in people: "The people dimension is the value added to the commodity. Many investors still don't fully appreciate this point, but high commitment and participation, and maximum flexibility and massive creative productivity are the most important strategies in People Express" (Whitestone & Schlesinger, 1983, pp. 9-10). To achieve these aims, he designed the organization to have minimal hierarchy and perks (Petzinger, 1995). There were only three levels of formal authority. Burr himself had no secretary, nor did others. All employees were expected to rotate between flight operations and staff functions. At a given moment, a customer service representative might load baggage while a baggage handler was handling reservations. Finally, all employees were expected to own shares in the company and were promised a lifetime career at the company. These were truly remarkable innovations in a generally staid industry in which human resources received limited attention. In conjunction with the company's strategy, the formula would lead to an initial period of enormous success, with the airline growing from nothing in 1980 to $1.2 billion in revenues by 1986. It would appear during this time in *The 100 Best Companies to Work for in America* (Levering, Moskowitz, & Katz, 1984). As Chen and Meindl (1991) have shown, the popular press saw Burr as the talented genius behind the venture: "Burr was an all-around ideal leader: charismatic, innovative, dedicated, and competent" (p. 534).

In *The Charismatic Leader* (1989a), Conger examined two of the roots of Donald Burr's vision. The first was Burr's experiment with supersaver or "peanut" fares at his previous employer, Texas International Airlines, which gave him a baseline of experience with a low-fare strategy. The second was the critical role of deregulation in the airline industry in 1978. This event allowed airlines to compete aggressively in both pricing and routing in national markets and also encouraged new entrants to the market. Without it, People Express's existence as a low-fare interstate carrier would not have been possible. Since Conger's publication, new documentation (Petzinger, 1995) has been published that sheds additional light on other factors that shaped Burr's process of envisioning People Express's low-price strategy and people philosophy.

It appears that Burr's first exposure to the potential advantages of a low-fare strategy actually came soon after he joined Texas International. With 6 years of specializing in airline securities in the mutual fund industry behind him, Burr joined Frank Lorenzo as co-chief executive officer at Texas International Airlines in 1973. At the time, a local competitor was Southwest Airlines. For reasons to be explained shortly, Southwest had limited itself to markets within Texas, whereas Texas International was an interstate operation. As a competitor, Southwest had more limited funding and a very small fleet of Boeing 737s. It had chosen to compete using a low-fare strategy. Given the vastness of the state of Texas and the significant distance between its cities, Southwest had targeted automobiles as its competitors, not other airlines. It priced its fares to compete with the costs of ground transportation. In Southwest, then, were the seeds to Burr's People Express, yet Southwest itself was not the originator of the low-price fare strategy. Instead, it was an airline called Pacific Southwest Airlines (PSA) based in California. For a $10 fare, an individual could fly between Los Angeles and San Francisco on PSA. Operating inexpensive, old aircraft solely within the state of California, the airline undercut the costs of driving between the two cities. By not flying over state lines, PSA had cleverly avoided restrictive federal regulations that would have prohibited its low pricing and high-frequency scheduling. PSA could charge whatever price it wanted, fly the schedule it chose, and use any airplanes it wished (Petzinger, 1995).

During PSA's heyday, an individual named Rollin King ran a charter air service in Texas for hunting parties and business executives. He called the company Air Southwest, and Herb Kelleher was his attorney. A friend of King had returned from a trip to California having flown on PSA and described the experience to King. A short time later, King and Kelleher met for cocktails. Over drinks, King explained the PSA strategy and suggested that Texas could support a similar airline, given the great distances between cities in both states. The target market would be businesspeople who made the 250-mile drive between Houston and Dallas. King marked on a napkin three dots that represented the cities of Dallas, Houston, and San Antonio. As he connected the dots, King drew a triangle that he explained was an ideal route structure for a commercial airline. He believed that the existing competition had limited schedules and poor service. By restricting itself to the state of Texas, Air Southwest could legally undercut the fares of the existing airlines such as Braniff and Trans-Texas (later to be renamed Texas International). On the cost side, it could beat the competition by flying turboprop aircraft (later Boeing 737s) rather than jets, which were more expensive to operate. At that moment, Southwest Airlines was born (Petzinger, 1995, p. 24).

Now we return to Donald Burr. Frank Lorenzo had taken over Texas International at a time when the airline was financially troubled. It was during this turnaround period that Burr joined the company. At the same time, Southwest was gaining momentum in 1973, adding a fifth and sixth Boeing 737 to its fleet. Although Texas International had routes outside Texas, both Lorenzo and Burr felt that the company had to cut costs to stay competitive with Southwest within the state of Texas. Simultaneously, a labor contract for the ground crews of Texas International had come up for renegotiation. Final negotiations yielded a package agreeable to all the parties. The very next day, however, Lorenzo backed out, claiming that he had not approved the arrangement. Angered, the union launched a strike against Texas International that would last 4 months. This strike, it now appears, was a turning point in the industry, serving as a reminder of the critical role of contextual events that lay the groundwork for a later vision (Petzinger, 1995, pp. 43-44).

One of the towns serviced by Texas International was Harlingen, a small agricultural town at the southern tip of the state on the border with Mexico. Given the town's remote location, air service was critical for Harlingen's residents. Texas International for years had a monopoly over Harlingen, which in turn allowed the company to charge reasonably high air fares. The strike, however, brought the town's air links to a standstill. Meanwhile, Lamar Muse, the chief operating officer for Southwest Airlines, saw Texas International's strike and its impact on Harlingen as a window of opportunity for his airline. The town was located close to an increasingly popular coastal resort called South Padre Island and therefore was a natural new destination for Southwest (Petzinger, 1995, pp. 44-45).

Lorenzo, however, decided to fight Southwest's entry into Harlingen. He began with an advertising campaign proclaiming that Texas International was the town's major link to cities all across the United States, carrying its passengers, cargo, and mail. Southwest, the ads pointed out, did not provide service beyond Texas and did not even carry U.S. mail. In addition, Lorenzo hired a new general counsel, Sam Coats, a former state representative whose childhood home was Harlingen. Despite these efforts, the support at public hearings for Southwest's application to fly into Harlingen was overwhelmingly for Southwest. Within a short time, the new route was approved, and tickets went on sale at $25 each way. Soon, Southwest's passenger load into and out of Harlingen was 1,000 individuals a day, in contrast to a few hundred at Texas International. Lorenzo and Burr were determined to stop Southwest's growth through a new pricing strategy (Petzinger, 1995, p. 45).

Gerald Gitner, who was Texas International's marketing director, and his assistant, James O'Donnell, were assigned to develop a pricing counterattack to Southwest. In a series of discussions with senior company executives, Gitner and O'Donnell argued for a radical solution that would also garner publicity. Half-price tickets, they believed, were the only solution. They demonstrated through their analyses that a full plane with passengers at half fare offered a superior return to one that was one-third full with full fares. Although several company executives had argued for a reduction of only 15% off existing fares, Lorenzo was convinced that the more dramatic pricing would bring results. One hurdle, however, stood in the way. As an interstate carrier, Texas International would face a regulatory challenge from the Civil Aeronautics Board (CAB). This agency had to approve the new fares. As a matter of sheer good timing, John Robson, a career Washington bureaucratic with no connections to the airline industry, recently had been appointed as head of the CAB. Robson was a reformer and wished to challenge many of the CAB's traditions that had supported the status quo of the industry. The timing was impeccable because Robson's predecessor, Robert Timm, wanted higher airfares, having himself set an agency goal of doubling the industry's rate of return. Timm also had permitted carriers to meet among themselves to jointly select the routes on which they would cut back. Under Robson, the rules were to be different. On November 3, 1976, Texas International petitioned the CAB for a 50% fare reduction in certain of its interstate markets. CAB approved Texas International's request for new rates—the first time in 40 years that an interstate airline was allowed to cut prices to respond to market conditions (Petzinger, 1995, pp. 4-7).

Passenger loads doubled on the first-day launch of Texas International's "peanut fares." At the end of the first week, the increase in loads was as much as 600%, with no advertising. Follow-up surveys showed that 30% of customers would have remained home without the new fares, and 25% would have made the trip in their automobiles. Lorenzo made the "peanut fares" the cornerstone of the company's marketing efforts (Petzinger, 1995, pp. 97-98).

Lessons from this experiment were what Donald Burr would take with him to start People Express in 1980. As is now evident, the ideas for a new form of airline service came not from within the leader but from the leader's observations of marketplace conditions, competitors, and Texas International's implementation of a similar strategy. None of this, however, would have been possible without the deregulation of the industry during the Carter administration and the timing of Robson's appointment to the CAB.

Also interesting is that Burr himself had a concern about this pricing cornerstone of his later vision for People Express. Cheap fares, he believed, would soon become widespread throughout the industry (Petzinger, 1995). Texas International itself would need to find an additional way to set itself apart from the competition. For Burr, this could only be through a company's culture. As a young man, he had developed a great attachment to a book titled *The Greatest Thing in the World*, written by Henry Drummond, a 19th-century Scottish clergyman. Drummond argued that individuals needed to build a foundation of love in every activity in their lives. Burr believed that this principle could be applied to the workplace. With Edwin Cathell, Jr., Texas International's chief of service, Burr produced a "people's program" for the company after many months of examining theories on motivation and the best practices of companies known for effective personnel management. Approval, however, was dependent on a meeting with Lorenzo and the rest of the company officers. A document describing the idea was sent out beforehand. In it were descriptions of a "leadership and love" program. There would be open work spaces, jogging trails, a new headquarters campus, indoctrination experiences, and so on. It argued quite simply that when low fares become universal, Texas International would be left in large part with the "people" equation as the chief component of competitive leverage. The emphasis had to shift to addressing emotional and psychological needs because manipulation of this variable could make it the most productive (Petzinger, 1995, pp. 97-98).

Although the new program would cost money, it proposed that every 1% increase in business resulting from happy employees would translate into $1,441,660 of additional revenues for Texas International. Some 10 minutes into an overview presentation of his people program, Burr was interrupted by Lorenzo and asked to follow Lorenzo to his office for a moment. Once inside the office, Lorenzo threw the presentation report down onto his desk and exclaimed, "This is complete bullshit!" At that moment, Burr's plan was dashed to the ground. Deeply disheartened, Burr would resign sometime later from Texas International, sensing that only out from under Lorenzo could he implement his people plan. These core ideas would then form the basis for the people side of his vision for People Express (Petzinger, 1995, p. 98).

In conclusion, we see from the Burr example that the visioning process involves multiple individuals, important events unfolding in the environment, and matters of timing. In our next example of Balfort Mount, we will see similar dynamics in a completely different context.

BALFORT MOUNT AND THE
ROYAL VICTORIA HOSPITAL

Dr. Balfort Mount was the visionary founder of the Palliative Care Service at the Royal Victoria Hospital in Montreal. He has been described as a charismatic leader in research by Westley (1992). He would introduce to his organization a remarkable innovation in care for the dying.

As Westley (1992) has shown, the seeds of Dr. Mount's vision were planted during an adult education evening at his church on the challenges of the dying. A film by an expert on death and dying was shown, and a panel composed of a minister, a nurse, and a surgeon discussed the film. Mount was chosen to chair the panel because of his medical specialty, which centered on the treatment of terminal cancer cases. During the discussion, the surgeon challenged Mount to survey his hospital's own patients and staff to determine the quality of death at the Royal Victoria. Piqued by the challenge, Mount wrote a grant proposal the very next day for funds to undertake the survey. The proposal was soon approved.

The initial vision (or "catalytic vision," as termed by Westley, 1992) then was the result of a challenge by a fellow physician. In addition, Mount had contracted a rare form of cancer of the testes during his last year as a medical student. In interviews, Mount described this experience as playing a role in his willingness to accept the challenge. For example, it would lead him to both study and practice surgery on cancers like his own. It also would lead him to identify with young patients who at times would die from the disease.

> Bal [Mount] was bright and good and certainly had a mind of his own. . . . He was interested in cancer of the testicle and was experimenting with radical surgery. He would do these extremely long, complicated operations which involved doing meticulous dissections. . . . He experienced a lot of disappointments in patients of his who did not make it. He saw a lot of dying and got very worried about how many were dying. (Senior hospital administrator quoted by Westley, 1992, p. 282)

Several months later, Mount's survey was administered. The results were surprising. It was revealed that dying patients were suffering often unnecessary physical and emotional pain. The survey would solidify Mount's interest.

> Perhaps the most meaningful thing of that summer (when the survey was conducted) was having Alan, this one student, coming in the afternoon. I

remember the first time it happened, him coming in and relating the story of a
patient on one of the surgical wards. It was just a horror story of inadequate care.
. . . And I said, "well, who is her surgeon" and Alan told me and he is a good
guy. . . . It set me back. . . . Well, the next day it was another patient. . . . In the
end, I reached two interesting and disturbing conclusions . . . one, that there was
a problem, and two, that people who worked here, whom I knew to be caring,
concerned, bright, industrious individuals were completely unaware of it. (Mount,
quoted in Westley, 1992, pp. 282-283)

As Westley (1992) has shown, Mount was faced with an anomaly—committed
caregivers not recognizing the need for care of a particular patient population.
What is important, however, is the manner in which Mount frames the problem.
It is not a matter of conscious neglect of care but rather of a *lack of awareness*,
so his mission became one of informing, not attacking (Westley, 1992), a far
more viable strategy for acquiring internal support.

Given his initial findings, Mount decided that something had to be done. He
began to research what was known about palliative care and discovered that an
intriguing team-based approach had been developed by Dame Cicely Saunders
at St. Christopher's Hospice near London, England. He visited the hospice and
returned to the Royal Victoria with many of the core ideas and principles of
palliative care that he had observed.

As in the case of Burr, we see that the core ideas behind the vision existed
elsewhere. Charismatic leaders are very adept at taking the lessons of others and
applying them to their own situation. In Mount's case, these steps also permitted
him to form a primitive blueprint of the palliative care process. With this, he
could improve his own articulation of the future vision and begin initiatives to
acquire support for the forming vision (Westley, 1992).

At the time, there were no hospitals in North America offering in-house
palliative care services. In a teaching, tertiary-care hospital such as the Royal
Victoria, the notion of palliative care was countercultural. Such hospitals focused on curing patients, on the training of health professionals, and on experi-
mentation and innovation. Mount's challenge was one of securing political
support and resources—in other words, *legitimization* of the vision. This is the
enlistment phase of formulating the vision. Mount turned his attention to the
individuals controlling resources:

So I looked around and realized that there were two or three people who had to
be convinced because they controlled the outcomes. I had to slowly work with
them; the rest didn't matter. Basically, I had faith that this is a hospital, an

organization which is willing to experiment. (Mount, quoted in Westley, 1992, p. 284)

His three resource brokers were the chief of surgery, the head of nursing, and the chief of professional services. Mount framed his initiative or vision such that it offered each individual something of personal interest. The initiative became a means to achieve their own agendas. For the chief of surgery, Mount emphasized the research aspects. For the chief of professional services, who was a deeply religious man, the initiative would be built around a concern for the whole person, including spiritual needs. For the head of nursing, the caregiving process would employ egalitarian teams, with nurses having equal standing to other care providers. As a colleague of Mount explained,

> But the secret about [Mount's] success was that he hooked into something spiritual, something emotional, something idealistic, that is in most doctors. Many were suspicious, but Mount packaged it in a way that was scientifically and intellectually acceptable. . . . Mount took great care to speak the language of his audience at all times. Once they felt engaged by his excitement, they rationally could say "this makes sense." Whether an individual needed scientific language, political language, or spiritual language, Mount was able to identify the "hooks" and use them to link key people to his larger purposes. (quoted in Westley, 1992, p. 286)

Through this process of attaining political support, Mount would receive both space and some funding for his program.

He would then begin to assemble his team. Two other doctors joined him, both of whom shared a deep Christian theology. As Westley (1992) points out, they were recruited by Mount on the basis of their personality and their qualifications—supporting Locke's (in press) thesis that often the leader simply hires followers who are already in alignment with his or her beliefs and goals. As we saw with both Burr and Grove, the actual "coming together" of the vision was shaped by these two doctors as well as by Mount. Mount himself recognized that he was not a "details" person and that he needed others to translate his ideas into day-to-day realities. For example, one doctor was influential in determining the egalitarian nature of the caregiving teams. The other doctor shaped the details of how the palliative care actually would be delivered. From her overview of the process, Westley (1992) comments:

Like artistic production, the production of a vision is a highly creative enterprise, requiring the participation of many people at different stages if it is to be recognized. . . . [It is not] the sole possession of the visionary. (p. 304)

Rather many critical elements of the vision, including those aspects for which the palliative care service were [sic] renowned (i.e., the volunteer service and the use of teamwork) were articulated and developed by others, if not conceived by them. Indeed it would appear that Mount was most centrally responsible for what could be called the legitimization and articulation stages of the vision. (pp. 301-302)

Through the examples of Balfort Mount and Donald Burr, we hope we have illustrated a response to the second debate we earlier highlighted—whether vision is largely a rational process or more of a fragmented, creative, and intuitive process. On one hand, authors such as Kouzes and Posner (1987) have suggested that vision is the outcome of creative intuition on the leader's part. Others such as Nanus (1992) have proposed that it is a largely rational, planned process. For example, in his book *Visionary Leadership*, Nanus offers readers a series of actual visioning tools built around reflective questions that will aid them in the development of an organizational vision. We believe that although such structured exercises are helpful for thinking more broadly about an organization's environment, they do not adequately depict the creative, opportunistic side of a leader's vision, which cannot be captured through formal brainstorming sessions. This is most evident in our two case examples, in which the leader's own motivations were crucial, opportunities and events in the larger environment played catalytic roles, and political and resource-related events determined initial support for the leader's ventures. The process of turning environmental and follower assessments into vibrant organizational visions is a remarkably complex one shaped in part by forces beyond the leader's immediate control.

In the next chapter, we turn our attention to exploring the role of the charismatic leader's vision, its content, and its dynamism. This vision not only provides strategic direction but also aims to align the leader's organization to its objectives. We also will examine how the leader articulates the vision in ways that garner follower commitment, provide meaning, and guide actions.

NOTE

1. Material from the interviews with Jim W. Dawson, President, ZEBCO Corporation, is used by permission of Mr. Dawson.

5

Aligning the Organization Through Vision

In this chapter, we explore the notion of vision as it relates to charismatic leadership. Defined by the *Oxford English Dictionary* as the "ability to plan or form policy in a far-sighted way," vision was a rarely used term in the literature on leadership until the 1980s. Weber himself used the terms *mission, order,* or *normative pattern* to describe the goals of the charismatic leader. Many of the changes in the business world described in our opening chapter would, however, encourage the popularization of the term by leadership researchers in the late 20th century.

Intense global competition and shortened development cycles for technology had disrupted the typical life span of corporate strategies. As a result, business leaders were called on to pay far greater attention to the *future* direction of their organizations as their products and strategies were rapidly outdated by competition. At the same time, efforts at organizational adaptation often produced downsizing of workforces. In many cases, the resulting layoffs shattered decades-old psychological contracts with employees concerning job security. This led to concerns of how to enlist and motivate employees under such difficult circumstances.

Academics searched for terminology that adequately described the goal-setting process used by leaders in addressing these twin challenges of providing direction that ensured both organizational adaptation and employee empowerment. With its generally constructive connotations around foresight and positive goals, the term *vision* seemed appropriate. From the vantage point of charismatic leadership theorists, *vision* appeared particularly suitable given that these leaders typically articulate very forward-looking goals for their followers.

In the discussion to follow, we will explore the topic of vision around four distinct areas. The first involves an examination of how the term has been defined to date by leadership theorists. We will discover that it is a primitive term whose imprecision presents certain dilemmas and opportunities. The second topic centers on the roles that vision plays in the charismatic leadership process. In addition to direction setting, the charismatic leader uses vision to accomplish multiple aims such as motivating and garnering follower commitment, aligning the organization, and building group identity. Third, we will turn our attention to understanding the basic character or content of a leader's vision. For example, there is some debate whether a vision can include strategic and tactical goals or whether it must contain only lofty and transcendent goals. We will attempt to answer this thorny question. In addition, there has been a tendency in the literature to assume that *vision* refers only to the leader's goal statements concerning future directions. We will argue for an expanded conception that includes communications beyond formal goal statements. Our fourth and final topic focuses on the articulation and communication of the leader's vision. In essence, the vision is given "life" through its description and manner of conveyance. How charismatic leaders actually articulate their visions is an important point of differentiation from other types of leaders.

In closing this introduction, we should add that there are schools of thought arguing that vision is not a critical component of the charismatic leadership process. For psychoanalytic theorists (Kets de Vries, 1988; Lindholm, 1988), the followers' psychological identification with the leader is sufficient in itself to foster followership. Through the process of transference (whereby individuals transfer unconsciously what they experienced in past relationships, often familial ones, to those in the present), followers endow their leaders with powers and omniscience that they attributed to their own parents in childhood. They come to idealize the leader and his or her personal qualities. This school argues that transference, not vision, forms the root of the leader's influence. The leader's vision plays at best a secondary or minor role in the influence process.

A second school—a social contagion theory proposed by Meindl (1990)—argues that the self-concept of many individuals contains a heroic social identity component. This is an image of the person positively involved in a righteous cause for which he or she is willing to expend extra effort and make personal sacrifices. Individuals essentially are waiting for a leader to appear whose cause will activate this part of their identity. In contrast to the majority of charismatic leadership theories, it does not matter who becomes the leader as long as it is someone who is reasonably exceptional and attractive. As a body of followers form, they influence one another through their descriptions and stories about the leader. The heroic characteristics associated with the leader are increasingly exaggerated, especially by followers who have no direct contact with the leader. These followers promote mythic perceptions of the leader. This process cascades and creates a social contagion phenomenon such that distant followers develop the notion that their leader is truly superhuman and extraordinary. As a result, it is this social influence process among followers and not the leader's vision itself that is the principal forces behind followership (Yukl, 1994).

Our own position is that vision does play an important role. We do, however, feel that it is not the vision per se that is the primary source of follower attraction and identification with the charismatic leader. Rather, as Weber (1947) has suggested, it is follower perceptions of the extraordinary character of the leader that are the foundations of attraction. It is through these perceptions that followers come to believe in the *viability* of the vision and the potential rewards that it offers. We also argue that a necessary component of all forms of leadership is the setting of direction and goals, and such processes cannot be divorced from the act of leadership. To be perceived as a leader, an individual must offer a set of task-oriented goals that followers willingly accept. Visions are simply goals that are more forward-looking and idealistic. To believe that vision as a form of direction setting plays a minor or no role in the leadership process is to overlook the structure of leadership itself. Visions serve important and multiple roles in the influence process of charismatic leadership and in the actual accomplishment of the leader's goals. For these reasons, it is essential that we grasp their nature.

DEFINING VISION

Vision is a problematic term with a silver lining. In the literature, the word is used principally in a heuristic manner rather than to define with precision a set of phenomena. According to the theory construction literature (Gibbs, 1972; Hage, 1972; Reynolds, 1971; Stinchecombe, 1968; Zetterberg, 1965), we can think of *vision* as a "primitive" term—primitive in the sense that it sensitizes us to phenomena without providing clear, specific hypotheses or ideas. For example, *vision* has been used to describe a leader's capacity to powerfully interpret industry trends; in other cases, it is applied to describe organizational goals that are future-oriented. Similarly, there have been no attempts to distinguish vision from company mission statements or from descriptions of strategic and tactical goals or from value statements. Quigley (1993), for example, uses the term *vision* to represent all three elements: values, missions, and goals. Even in an allied literature on business strategy, the term's usage varies. There it is used similarly to describe either "a well-articulated point of view about tomorrow's opportunities and challenges" (Hamel & Prahalad, 1994, p. 74) or the strategic dynamics of a visionary individual (Westley & Mintzberg, 1989).

Although this looseness around the term's boundaries confounds its application, primitive terms such as *vision* do have distinct advantages. They can and do (1) expose the multidimensionality and complexity of phenomena that otherwise would be treated too simply, (2) integrate for more effective analysis what appear to be disparate ideas, and (3) lead to more precise, well-defined terms (Bacharach & Lawler, 1980, pp. 13-14). For us, *vision* is inherently, and will most likely remain, a primitive term much like the concepts of power or even leadership. It serves us best in this capacity because we are able to capture a range of phenomena under this umbrella concept that, as we shall shortly see, reflects complexity and a contextually dependent character.

Despite this imprecision, there are areas of overlap among the many researchers' descriptions of the term. Specifically, the leadership field tends to define vision around future-oriented goals that are highly meaningful to followers. For example, Tichy and Devanna (1986) describe vision as "a conceptual roadmap or set of blueprints for what the organization will look like in the future" (p. 128). We define vision as a set of idealized future goals established by the leader that represent a perspective shared by followers. Similarly, Bennis and Nanus (1985) explain that vision "articulates a view of a realistic, credible, attractive future for the organization, a condition that is better in some important ways than what now exists" (p. 89). They conclude that it "may be as vague as a dream or as precise as a goal or mission statement" (p. 89). To Kouzes and Posner (1987), the term implies an image of the future that provides a sense of direction, a set of ideals, and feelings of uniqueness for the organization. For House (1995), vision reflects "cherished end values shared by leaders and followers. It is a vision of a better future to which followers have a moral right; thus, it embraces a set of ideological values . . ." (p. 416). As one can see, these definitions tend to hold in common the notion that vision is distinguished by future goals that are seen as attractive for followers. In a recent review of the limited literature on vision, Nutt and Backoff (1997) similarly concluded that vision was generally interpreted to be "a mental model of an idealistic future or future perfect state, which sets standards of excellence and clarifies purpose and direction" (p. 312). Moreover, descriptions shared the following properties of "inspirational possibilities that are value centered and realizable, with superior imagery and articulation" (p. 312).

Where we begin to see differences is in the precise nature of the goals—whether they can include strategic and tactical goals or whether they must incorporate a higher social purpose and ideology to be classified as a "vision." For example, some categorize "being the number one company in market share in xyz industry" as a vision in the same manner as "revolutionizing the way children learn through our company's innovative products." Clearly, the latter has more affective and inspirational content than the former, yet the former has been the historical vision of one of today's most visible charismatic leaders, Jack Welch, the CEO of General Electric.

A second area of diverging viewpoints relative to defining vision is its use among certain writers to describe an individual's special capacity to be visionary (e.g., Sashkin, 1988). This attribution is particularly commonplace in the popular press. We are strongly disinclined to use the term in this context. As we showed in the previous chapter, the formulation of the visions of charismatic leaders is rarely if ever the product of a single individual. Defining vision as a unique individual capability reinforces the mythology about "divine insight" (Weber, 1947) and plays to highly romanticized notions of leadership (Meindl, 1990). Although this is often the attribution made by followers, it does not reflect reality. For this very reason, we define vision around future-oriented goals and communications that are meaningful and challenging to followers. Where the charismatic leader does possess a special capacity vis-à-vis other types of leaders is in their ability to *articulate* a vision. As we shall illustrate later in this chapter, charismatic leaders are able to construct highly meaningful visions through their choice of words, descriptions of images, and well-constructed justifications. They are more the masters of language and opportunists than the divine recipients of future insight.

VISION'S ROLE

In our theory of charismatic leadership (Conger & Kanungo, 1988a, 1994), we proposed that charismatic leaders increase their "likable" qualities in the eyes of followers (Byrne, 1977; Rubin, 1973) by formulating a set of idealized, future goals that represent an embodiment of a perspective shared by followers and that appear to satisfy their needs. The more idealized the future goals advocated by the leader, the more discrepant they become in relation to the status quo, and the greater the discrepancy of the goal from the status quo, the more likely is the attribution that the leader has extraordinary vision, not just ordinary goals. The idealized vision therefore serves to further highlight the uniqueness of the charismatic leader, making him or her more admirable and worthy of both identification and imitation by followers. We argue that this idealized quality of the charismatic leader's goals—supported by appealing rhetoric—is what distinguishes him or her from other leaders.

The idealized quality of the vision plays an additional role. By presenting very discrepant and idealized goals to followers, the leader provides a force for change. For example, we know from the attitude change literature that a maximum discrepant position within the latitude of acceptance puts the greatest pressure on followers to change their attitudes (Hovland & Pritzker, 1957; Petty & Cacioppo, 1981). Because the idealized goals of the leader's vision represent a perspective shared by followers that promises to meet their aspirations, it tends to be within this latitude of acceptance despite its often extreme discrepancy. As a result, the vision aligns the attitudes and behaviors of organizational members to achieve its objectives.

In *The Charismatic Leader*, Conger (1989a) went on to expand on the roles that vision played. Drawing on in-depth case studies of charismatic leaders, he described two additional roles unrelated to the identification and change process described earlier by Conger and Kanungo (1988a). One involved vision's usefulness in aligning the organization to its strategic direction, and the other concerned the motivational role of the goals themselves.

In the first role, the vision of charismatic leaders provides a "strategic umbrella" (Mintzberg & Waters, 1985) in the sense that their goals describe a clear strategic direction in overarching terms for the organization. The quality of "overarching" is important in that general goals allow for more specific, tactical goals to be worked out as opportunities arise and barriers appear. The vision then is an alignment device in the sense that it provides broad action guidelines for followers. In contrast, detailed strategic and business plans—the more traditional means of aligning—often are not well understood beyond executive levels of the corporation. As such, a well-articulated vision provides organizational members at all levels with a simple memory tool to align their values, actions, and decisions with the organization's strategic objectives. Its simplicity also promotes clarity of focus. Through minimization of the number of goals, organizational resources are more likely to be focused. Resources also are more effectively deployed given that only a few major strategic goals can be absorbed by an organization at any one time because of resource commitments and ongoing momentum (Quinn, 1980). In addition, the charismatic leader typically articulates a compelling rationale for the strategic aims of the vision and describes follower roles that further aid implementation.[1]

Similarly, the goals of the vision clarify performance outcome expectations and aid in goal implementation, which in turn heighten performance. Studies from both the field and the lab show consistently that when a manager sets specific, clear, and challenging goals rather than vague or no goals, the performance of subordinates is higher (Locke & Latham, 1990). We also know that performance is improved with specific goals because they focus subordinate efforts, whereas challenging goals energize a higher level of effort (Earley, Wojnaroski, & Prest, 1987). As a rule, goals exceed needs, values, and tasks in shaping an employee's intent to work long and hard because of the utilitarian and calculative side of human nature (Locke & Henne, 1986).

The motivational role of vision is achieved through the selection of goals meaningful to followers. For example, Mary Kay Ash articulates her company's mission as enhancing women's roles in the world and empowering them to become more self-confident. This is a highly appealing message to an organization comprising women for whom selling Mary Kay Cosmetics may be their first working career. As Shamir and colleagues (1993) point out, the vision usually is portrayed as a *unique* set of goals heightening the followers' sense that their endeavor is a special one. As such, the charismatic leader's vision creates for followers the perception that they are at an active center in the social system—those rare and remarkable arenas in society where change and innovation are taking place (Bennis & Nanus, 1985; Eisenstadt, 1968).

In addition to these various roles, we understand today that vision also reinforces followers' sense of collective identity (Shamir et al., 1993). By stressing the vision as the basis for the group's identity and by highlighting the necessity of collective effort to realize its goals, the leader reinforces the notion that individuals must subordinate their own needs for the larger group. As Meindl and Lerner (1983) have proposed, a shared identity can heighten the sense of a collective "heroic motive" and increase the likelihood that self-interested pursuits will be abandoned voluntarily for more self-sacrificing and collective behavior—all of which may be necessary to achieve the idealistic goals of the vision (Shamir et al., 1993). This is illustrated by comments from Mary Kay Ash to her sales force at the company's annual convention:

> Back in the days of the Roman Empire the legions of the emperor conquered the known world. These soldiers moved from nation to nation bringing into subjection people from the coasts of Spain to the borders of India. There was, however,

one band of people that the Romans never conquered. These people were the followers of the great teacher from Bethlehem. Historians have long since discovered that one of the reasons for the sturdiness of this folk was their habit of meeting together weekly. They shared their difficulties and they stood side by side. Does this remind you of something? The way we stand side by side and share our knowledge as well as our difficulties with each other at our weekly unit meetings? I have so often observed when a director or unit member is confronted with a personal problem that the unit stands together in helping that sister in distress. What a wonderful circle of friends we have. Perhaps it is one of the greatest fringe benefits of our company. . . . The simple fact of life is that no one is independent. We stand on the shoulders of countless people who have gone before us. Every time we eat a meal, we gain from the labor of another. Each visit to our doctor utilizes the sacrifices of people who have struggled with the complicated secrets of illness and disease. Every trip in our automobiles or in an airplane makes us debtors to courageous explorers and the pioneers of science. We are the recipients of countless gifts from friends of the past. We remember these friends with gratitude and try to pass on to others something of what we have received. (Ash, 1989)[2]

Through this analogy, Mary Kay (as Ash is commonly known) links collective support in the company to a courageous period in Christian history as well as to noble professions such as medicine and to remarkable 20th-century inventions. These connections elevate the sense of a heroic motive, as Meindl and Lerner (1983) have suggested. Her opening lines imply that it was only through collective support that early Christians were the sole people able to avoid conquest by the mightiest empire of the time. By implication, Mary Kay is saying that collective unity literally can work miracles in overcoming any odds. Reinforcing such collective behaviors is essential to Mary Kay's organization. The large majority of her employees are independent salespersons. Daily they face the challenge of direct selling. To ensure that their esteem and confidence remain intact (and to achieve the company's goals) in the face of customer rejection, an emotional support system of fellow organizational members is crucial. They must be heroic in their support for one another.

In summary, we see that vision is not simply a set of future-oriented goals that set direction for the charismatic leader's organization. Instead, it is a more complex mechanism through which the leader builds identification with himself or herself and the organization, heightens follower perceptions of the leader's extraordinary character, aligns organizational actions and strategies, enhances follower motivation and commitment, and builds collective identity.

THE CONTENT OF VISION

To simply possess a "vision" is insufficient; the content of the vision is crucial in determining whether its multiple aims will be achieved. For example, Conger (1989a) has shown that the home-banking vision of Robert Lipp, former president of Chemical Bank, and the product vision of the SX-70 instant camera of Dr. Edwin Land, inventor of the Polaroid, both failed because of poor market demands. Similarly, a leader could articulate a set of vision goals that were relatively meaningless to followers and therefore fail to garner sufficient commitment. Such examples lead us to ask, "What can we generalize about the *content* of the visions of successful charismatic leaders?" Here we encounter a problem. What is considered a "vision" is an area of debate (Bryman, 1992) in large part because of a lack of systematic research. Most of the research looking at the content of the visions of charismatic leaders has been limited to a select number of individual case studies (e.g., Conger, 1989a; Kotter, 1990; Westley, 1992; Westley & Mintzberg, 1989). The research has focused primarily on entrepreneurs such as Steven Jobs of Apple Computer, Mary Kay of Mary Kay Cosmetics, and Anita Roddick, founder and CEO of The Body Shop, and secondarily on organizational change agents such as Lee Iacocca at Chrysler, Jan Carlzon of Scandinavian Airways, or Jack Welch at General Electric. These are highly visible charismatic leaders in a handful of industries with generally positive track records. We cannot be completely certain that they are truly representative.

To date, only one large-scale empirical study (Larwood, Falbe, Kriger, & Miesing, 1995) has attempted to generalize the content of vision. Unfortunately from our standpoint, it was not directly linked to charismatic leaders. Instead, it relied on assessments from chief executive or chief operating officers of their own organizational visions. No determination was made whether the respondents were either charismatic leaders or leaders beyond their formal leadership positions. It is, however, the only large-sample survey of organizational visions to date and offers some confirmatory evidence of the vision characteristics we have been describing. Specifically, the research asked respondents to complete an evaluation of their company "vision statements" employing a 26-item self-evaluation list of vision descriptors. They rated each item from 1 = *very little* to 5 = *very much*. Items receiving the highest affirmative responses included "action-oriented," "responsive to competition," "long-term," "purposeful," "bottom-line oriented," "product of leadership," "focused," and "strategic." Items receiving low evaluations (that were not characteristic of their visions) included "difficult to describe," "conservative," "risky," and "general." Most of the descriptors reflect a proactive, goal-focused character that involves leadership.

Of the low ranked descriptors, only "risky" would appear to be at odds with theories about charismatic leadership given the lofty and therefore difficult-to-achieve visions such leaders commonly articulate. There are two possible explanations for this discrepancy. First, the sample may in reality contain only a small number of actual charismatic leaders. The majority of respondents therefore are either more traditional leaders or simply managers who advocate non-risky goals. The second possibility is that the assessors themselves do not perceive or do not wish to interpret their visions as risky. As we have proposed with charismatic leaders, the goals of the vision are always described as attainable, and to convey this effectively the leader may wish to downplay the presence of risk.

From a factor analysis of their data, the authors of the study drew the general conclusion that vision is interpreted by most as involving far-reaching strategic planning along with the ability and willingness to share and communicate the vision with organizational members—confirming our earlier assertions about the characteristics shared by the majority of conceptualizations in the field. Unfortunately, this type of study has several shortcomings. Beyond the fact that it relies entirely on respondent self-assessments, the study is context-free and stationary in time. As a result, it overlooks the fact that visions are shaped by contextual forces that cause them to be dynamic and evolutionary. Instead, the research tends to reinforce notions of vision as a step-by-step rational process involving the deployment of certain types of descriptors. The assumption is that the employment of these contextually sanitized descriptors increases the likelihood that an organization can devise an effective vision. As we argued in the previous chapter, we believe that this creates a misleading portrait of this complex phenomenon in opposition to those who see it as only a rational, planned process (Nanus, 1992).

Although the Larwood et al. (1995) study does confirm interpretations of vision as strategic goal setting, there still remains the important question of the exact nature of a vision's goals. For example, in recent years, we have tended to think of the visions of charismatic leaders more in the light of The Body Shop's lofty mission "to dedicate our business to the pursuit of social and environmental change" (Baker & Duncan, 1995, p. 1) or the Mary Kay organization's articulated mission of helping women develop into "the beautiful women that God intended them to be" (Conger, 1989a). Are such transcendent visions the norm for charismatic leaders in business?

Although there are charismatic leaders who articulate cause-related missions for their organizations, it would appear that there are an equal number of charismatic leaders who do not articulate aims of such higher purposes as helping society or the environment or an underprivileged group. For example, Richard Branson, a charismatic British entrepreneur, has built a diversified, multibillion dollar business whose unifying themes are entertainment and the brand name of the enterprise. There are few if any truly transcendent ideals as one traces the history of his organization. His first successful business venture was a mail-order business offering discounted records to young people. From someone's suggestion, he teasingly named the enterprise Virgin both to acknowledge his innocence in business and to be in sync with the anti-establishment sentiment at the time. From there, he built businesses in record production, retail music, tour operations, nightclubs, broadcasting, and publishing, along with an airline. In recent years, he has simply leveraged the Virgin trademark, given the company's high visibility throughout Europe. This has led to a joint venture in beverages with a cola named Virgin Cola and a retail chain called Virgin Bride for wedding arrangements. Other ventures are in the works. In Branson's case, the notion of a vision as a set of transcendent organizational goals is diffuse at best. As well, his company vision is to be found in his operating philosophy rather than in a well-articulated company vision statement. For example, as Kets de Vries and Dick (1995) have shown, Branson's organization is guided by certain fundamental values that are widely understood and shared by employees. First among them is the notion that organizationally "small is beautiful." Branson seeks to cultivate an entrepreneurial atmosphere within all the company's enterprises. When one unit grows too large, it is split apart. Each operating manager is given enormous autonomy and the potential to become a millionaire through partial ownership in the venture he or she oversees. The company is at the same time a venture capital firm. Branson provides seed capital to individuals with solid ideas for new ventures like Virgin Bride. This also reflects company values supporting organic growth rather than growth through acquisition (Kets de Vries & Dick, 1995). Internal growth guards the Virgin culture and allows Branson to provide continual upward career opportunities for employees. Another guiding value is customer service. The organization goes to great lengths to provide the highest level of value to customers. For example, Virgin Airways is a consistent innovator in airline service. Its first-class passengers are provided with massage and manicure services, its business and first-class passengers have limousine service door to door, and coach passengers have extensive video selections on personal monitors normally reserved for first-class passengers at other airlines. Each of the above values comprises a set of organizational ideals that the company strives to attain. These in essence shape the "vision" of the Virgin Group.

Another well-known charismatic business leader who offers no transcendent goals is Herb Kelleher, CEO of Southwest Airlines. His company's vision is essentially to be a friendly, efficient "flying car": nothing more, nothing less. Like Virgin, the company strives to be the best in its class, playing to the theme of the underdog challenging industry giants such as United and American airlines. Otherwise, the Southwest Airlines vision is shaped more by the attainment of certain values around teamwork, friendly service, speed, and competing against industry giants than it is a social mission. These two examples of Virgin and Southwest Airlines illustrate that in the business world, the visions of charismatic leaders are less likely to be cause-driven and transcendent than, say, in the arenas of politics, religion, and social movements.

Given the above examples and the wide range of visions that we ourselves have observed, our preference is to be broadly inclusive about what constitutes the content of a vision. We simply use the term *idealized*, which is an interpretive one similar to *charisma*. As such, it is quite conceivable that strategic goals that are highly challenging could be perceived by organizational members as idealized. Furthermore, broadening the term to include messages about strategy is important given the leader's task of using organizational goals (Kotter, 1990; Pascale, 1989) to align the behaviors, values, actions, and decisions of followers. For example, in the early 1980s, as he took over the helm at General Electric, charismatic leader John F. (Jack) Welch outlined four basic strategic goals as the company's vision for operating groups, as described by Tichy and Sherman (1993, p. 90):[3]

1. *Market leadership:* Each division must be either number 1 or 2 in share in their respective markets.
2. *Well above average real returns on investments:* Although Welch preferred flexible targets, one measure that was considered a threshold was the company's 18% to 19% return on shareholder equity.
3. *A unique competitive advantage providing value that no competitor can match.*
4. *Leveraging on GE's distinctive strengths:* In other words, focusing on opportunities that involve complex, large-scale pursuits requiring large capital investments, professional management, and staying power.

An additional pitfall for leadership researchers in determining what constitutes a vision has been to assume that the leader's vision is encapsulated entirely in formal statements. For example, there has been a tendency in the leadership literature to view vision as an "articulated directional masthead" or set of phrases that the leader uses repeatedly—much like an organizational mantra. This has shaped what researchers assume to be the content of a leader's vision. Most of the charismatic leaders we have studied do indeed have a formal "vision statement," but it would be a mistake to assume that such a statement is the sole contents of "the vision." Taking such a narrow perspective on vision overlooks the reality that charismatic leaders employ a wide range of communications, which are like supporting scripts for the vision. These may include descriptions of behaviors, values, activities, and immediate-term goals necessary to achieve the idealized, future goals. They may or may not be included in the leader's formally stated vision and often are communicated through a variety of channels other than official forums. For example, the charismatic leader may use hallway chats, formal and informal meetings, one-on-one discussions, reports, memos, and so on to convey them.

These communications can tell us as much, if not more, about the leader's vision than formal statements. Researchers to date, however, have tended to focus primarily on the official pronouncements. As a result, researchers have concluded that "non-charismatic leadership" emphasizes proximal specific goals, and "charismatic leadership" emphasizes values and distal goals and utopian outcomes (Shamir, Arthur, & House, 1994, p. 28). We believe this is an inaccurate description of charismatic leaders and the range of goals they articulate. It is assumed that they rely almost entirely upon broad, idealistic goals rather than more tactical ones. As we shall see, there are numerous examples in which supporting scripts incorporating values, tactical and strategic goals, and pre-scribed behavior came significantly before the articulation of an official vision. For these very reasons, it is important that *vision* remain a primitive term. Guarding its breadth allows us to capture a range of related phenomena that might otherwise be overlooked. In addition, focusing research solely on the leader's articulated vision may cause us to overlook tactical goals that are essential for the vision's success or else forerunners to the formulation of an official vision. To illustrate such a point, we will draw on the example of charismatic leader Charlotte Beers.

Beers was the CEO and chairman of the New York advertising firm Ogilvy & Mather. The firm had lagged behind in addressing fundamental marketplace trends unfolding in the 1980s, when clients began to demand lower fees and greater service. As a result, the company's performance sagged, and the quality of its services diminished greatly. Called in from an outside advertising firm, Beers took over in early 1992. Within a few years, she had staged a remarkable turnaround and revitalized the firm (Sackley & Ibarra, 1995).

To a large extent through client feedback and in-company committees, she would develop an initial vision for the firm in 1993 (Sackley & Ibarra, 1995): "The purpose of our business is to build our clients' brands." This would soon be followed by a later refinement: "To be the agency most valued by those who most value brands." On the surface, these vision statements contain very concrete and almost mundane goals—hardly transcendent. Beers, however, was able to transform them into idealized goals for her organization by arguing that few if any advertising firms in the world had achieved the capacity to consistently create and build corporate brands. Ogilvy & Mather, she argued, would achieve that stature.

What the vision statements fail to capture are the supporting scripts and initiatives that, in Beers's case, were more instrumental than the vision statement itself in the company's turnaround. Although both statements clearly focused the firm on building an expertise in branding, the Ogilvy & Mather "visions" are at such an abstract level that they lack an explicit tactical side—or answers to "how do we do this?" Given the desperate condition of the firm during the turnaround period, such visions would have been of little value in guiding the day-to-day actions of organizational members. Organizational members needed more concrete and clear objectives to realize the "valued brands" goal. Crafted in a company memo, Beers provided the following set of simplified strategic goals to guide the turnaround before she articulated a refined vision:

> I think we have hit bottom and are posed for recovery. Poised but not assured. Our job is to give direction for change. So here is where I start. For 1993, we have three—and only three—strategies. They are:
>
> 1. Client Security. Let's focus our energy, resources, and passion on our present clients. It takes three years to replace the revenue from a lost client. Under strategy one, there's a very important corollary: We must focus particularly on multinational clients. This is where we have our greatest opportunity for growth and where our attitudes, structure, and lack of focus have been obstacles.
>
> 2. Better Work, More Often. Without it, you can forget the rest. Our work is not good enough. Maybe it will never be, but that's O.K.—better to be so relentless about our work that we are never satisfied. You tell me there's nothing wrong with our credo, "We Sell, or Else," but you also say we need some fresh thinking on how to get there. We must have creative strategies that make the brand the central focus.
>
> 3. Financial Discipline. This has been a subject of high concentration but not very productively so. We simply have not managed our resources very well, and that must change. (Sackley & Ibarra, 1995, p. 10)[4]

These goals are largely strategic and tactical—certainly not visionary—but they were essential in drawing attention to the core goals that Ogilvy & Mather required to achieve its vision theme. What also is apparent is that they are simplified rather than complex organizational plans, a trademark of the charismatic leader. The simplification ensures widespread comprehension throughout all levels of the firm. We would suggest that discussions of a leader's vision also must include these types of communications if subordinates are to fully understand how the leader sets direction and mobilizes the organization. These in essence become supporting elements of a vision.

In addition to these articulated goals, the vision initially was given life through an operational initiative Beers undertook called Brand Stewardship (Sackley & Ibarra, 1995). A process called "brand auditing" was developed whereby a company's product brand was carefully examined by Ogilvy & Mather teams to reveal both its logical and emotional significance from the consumer's perception. This process in turn led to a capsule statement of the brand called a BrandPrint, known as the brand's unique "genetic fingerprint." such as "A Jaguar is a copy of absolutely nothing—just like its owners." One cannot understand the viability of Beers's vision divorced from these types of concrete initiatives as well as the supporting vision scripts conveying tactical and strategic goals.

To summarize, in our earlier thinking about the visions of charismatic leaders, we assumed like our colleagues that vision or mission statements had to contain transcendent and ideological goals to ensure their appeal and meaningfulness. Increasingly, we believe that many of the vision goals articulated by the leader can be simply strategic, especially in the business world. More often than not, however, they are strategic *ideals* that followers find deeply challenging. In addition, we now believe that to truly understand the effectiveness of a leader's vision, we must turn our attention to supporting communications and operating initiatives as well as to the formally articulated vision.

Visions Are Contextually Dependent and Dynamic

As we observed in the last chapter, a leader's vision generally evolves in interaction with a larger environment or context. Although most writers acknowledge that the charismatic's vision must reflect the shared concerns of followers, there have been fewer links drawn to the environment beyond the organization. Both, however, shape the vision. For example, the vision of The Body Shop, a British retailer, cannot be divorced from its larger environment. During the company's greatest growth period in the 1980s, the environmental or Green movement swept across the nations of Western Europe. The Body Shop's simple packaging, recycling of product containers, and natural ingredients matched a societywide environmental sensitivity, despite the fact that those initiatives originally were undertaken to contain costs, not to be social statements (Bartlett, Elderkin, & McQuade, 1991).

One of the most apparent examples of a vision being shaped by immediate events within a larger context is Lee Iacocca's vision for the turnaround of Chrysler. Westley and Mintzberg (1988) have shown how Lee Iacocca constructed a vision for the failing Chrysler corporation that justified a crucial large-scale government bailout. Specifically, he portrayed Chrysler through the analogy of a loyal, hardworking American family, of which Iacocca himself was the father, struggling in the face of famine and war. He created images and stories that were rich in justifications that would encourage his potential opponents (legislators, bankers, unions, and employees) to shift their stance to becoming a community of supporters. For example, he described the company's character to appeal to American myths about entrepreneurship and to overcome arguments that the company was simply a bureaucratic dinosaur:

> We explained that we're really an amalgam of little guys. We're an assembly company. We have eleven thousand suppliers and four thousand dealers. Almost all of these people are small businessmen—not fat cats. We need a helping hand—not a hand out. (Iacocca & Novak, 1984, p. 212)

In this description, he plays to American themes of small enterprise and of individuals needing temporary support rather than corporate welfare. The "helping hand" theme is reminiscent of early American pioneers who assisted one another to ultimately prosper in a new land and so plays to an important and deeply held American value.

Iacocca goes on to say that his own role was to doctor to health the war-torn organization by making tough personnel decisions: "I felt like an army surgeon. The toughest assignment in the world is for the doctor who's at the front during the battle . . . it's a question of priorities. . . . They would pick the ones who had the best chances of survival" (Iacocca & Novak, 1984, p. 186). Through this description, Iacocca becomes a well-intentioned surgeon who has little choice but to abandon some individuals (through layoffs) to save others. Casting himself in the father role to induce sympathy, he explained, "Our struggle also had its dark side. To cut expenses, we had to fire a lot of people. It's like a war—we won, but my son did not come back" (Iacocca & Novak, 1984, p. 230). The underlying message was that each Chrysler employee was like his own child. The company's widespread layoffs had the emotional impact on him of a parent losing a child in a war—but a war designed to save the nation. It portrays the situation in varying degrees of valor, tragedy, and necessity. This construction of the Chrysler vision was largely to secure government aid and employee support during a singular moment in Chrysler's history. In both of these areas, it succeeded.

As the above examples illustrate, one cannot divorce the content of a leader's vision from the context, nor from the leader's own ability to use language skillfully in depicting goals and providing convincing rationales. For example, an organization might adopt through brainstorming efforts a "vision" statement that pronounces its mission to "pursue social and environmental change." In this case, let us say that the company has no prior history of such interests. Without the supporting contextual dynamics akin to The Body Shop, this so-called vision would likely lack credibility, appearing artificially constructed and manipulative in the eyes of organizational members.

Because visions are contextually shaped, they tend to have a dynamic character. If we look longitudinally at the visions of many charismatic leaders, we will see that they evolve over time. This is an outcome of the shifting concerns of the leader and the organization, which are shaped either by accomplishing goals or by new opportunities that present themselves in the larger environment or in internal organizational forces that demand change.

To illustrate this dynamism, we will use two examples of Jack Welch's visions for the General Electric Corporation from different time periods. His early 1980s vision for the company consisted of four goals: (1) market leadership (either number 1 or number 2 in an industry), (2) well above average returns, (3) a unique competitive advantage, and (4) leveraging of the company's strengths. Over the decade, this vision would drive a remarkable transformation within the company. It would lead GE to sell or close approximately $10 billion worth of businesses and product lines that were not market share leaders. The remaining 350 businesses and product lines would be consolidated under a group of core operating companies. In addition, some $18 billion worth of acquisitions would be made to build market share in the new core businesses. These strategic moves would ensure that by the end of the 1980s, each of GE's businesses would rank first or second in its worldwide market. From 1980 to 1989, GE's stock value would rise from $12 billion to $58 billion, making it the number 2 company in equity valuation in the United States as net earnings rose for 40 straight quarters over the decade.

Having accomplished his original vision, Welch began to focus the corporate vision in 1990 around a new set of goals that addressed intracompany cooperation, customer relations, and the company's internal bureaucracy. First among his goals was the notion of the "boundary-less" organization. As Welch explained, a distinct character was needed at General Electric:

> In a boundary-less company, suppliers aren't outsiders. They are drawn closer and become trusted partners in the total business process. Customers' vision of their needs and the company's view become identical, and every effort of every man and woman in the company is focused on satisfying those needs. . . .
>
> The boundary-less company blurs the divisions between internal functions; it recognizes no distinctions between "domestic" and "foreign" operations; and it ignores or erases group labels such as "management," "salaried," and "hourly" which get in the way of people working together. . . .
>
> How do you get rid of these boundaries? The vertical ones—layer after layer of management—are relatively easy targets and, as I mentioned, we reduced or compressed them substantially in the eighties. We have more to do in the nineties. The horizontal ones, primarily between functions, are more difficult. The barriers between them grow, basically because of insecurity. People who spend their days working in the smog of bureaucracy have difficulty making the connection between what they do all day and whether the customer is served and the Company wins or loses. Their sense of security—which we all need—must come from their place in the bureaucracy and their sense of importance from owning a piece of organizational turf and defending it with jargon, channels, approvals, and other symptoms of what we call "functionalitis."
>
> How do you change a mindset that is more than a century old? We know the answer—the antidote. . . . It's self-confidence. Give people the chance to make a contribution to winning, let them gain the self-confidence that comes from knowing their role in it, and before long they abandon the paraphernalia of status and bureaucracy. They simply don't need it anymore. (Welch, 1990)[5]

This new vision of the "boundary-less" organization was intended not only to facilitate more powerful partnerships between the company and its suppliers and customers but also to leverage resources and ideas across the company's now 13 core businesses and to undermine bureaucracy. Welch realized that an enormous potential existed to share knowledge, best practices, and human resources across GE's divisions. What is intriguing is the solution that Welch offers to overcome bureaucracy at GE—instill greater self-confidence in the workforce. As we will see shortly, this plays to themes of promoting collective support and strengthening follower self-esteem that typically are associated with charismatic leaders.

We have found similar patterns of dynamism in other visions that we have studied. To retain their effectiveness, visions generally must have an evolutionary rather than a static character, reflecting an ongoing interaction between the leader and evolving organizational and marketplace demands.

A final issue related to the evolution of a vision is whether charismatic leaders formulate a rather well-defined vision at the onset of their mission. In the case of Charlotte Beers (Sackley & Ibarra, 1995), we see to the contrary that crystallization of a vision took her more than a year after her arrival. Many researchers nevertheless have assumed that charismatic leaders do indeed possess a vision early on that contains at least formative ideals and a meaningful purpose beyond normal business requirements.

Recently, however, we examined the history of several charismatic entrepreneurial leaders who started out with rather mundane goals. In these cases, either the leader, organizational members, or outsiders engaged in retrospective sense-making that attributed a well-formed vision early on to these leaders despite reality. For example, in the case of Anita Roddick of The Body Shop (Bartlett et al., 1991), we know that her earliest goal—like most entrepreneurs—was simple survival. No lofty vision was articulated at the onset. Instead, necessity guided Roddick's action and at the same time laid the groundwork for a later, substantive vision. Roddick has explained that the company's style was "developed out of a Second World War mentality of shortages, utility goods, and rationing. It was imposed by sheer necessity and the fact that I had no money" (Roddick, 1991, pp. 19-21). As a result, what would later become company trademarks of social and environmental sensitivity were begun by happenstance (Bartlett et al., 1991). Cash flow problems prevented Roddick from purchasing more product bottles, so she turned to a simple refill service for clients, offering them a discount in return—in essence, creating a recycling service. The extensive information on product labels was initiated because the product ingredients were unfamiliar to many customers. This step later would be interpreted as a company initiative to meet consumer needs for greater awareness of ingredients. The Body Shop's trademark color of green was chosen to hide moisture coming through the store walls in the company's first shop. Later, this color would become a symbol of the company's environmental concerns.

It was only as the company became more and more successful that Roddick began to envision a higher purpose for her organization:

Since 1984, the year The Body Shop went public, as far as I am concerned, the business has existed for one reason only—to allow us to use our success to act as a force of social change, to continue the education of our staff, to assist development in the Third World, and above all, to help protect the environment. (Roddick, 1991, p. 24)

Her principle-driven character and iconoclastic attitude toward traditional practices of the cosmetics industry lent themselves to the creation of a company
vision that was part social movement (Bartlett et al., 1991). For example, shortly
after the public trading of company stock, Roddick formed an alliance with
Greenpeace and initiated a "Save the Whales" campaign in 1986 within Body
Shop stores. Roddick saw the link as a natural one—after all, Body Shop
products used jojoba oil, a plant-based product that could be substituted for the
sperm whale oil used elsewhere in the cosmetics industry. Following this
campaign, similar annual initiatives became the norm. Projects were launched
to campaign for acid rain prevention, support for the homeless, protection of the
ozone layer, banning of animal testing, voter registration, and so on. In 1987,
she would establish The Body Shop's "Trade Not Aid" program, the sole purpose
of which was to trade with peoples of less developed countries to produce or
harvest the ingredients used in Body Shop products. An ongoing in-house
program of 300 "environmental advisers" was formed, drawing on employees
who volunteered to audit the company's performance in energy efficiency, water
usage, and waste management annually. These various initiatives would lead her
to crystallize the company's grander vision of "the pursuit of social and environmental change." Seen at two different points in time—the company's begin-
nings and its later success—the organization's goals evolved from simple tactical
goals to a lofty vision as resources, personal inclinations of the leader, and social
movements within society coalesced into The Body Shop's mission of today.

ARTICULATION AND
COMMUNICATION OF THE VISION

As Pondy (1978) notes, one of the most vital roles of a leader is to make activity
meaningful largely through language. In other words, what effective leaders do
is provide an understanding to their followers of why they are doing what they
are doing. In addition, as Morris (1949) pointed out some time ago, "Sharing a
language with other persons provides the subtlest and most powerful of all tools
for controlling the behavior of other persons to one's advantage" (p. 214).
Through choice of words and portrayals of future organizational outcomes, the
charismatic leader uses language to create meaning and a shared identity and
community vocabulary. For these reasons, it is critical that we understand how
charismatic leaders communicate to followers.

In our original theory (Conger & Kanungo, 1988a), we focused on leaders' communication of their vision and proposed that its articulation involved two separate processes: a description of the context and an articulation of the leader's own motivation to lead. Since that time, we have expanded our understanding of the role of language. Specifically, we see three major roles for the leader's use of language as they pertain to followers: (1) meaning-making and motivating; (2) aligning actions, behaviors, and values, and (3) and credibility building. Our two original roles are now subsumed under these categories.

Language That Shapes Meaning

The first role—meaning-making and motivation—is the most complex and perhaps most important in the influence process under charismatic leadership. Unfortunately, there has been little theory building and research on the use of language in motivating others (Sullivan, 1988). The theory that does exist focuses almost exclusively on the role of language to reduce uncertainty among organizational members. It assumes that employees are uncertain about how to accomplish goals, satisfy their needs, and act accordingly. Communications on the part of superiors can convey information necessary to lessen these uncertainties. For example, operant conditioning and expectancy theories explain how information is employed to reduce uncertainties about reward outcomes for performance efforts (Mitchell, 1982). Almost no attention has been directed to understanding language's use in meaning-making aimed at motivation. Below we offer a rudimentary model as it pertains to charismatic leadership.

We begin with the fundamental assumption that charismatic leaders are especially adept at employing language as a tool to help followers construct mental models of their world that give strong intrinsic meaning to their work and convincing justifications for action. As Sullivan (1988) has pointed out, organizational members want to construct an interpretation of their workplace reality that makes sense for them. Charismatic leaders are very effective at fostering such meaningful interpretations—often by imparting an idealized purpose for their organizations beyond the simple production of products or the provision of services. This facility is captured in sentiments expressed by Anita Roddick:

> Most businesses focus all the time on profits, profits, profits . . . I have to say I think that is deeply boring. I want to create an electricity and passion that bonds people to the company. You can educate people by their passions, especially

young people. You have to find ways to grab their imagination. You want them
to feel that they are doing something important. . . . I'd never get that kind of
motivation if we were just selling shampoo and body lotion. (Burlingham, 1988,
p. 42)

To understand how the charismatic leader uses language to make meaning
that is highly motivational, we must turn to the concept of framing. Goffman
(1974) noted that individuals use personal schemata of interpretation or "frames"
to understand events as elements of a larger, more coherent picture of life. In
essence, we organize experiences to make them meaningful and in turn use these
resulting scripts or frames of meaning to help guide our actions (Snow, Rochford,
Worden, & Benford, 1986). Similarly, leaders frame or interpret events so as to
make them meaningful to their followers.

In their analysis of social movements, Snow and colleagues (1986) describe
a process called *frame amplification* that involves the amplification of specific
values or beliefs by movement leaders to ensure follower participation. Values
in this case are defined as certain states of existence or modes of conduct that
are worthy of promotion and protection (Rokeach, 1973; Turner & Killian,
1972), and beliefs are relationships presumed to exist "between two things or
some thing and a characteristic of it" (Bem, 1970, p. 4). We believe that a similar
process occurs under charismatic leadership.

In value amplification, the charismatic leader essentially chooses to amplify
or elevate or idealize values that are held in regard by followers. By framing a
vision around appeals to these values, the leader provides a meaningful endeavor
and builds identification with the mission. For example, Snow and colleagues
(1986) use the example of the peace movement in the United States, in which
movement leaders and followers amplified the values of justice, the sanctity of
human life, equality, and freedom of speech (deeply held American values) to
enlist participation. Belief amplification is an extension of value amplification
in the sense that beliefs are "ideational elements that cognitively support or
impede action in the pursuit of desired values" (Snow et al., 1986, p. 470).

To illustrate how charismatic leaders more effectively employ framing (particularly to provide interpretations of events or goals that raise their intrinsic
value or meaningfulness in the eyes of followers), we will contrast two speeches—
one by a noncharismatic leader, the other by a charismatic one. Both are
articulating goals for their organizations, yet they use radically different frames.
Below is a portion of a speech delivered by a noncharismatic leader to his
company, a Fortune 500 company, in which he outlines the steps to realize the
organization's vision.

There's no question on management's part that even in the face of greater competition we can realize Vision 2005. We have three key goals:

1. One, grow in North America. The more growth we can gain in our home markets, the greater our worldwide growth will be. Our American operations are the shoulders upon which our international business grows.

2. Two, continue the kind of financial performance that marked last year's performance.

3. Three, continue to focus on adjusting the short term to ensure our long-term growth. This includes activities like our recent streamlining of the organization. Our vision is both a blend of the bottom line and the high ground. We will pay for it as we move from quarter to quarter and year to year with strong overall performance. I believe it is essential that everyone understand this quality of the vision—the blend of bottom line with high ground. Realizing Vision 2005 will be through the day-to-day activities as we cope with tough competition, economic downturns, and the increasingly more demanding expectations of our customers.

What we hear is a straightforward exposition of general goals—increase North American business, repeat the previous year's financial performance, and continue a focus on short-term initiatives. The values that are articulated are rather mundane (e.g., growth is good for a company), and beliefs are simple and business related (e.g., growth in our home markets will ensure growth abroad). The implicit rewards for organizational members appear to be financial and presumably career related (e.g., greater company growth will lead to greater job creation and presumably increase upward mobility in positions and salaries).

Contrast this framing of organizational goals with Mary Kay Ash, who similarly articulates the steps necessary to achieve her company's goals:

As I was preparing to address you today, I was thinking back over the past of what has made us great—and I thought it might be good to review once again those principles on which our company was founded.

First of all, we succeeded with a foundation built upon the golden rule and a philosophy of "God first, family second, and career third"—giving women a chance to keep their lives in proper perspective, a chance to have it all. These principles are not just important to our success. They form the foundation upon which our company was built.

Second, success comes from providing a product second to none, sold at a reasonable price. We started with a wonderful product, one that I had used personally, that simply provided better skin care than any other product I had seen at the time. . . .

We have succeeded through customer focus. If there was a single term that could capture the element that sets top performers apart, it would probably be customer focus. She makes their needs her goals. . . . The best sales people become facilitators for their customers, creating a partnership with them. It makes great business sense, because it costs five times as much to attract a new customer as it does to maintain an established one. . . . In direct sales, probably more than any other business, customer focus is truly the key. It's the real test of service, and service is the real heart of our business.

And finally, . . . quality growth comes from learning how to turn failure into success. It was Keats who said, "Failure is, in a sense, the highway to success inasmuch as every discovery of what is false leads us to seek earnestly for that which is true, and every fresh experience points out some form of error which we shall afterwards carefully avoid." That quotation has stood the test of time. . . . In the founding days of our company, when I took that legal pad and wrote down the problems that I had experienced, and challenged myself to find solutions for them, I was seeking ways to turn failures into successes. . . .

Our business, more than any other, is people-driven and people-dependent, and that gives us, at once, a great opportunity as well as a great responsibility. . . . Success is not a selfish objective. There is no way you can succeed unless you find a need and fill it, find a hurt and heal it, find a problem and solve it. If you are in business, people aren't going to come to your store because of your name and fame. They will come only if you can help them. (Ash, 1989)[2]

Mary Kay begins her address with a message similar to the Fortune 500 executive—"to continue our success, we must repeat certain things." Whereas the executive refers to business goals, Mary Kay describes a mix of activities, values, and beliefs. Similar to social movements, values are amplified early on: "God first, family second, and career third." Here we see Mary Kay building values-driven identification with her organization. Most of the company's members are part-time salespeople with families. Many are also deeply religious. The articulated values align with their own sense of priorities as if to say, "You can live out your values by working for Mary Kay; you do not have to sacrifice either God or family to be successful here." She then moves on to reinforce a belief—"a customer focus is the key to success." She heightens its importance by describing it as the *distinctive competency* of "top performers," as if this were the secret yet accessible ingredient that can be mimicked, leading to success.

Failure, interestingly, appears as an important topic in Mary Kay's speech. If we think about the Mary Kay organization, it is sales driven. Failure is part of her sales force's daily experience as potential clients turn down sales offers. Mary Kay challenges popularly held notions of failure through a justification that they are simply part of the path to success. She makes this belief appear highly plausible as she ties her own early start to learning from failure (the logic being that she herself learned and as a result has become enormously successful) and to the writer Keats, who is similarly seen as a highly successful and well-informed individual. Mary Kay is in essence providing staff with permission to fail as long as they learn—"[I] wrote down the problems that I had experienced, and challenged myself to find solutions for them."

Finally, she addresses a certain concern that some of her salespeople may have about "selling"—is it an admirable profession? Her aim is to elevate their role in society, to make it an honorable profession—in essence, raising the intrinsic worth of selling to build the self-esteem of her salespeople. She does this through the notion of *helping others*. With her statement "find a hurt and heal it," she implicitly ties selling to two honorable activities—parenting and medicine. In summary, the charismatic leader, Mary Kay, is far more adept and masterful at framing than is the Fortune 500 executive; she amplifies values and beliefs with which her organization readily identifies and that build follower esteem.

Through the framing of the vision around highly meaningful and empowering goals, the charismatic leader addresses two motivational challenges—one to motivate the followers' desire for the vision itself, and the second to motivate the followers' willingness to expend great personal efforts on achieving the vision. We draw this twofold distinction because it may be possible to have a situation in which followers find the vision motivational but are unwilling to expend a great deal of personal effort to attain it.

In addition to amplifying values and beliefs, the charismatic leader further seeks to achieve these dual motivational outcomes through descriptions of the status quo and the future state promised by the vision. Through frames of sharp contrast, the leader attempts to heighten the attractiveness of the future state such that it enhances follower commitment and performance efforts. The leader essentially constructs images of reality that emphasize the positive features of the future vision while simultaneously highlighting the negative features of the current context. The aim is to depict the status quo as so unattractive or threatening that it creates disenchantment. This portrayal unfreezes attachments to the current state and in turn lowers resistance to whatever changes the leader is advocating. It heightens the probability that followers will abandon behaviors, values, and beliefs that are perceived as ineffective in reaching the new order (Beer, 1980). Research in the organization change literature (Beckhard, 1969; Beer, 1980; Greiner, 1967) supports this notion of effective leaders creating dissatisfaction with the current situation so as to overcome the resistance of organizational members who face costs in terms of their own status, power, security, skills, and identity.

Jack Welch has been highly effective in this regard, powerfully interpreting the status quo of General Electric as threatening or detrimental. For example, in his 1989 address to shareholders, he initiates his discussion by describing a dire status quo in which fierce competitors from several continents are staging onslaughts:

> Our view when we entered the 80s focused appropriately on one powerful competitor: Japan Inc. As we stand on the threshold of the 90s, we face not only an even more powerful Japan but a revitalized, confident Europe moving closer together and led by bold entrepreneurs of the kind we simply didn't encounter in the 70s and 80s. . . . Korea and Taiwan . . . enter the 90s as innovative manufacturing powerhouses challenging the world in electronics, autos, steel, and a dozen other industries. Behind them on the same path come the other nations of the Far East including a potential colossus of the next century . . . China. The global market pie is not growing at nearly the rate necessary to satisfy the hunger of all those after it. (Welch, 1989)[6]

By implication, Welch suggests that these new competitors must eat from the same global trough as GE. He wants his organization to understand profoundly that although the previous decade had only one serious competitor, today there are many more of equal strength. The status quo is portrayed as a highly threatening world demanding high performance standards from GE employees to remain successful.

Charlotte Beers, at Ogilvy & Mather, is another illustration of how the charismatic leader depicts the status quo to garner commitment to the future vision (Sackley & Ibarra, 1995). Beers spent her initial months at Ogilvy & Mather studying how the organization's services had deteriorated. After extensive fact-finding visits with clients, she shared what she had learned with senior management in a series of meetings. There she revealed customer perceptions about the firm:

> Clients stunned me by rating us below other agencies in our insight into the consumer. Clients view our people as uninvolved, distant, and reserved. We have organized ourselves into fiefdoms, and that has taken its toll. Each department— Creative, Account, Media, and Research—are often working as separate entities. It's been a long time since we've had some famous advertising. (Sackley & Ibarra, 1995, p. 7)[4]

Through these meetings, she dramatically raised awareness that the firm was failing customers—in essence, highlighting the intolerable state of the status quo and implying that the firm's future was in serious jeopardy.

At the same time, by portraying future goals as the most attractive and as attainable, a charismatic leader seeks to create a strong identification among followers with the vision. This increases the willingness of followers to expend significant personal efforts to ensure the organization's passage to the future. As Shamir and colleagues (1994) similarly argue, these outcomes are produced by the leader's ability to heighten the intrinsic value of follower efforts and commitment and to show that such efforts will result in realizing the vision.

We returning to Beers to demonstrate our point. Beers proactively portrayed the future of Ogilvy & Mather as a great opportunity and as a vehicle that would enhance employee work life (Sackley & Ibarra, 1995). This was eloquently captured in a letter she sent to company employees titled "Statement of Vision and Values":

> The winds of change are blowing through Ogilvy & Mather. We are raising the sights of everybody in the company to a sweeping new vision: TO BE THE AGENCY MOST VALUED BY THOSE WHO VALUE BRANDS.
>
> Not that we have ever been unmindful of the importance of brands. Quite the contrary. Our new thrust gets a big boost from ingrained Ogilvy & Mather strengths. . . . We have always aimed to create great campaigns with the spark to ignite sales and the staying power to build enduring brands.
>
> What's new is a restructuring of resources, an arsenal of modern techniques, and an intensity of focus that add up to a major advance in the way we do business. We call it BRAND STEWARDSHIP—the art of creating, building, and energizing profitable brands. . . .
>
> This will affect the working habits of every professional in the agency, to the benefit, I am convinced, of every brand we work for. I predict that it will bring out the best in all of you—creatively and in every other aspect of your work—and add a lot to the pleasure and satisfaction you get out of your jobs. . . .
>
> All vital cultures—national, artistic, corporate—tend to evolve as conditions change, preserving valuable old characteristics as new ones come into the spotlight. In just that way these Shared Values [of Brand Stewardship] now take their place at the forefront of the dynamic culture of Ogilvy & Mather. (Sackley & Ibarra, 1995, p. 19)[4]

As we would predict, Beers frames the future vision not only as a restoration of the firm's former greatness but also as a move into a new era of advertising that Ogilvy & Mather will be leading. She attempts to create a strong identification with the vision by offering a very positive future and by appealing to employees' self-concepts—"it will bring out the best in all of you."

Language That Aligns

As we mentioned earlier in the chapter, the leader's vision plays an important role in aligning not only the strategic initiatives of the organization but also the behaviors and values of followers so that they focus on achieving company goals. For this very reason, the charismatic leader invests considerable time in communicating what are appropriate follower attitudes, behaviors, and values. These are framed as necessary to achieve the vision or mission of the organization. For example, Mary Kay spoke about the need to provide collective support for one another:

> I have so often observed when a director or unit member is confronted with a personal problem that the unit stands together in helping that sister in distress. What a wonderful circle of friendships we have. Perhaps it's one of the greatest fringe benefits of our company, in making so many friends, beginning with our customers and going on through our association with our unit members. People who lead happy and exciting lives are those who work at making friends. Somehow difficult times are easier to handle when you don't have to handle them alone. (Ash, 1989)[2]

We will draw on one particular example to illustrate our point about alignment. The charismatic leader in this case is Orit Gadiesh, the vice chairman of Bain & Co., a well-known Boston management consulting firm (Rothbard & Conger, 1993). Founded in 1973, Bain was a remarkable success story, growing from $750,000 in revenues in 1975 to $175 million by 1991. Its founder, Bill Bain, and his original partners decided in 1985 and 1986 to harvest their success by selling 30% of the company to create an employee stock ownership plan. In return, the partners received for themselves a total of approximately $200 million in notes and in cash, which the company had to borrow. In the end, the company was burdened with great debt and high interest payments, and the valuation of the firm itself became controversial—after all, it was based on exponentially increasing future revenues and profits. By 1988, interest payments skyrocketed and competition intensified, forcing Bain into its first-ever layoffs. Morale within the organization slid dramatically. To resolve the growing crisis, a compromise solution was reached in 1991 whereby the founders agreed to return approximately $100 million to the firm, along with 70% of the stock. By 1992, the company's profits and revenues had climbed back to pre-1990 levels. In that same year, Orit Gadiesh was named vice chairman of the firm.

Having joined the firm in 1977 after graduate school, Gadiesh rapidly garnered a reputation as a savvy consultant, which led to rapid promotions. By early 1982, she already had become a vice president and soon progressed to executive vice president and company director. With her unconventional dress, funky jewelry, and purple hair, Gadiesh projected an air of confidence and command within the firm. She had become a legendary figure. As one former Bain consultant explained:

> Orit stories abound both inside and outside of Bain. Supposedly, the day after she made partner, she showed up with purple hair, and it's been purple ever since. When she walks into a room, you feel it. Her flamboyant risk-taking style makes her one of the most charismatic individuals I've ever met. (Rothbard & Conger, 1993, p. 16)

As a senior leader of the firm, Gadiesh had become deeply concerned about morale issues at Bain. Although the financial picture of the company had turned around, she sensed that the organization had lost pride in itself. She chose the company's annual meeting in August of 1992 to convey in words what she felt the organization had to realize—that a "pride turnaround" was a necessity. In interviews we conducted at Bain, her speech would be attributed as the turning point at which morale moved upward dramatically. Below is a partial transcript of what she told her audience:

> I want to talk to you today about confidence and pride in what we do. I know this sounds a little strange, but bear with me for a moment. Let me give you a sense of where this comes from.
>
> A couple of months ago, I had dinner with a business-school professor who is a friend of mine. In the course of the dinner, somewhat to my surprise, he asked me what I liked the most about what I do, and what I found most frustrating. The answer to the first part came easily, and I can summarize it here in one sentence: What I love most about my work is the fact that I am part of a team that produces the most extraordinary work, and continuously beats the odds and does the impossible in everything we put our minds to. I really believe it. . . .
>
> "Gee," he said, "that's an awful lot of self confidence from someone who has just gone through what you all have . . ."
>
> "That," I said, "is my biggest frustration—the fact that some people actually believe that the last year and a half—while distracting on many dimensions—would distract us from doing what we do best, or from feeling very proud about it."
>
> My answer was so instantaneous, so much from the gut, that I actually had to stop and think about it: What did I mean when I said pride?
>
> I realized that by pride I meant a conviction that what Bain & Co. set out to do was worth doing. And that for a year and a half, many of us believed that if

we could just cut through all the bull, we would get back to it. A conviction that enough of us were still passionate about what we do, and that shared passion was what had made this place great. And that we could do it again. In fact, that was precisely what carried us through what were undeniably hard times.

My friend the professor was startled. "Wow," he said. "If enough people feel like you do, Bain & Co. is going to be truly unstoppable."

I've been thinking about this ever since. I guess we stopped projecting self confidence . . . [but] I think very few—if any—of us ever really lost our pride in what we were doing individually in our work. But for a while there, we lost our collective pride. That thought kept bugging me. There is a fine line between arrogance and pride, and believe me, we've crossed that line in the past. But, boy was it powerful when we stayed on the right side of this line and projected it!

I talked about it with a number of you. People got it. It was hard to put a finger on what it meant, but it resonated . . . We really turned around everywhere our competitors said we would not be able to.

We've turned around financially, and we've turned around the business—and even our competitors are beginning to acknowledge that. Now it's time to turn around what they really fear, what they have always envied us for, what made them most uneasy—as crazy as this sounds. It's time to turn around our collective pride in what we do! (Rothbard & Conger, 1993, pp. 12-13)[7]

Gadiesh spoke for another 35 minutes, focusing on the accomplishments of the past year. She shared anecdotes that demonstrated how impressive the work of the various teams had been and how much clients had deeply appreciated their efforts. In one example, she read aloud a letter, written by the division president of a large financial services company, that was addressed to every member of the team complimenting them on their outstanding work. She stressed how these examples had come from all levels of the organization and that cumulatively they were having an impact on the building of powerful relationships with clients. With a few minutes remaining, she concluded:

I've asked you to listen to what people say about the power of what you do. I've asked you to look at each other and not take for granted what others envy us for. Our clients don't—they love it!

Our competitors don't—they fear it! It's time for us to project it again: Internally among ourselves because we will have more fun, and externally to the world.

Each and every one of us is an ambassador of our company. Each and every one of us is part of the team. Whether you are in the administrative staff convincing someone to apply for a job, or helping a colleague get through a bad day. Whether you are a consultant or an associate consultant, striking up a conversation or on a plane or celebrating your friends' successes in your area.

Whether you are talking to a potential employee or client, or working with your team—who you are and what you believe comes through. You can only say what you believe. You can only project what you feel. That's all I ask.

I told you how I feel. I told you why I'm proud. I hope you share some of it. Because when we believe in ourselves the way others do, our turnaround will be complete. And when we collectively project it, we are—as my friend the professor said—truly unstoppable. (Rothbard & Conger, 1993, pp. 12-13)[7]

Throughout her speech, Gadiesh uses language powerfully to create justifications for why the firm has restored itself completely with the aim of aligning employees' feelings to match a portrayed reality of success. She is in essence giving permission for her colleagues to return to earlier feelings of deep pride. Now is the time, she argues—"We are already back to our former greatness—do not be in doubt about this." Her recounting of recent success stories and the letter of praise from the financial services executive serve as evidence of her assertions, much like courtroom evidence. To heighten credibility, she uses an outside expert—the business school professor—to draw the conclusion that she wants her audience to reach—if we restore our confidence in ourselves and the organization, these feelings will provide us with a remarkable competitive advantage ("If enough people feel like you do, Bain & Co. is going to be truly unstoppable."). The implicit assumption is that if a credible source and expert in business perceives such a link, it must be a valid one.

What also is clear from our interviews (though impossible to convey in the printed text of her speech) is the affective side of her message. Throughout her presentation, Gadiesh used strong emotions conveying pride and confidence in the organization. The exhibition of such feelings "on stage" in essence becomes a model for the company of "pride refound"—the central theme of her talk. Finally, her delivery was conducted with great sincerity and conviction, which heightened the credibility of her arguments. In conclusion, Gadiesh is an excellent example of how charismatic leaders use language to align.

Language to Build Credibility

We proposed in our original theory (Conger & Kanungo, 1988a) that charismatic leaders model their commitment and confidence in their visions of the future through both verbal and nonverbal behavior. Through the use of rhetoric, they project their assertiveness, conviction, expertise, and concern for follower needs. These actions in essence make the charismatic leader and his or her vision appear credible. For example, sometime into the formulation for the new vision for Ogilvy & Mather, Beers encountered a moment during a senior management retreat when one person questioned the emerging idea of brand stewardship (Sackley & Ibarra, 1995). The executive commented, "There's nothing new here. I don't see how Brand Stewardship can be unique to Ogilvy." This stirred considerable debate within the group. The very next morning, Beers, who by this time had become convinced of the new vision, stated to the group:

> Certainly, the individual pieces of this thinking are not new. But to practice it would be remarkable. I have heard that in any change effort, one third are supporters, one third are resistors, and one third are apathetic. I'm in the first group. Where are you? (Sackley & Ibarra, 1995, p. 12)[7]

This sense of confidence and challenge to the group served as a catalyst. Shortly thereafter, the group reached a consensus that brand stewardship was indeed the right direction (Sackley & Ibarra, 1995, p. 12).

In any communications act, an audience must ascertain whether the speaker is trustworthy and the message credible. In the case of the charismatic leader, many factors in addition to language shape follower perceptions of the leader's credibility—for example, the leader's prior successes, demonstrated expertise, and history of relationships with followers. Charismatic leaders use language to reinforce further the credibility not only of themselves but also of the initiatives they advocate. The example we cited of Charlotte Beers verbally exhibiting confidence in her goals is one illustration.

We know from persuasion theory that audiences place trust in a speaker's message depending on their interpretations of the individual's character (Hauser, 1986), which is discerned in part by the habits they reveal about themselves through their communications. As Miller (1974) has shown, habits are discerned by the causes an individual advocates, the values he or she endorses, and the actions he or she advises to be undertaken. Charismatic leaders typically align themselves closely with follower sentiments or vice versa in all three of these areas so as to reinforce positive perceptions of their character and in turn their credibility.

We also know from persuasion theory that audiences evaluate a speaker's credibility by assessing three specific categories of habits that manifest themselves in intellectual, moral, and emotional qualities. The more admirable an audience finds these qualities in a presenter, the more credible that individual will appear (Hauser, 1986). Specifically, intellectual or mental habits are revealed through the appearance of the speaker being well informed, skillful at reasoning, and able to overcome objections by providing compelling evidence.

For example, as Hauser (1986) points out, John F. Kennedy was able to convey strong intellectual habits in his rhetoric through various means. He appeared extremely well informed by possessing a great command for retaining and using facts. He consistently employed the rhetorical device of antithesis ("not this, but that"), which projected a sense of analytic precision and therefore intellect. Finally, he was a quick thinker, able to rapidly turn a question back on to the questioner with charm and wit. We hypothesize that charismatic leaders will project similar verbal behaviors in their communications to a greater degree than noncharismatic leaders.

Moral habits are demonstrated by speakers through the confidence they exhibit in understanding what is right, through their courage of convictions, and through the virtues and values they extol. Hauser (1986) again provides an illustrative example, this time with Edward Kennedy, who in his 1980 address to the Democratic Convention was attempting to defend the viability of political liberalism:

> The commitment I seek is not to outworn views but to old values that will never wear out. Programs may sometimes become obsolete, but the ideal of fairness always endures. Circumstances may change, but the work of compassion must continue. It is surely correct that we cannot solve problems by throwing money at them, but it is also correct that we dare not throw national problems onto a scrap heap of inattention and indifference. (pp. 98-99)

What we see is that Kennedy makes no assertions that he himself is a virtuous individual. The values he pleads for, however, encourage listeners to see him as such. For example, he plays to important societal virtues such as justice ("the ideal of fairness"), generosity ("compassion must continue"), and temperance ("cannot solve problems by throwing money at them"). For audience members wishing to believe him, his rhetoric provides a rationale to see him as an individual of good character and to trust his platform.

Returning to Anita Roddick (Baker & Duncan, 1995), we see in her articulation of a hard-line stance against the traditional practices of the cosmetics industry a similar moral habit:

> It turned out that my instinctive trading values were dramatically opposed to the standard practices in the cosmetics industry. I look at what they are doing and walk in the opposite direction. . . . (Baker & Duncan, 1995, p. 3)

> [In contrast to industry promotional materials] You cannot change your body shape. We won't use sophisticated photographic images, and we won't make exaggerated claims about our products. We just talk about the ingredients. We are quite puritanical about this. (Baker & Duncan, 1995, p. 3)

In both examples, Roddick powerfully articulates her convictions— "I . . . walk in the opposite direction." By doing so, she creates an appearance of great courage and risk taking, particularly because traditional industry practices have proven to be wealth builders for cosmetics companies. Her own success as an outlier, however, heightens perceptions of the "rightness" of her convictions and the extraordinary quality of her vision. As well, there are virtues of prudence and honesty embedded in her position that strengthen perceptions of her moral character. We believe that most charismatic leaders will similarly build credibility in their moral character through the sheer strength of their convictions and the types of virtues and values they advocate in their communications.

Finally, a speaker's emotional habits are discerned through the disposition of either goodwill or ill will toward the audience. Goodwill typically is demonstrated through a speaker's concern for the audience's interests. Hauser (1986) highlights the types of expressions that audiences typically will interpret as reflective of a speaker's goodwill:

> They are angry at people who insult us or harm us; they are fearful of impending dangers; they are joyful at our successes and counsel us to emulate others who have succeeded. We further test the sincerity of their feelings in terms of the personal stakes they might have in the outcomes. We know people are well disposed when their advice is not necessarily in their best interests, though it is in ours. (p. 99)

We would postulate that charismatic leaders will consistently demonstrate goodwill in their communications toward followers, along with depictions of personal sacrifices for the good of the organization.

As we have described in this chapter, vision and its articulation are essential components of the charismatic leadership process. They not only build identification with the leader and his or her mission but also serve to align the followers' attitudes, values, and behaviors toward the realization of the vision. Vision, however, is insufficient in itself. The charismatic leader must demonstrate through strategic choices and actions the *viability and appropriateness* of these future goals. In addition, the leader must establish the requirements for implementing the vision as well as model the values and behaviors necessary for its achievement. In the next chapter, we will examine this daunting challenge of turning the vision into a reality—the implementation phase.

NOTES

1. For example, Alexander (1985) found in a study of 93 medium-sized to large companies that strategic decisions were more successfully implemented when senior managers clearly explained the rationale for strategic decisions and defined employee roles and responsibilities.

2. Excerpts from *A Festival of Friends*, a speech given by Mary Kay Ash in 1989 to the annual Mary Kay Cosmetics Seminar in Dallas, Texas, are used with permission.

3. Excerpt from Tichy and Sherman, 1993, is used with permission from John F. Welch, Jr.

4. Material from Sackley and Ibarra, 1995, is used with permission from Charlotte Beers.

5. Excerpt from Welch, 1990, is used with permission from John F. Welch, Jr.

6. Excerpt from Welch, 1989, is used with permission from John F. Welch, Jr.

7. Excerpts from this transcript are used with permission from Orit Gadiesh.

6

Implementing the Vision

In the implementation phase of the organization's vision, the charismatic leader faces three fundamental challenges: (1) ensuring high levels of follower commitment and performance; (2) instilling in followers the values, beliefs, and behaviors necessary for the vision's realization; and (3) devising and executing strategic initiatives that further the vision in the marketplace. All these activities are necessary to ensure that the lofty and demanding goals of the vision will be accomplished. In this chapter, we examine how the charismatic leader achieves these outcomes. Specifically, we will look at the role of the leader's exemplary acts, the use of empowerment approaches, the promotion of cooperative behavior among followers, and the deployment of innovative strategies for achieving the vision.

ROLE-MODELING EXEMPLARY BEHAVIOR

Charismatic leaders use role-modeling behavior for several purposes: (1) to demonstrate their own commitment to the vision and to followers; (2) to emphasize the beliefs, values, and behaviors that are essential to realizing the organization's vision; and (3) to provide a vicarious empowering experience for followers. Role modeling therefore aims to build follower trust, provide examples of required behavior, and promote a sense of self-efficacy. Preliminary studies (e.g., Agle & Sonnenfeld, 1994) suggest that such behavior has a strong effect on follower performance.

The first objective of role modeling—demonstrating the leader's commit-ment—is essential to creating a foundation of trustworthiness. This foundation will allow the vision and role-modeling behaviors of the leader to be accepted and internalized by followers. It also fosters cooperative or "good citizenship" behavior among followers (Podsakoff et al., 1990). In addition, the leader's past accomplishments and successes work to build this foundation of trust. In essence, success validates the leader's charisma and affirms his or her extraor-dinary abilities. Failure, on the other hand, suggests flaws in the leader's plans and abilities and strips away the aura of extraordinariness. At the same time, a continual demonstration of the leader's abilities and commitment is crucial to promoting ongoing follower trust.

Specifically, charismatic leaders seek to show that they have a total dedication to the cause they share with followers. Through actions that are seen by followers as involving great personal risk, cost, and energy (Friedland, 1964), these leaders create strong perceptions that they are highly trustworthy, which in turn solidi-fies follower commitment to them and their mission. In the business world, many of these behaviors take the form of the leader's willingness to forgo special entitlements and rewards.[1] Southwest Airlines's CEO Herb Kelleher, for exam-ple, requested that his office have no windows. This is in sharp contrast to status norms in the business world, where senior executives always have window views, often spectacular ones. Kelleher decided that he would send a message quite to the contrary by creating a lower-status office for himself. In other cases, he has forgone significant financial rewards. For example, in the 1980s, follow-ing deregulation, the airline industry underwent a series of mergers as companies sought to attain "critical mass." Some 20 major airline mergers took place during the 8 years following deregulation, creating a total of 10 airline holding compa-nies that operated nationally (Petzinger, 1995). Together they dominated 95% of the U.S. market. Southwest was the smallest, at number 10 on the list. As such, it was a natural target for acquisition. Although he stood to reap significant financial rewards, Kelleher vehemently defended Southwest against takeovers. He adopted a "poison pill" and other takeover defenses (Petzinger, 1995). At one point, he was visited by a Wall Street investment banker who commented how attractive Southwest was as a takeover target. Kelleher rose from his chair and backed the young man against the office wall. "You're too young to know what scorched earth is," stated Kelleher, who explained how the Russians chose to destroy their property rather than leave it intact for advancing Nazi troops. "Anybody who buys this company is going to have ashes, soot, and cinders. Those who build something know best how to destroy it!" yelled Kelleher as his hands held firmly to the man's shoulders, which were pushed against the wall. As the investment banker raced out of the office, Kelleher's executive assistant

Colleen Barrett asked what had happened. Kelleher responded, "I just sent a message to Wall Street." That year, on the cover of the company's annual report in bold yellow letters against a black background, read the words "In 1986, we didn't merge."[2]

In Chapter 4, we discussed how Jim Dawson of Zebco employed various initiatives to undo the status barriers between the company's executives and its workforce by removing time clocks and executive-level perks such as reserved parking. While running the airline Linjeflyg, Jan Carlzon closed the executive dining room:

> I realized immediately that the executive dining room had to go. Linjeflyg, a small company, was sending out the wrong signals by having such a pretentious dining room. If I began eating there myself, my actions would tacitly condone an image I don't like. . . . [Closing the dining room] was an unmistakable sign that we were all at Linjeflyg to work together. (Carlzon, 1987, p. 29)

At SAS, Carlzon would fly coach class rather than what was customary for company executives—first class. He used such acts to model his own willingness to forgo executive perks and to remind employees that customers were the company's number one priority. He observed that "the cabin crew interprets these tiny, symbolic gestures in this way: 'Even top management is helping give the passengers good service. That shows respect for *our* jobs' " (Carlzon, 1987, p. 30).

In summary, these examples of leader role modeling aim to demonstrate that the leader is on "equal footing" with followers in terms of their status and the rewards they share. As such, they show that the mission is not about improving the leader's own personal lot. Instead, they become visible "proofs" that the leader puts activities furthering the mission ahead of opportunities to profit personally from successes. Moreover, they prove that the leader is willing to forgo rewards normally associated with leader status to demonstrate that indefatigable commitment to the cause. This aspect of modeling also sends a clear message to followers that they too must be prepared to sacrifice for the good of the mission—that every member must place the organization's goals ahead of his or her own self-serving goals.

From the standpoint of the second aim of role modeling—instilling beliefs, values, and behaviors—the leader serves as a "representative figure" (Bellah, Madsen, Sullivan, Swidler, & Tipton, 1985). Leaders embody for followers the characteristics that are important to be emulated and internalized if the organization's mission is to be achieved. As Shamir and colleagues (1993) note, followers learn vicariously through the relevant messages [that] are inferred by followers from observation of leader's behavior, life style, emotional reactions, values, aspirations, preferences, and the like . . . [such that the leader becomes] a symbol which brings together in one concentrated image the way people in a given social environment organize and give meaning and direction to their lives. (p. 584)

Returning to Herb Kelleher as an illustration, his actions model many of the important behaviors and values associated with the company's vision, such as cooperative behavior and having "fun." He can be seen helping flight attendants to serve passengers or bringing doughnuts to maintenance crews at three o'clock in the morning. To model the importance of fun and playfulness, he can be found wearing a leprechaun costume on St. Patrick's Day or a bunny outfit on Easter. On occasion, he has greeted new corporate staff members in his office wearing a wig and sunglasses, posing as Roy Orbison (Petzinger, 1995). He has appeared in company commercials with a paper bag over his head, exclaiming "If you're embarrassed to fly the airline with the lowest customer complaints in the country, Southwest will give you this bag." Removing the bag, he states, "But if you're not, we'll still give you this bag—for all the money you'll save."

Richard Branson of the Virgin Group models through his dress and actions the importance of informality and a nonhierarchical work environment. He dresses in sweaters and slacks, uses few memos, is accessible to company managers, has a relaxed demeanor, and hosts company events at his family home in Oxfordshire (Kets de Vries & Dick, 1995). To model his aversion for bureaucracy, the company has no real "corporate offices"; instead, for much of the company's history, Branson had his office in a canal houseboat in London. One bedroom served as the secretaries' office, and Branson's desk was a dining table in a small sitting room of the boat (Kets de Vries & Dick, 1995). The headquarters of his companies are for the most part in townhomes throughout London rather than in corporate office towers.

The third role of leader modeling is to vicariously empower followers.[3] Branson is particularly noteworthy in this regard. He strongly encourages entrepreneurship and risk taking among his employees. His own entrepreneurial track record is remarkable in that he built a $1.5 billion enterprise from nothing. Encouraging decisiveness among staff, he demonstrates an action orientation in the manner in which decisions are made at Virgin: "We can decide something in the morning and have it in operation in the afternoon" explains Branson (Kets de Vries & Dick, 1995). He models risk taking not only through his own many ventures but through daredevil adventures. In 1985, he attempted to cross the Atlantic Ocean in a high-power speedboat to win the Blue Riband prize for the fastest crossing. His first vessel sank, but a second attempt the next year succeeded. In 1987, he sought to achieve the fastest trans-Atlantic balloon crossing with an expert balloonist, Per Lindstrand. They both barely escaped the experience alive. Nevertheless, in 1990, he attempted the first-ever trans-Pacific balloon crossing, which was successful (Kets de Vries & Dick, 1995). He has used these events not only to generate enormous publicity for his company but also to model the importance of risk taking for his organization. In each case, however, he sought out international experts such as Lindstrand to assist him in undertaking the adventure and in enforcing stringent equipment requirements, thereby modeling risk taking that is calculated and carefully thought out.

In addition to daily behavior, stories about leaders' early history may circulate in their organizations and provide models about hardships they have faced and overcome—in essence, modeling how leaders themselves were empowered. For example, one common story in the Mary Kay organization is how Mary Kay, early in her working life, had to raise a family without a husband and yet succeeded despite difficult financial conditions. The story conveys an essential message that persistence, an eye for opportunity, and an astute sense of women's needs were the characteristics that enabled her to triumph over tough circumstances. These, of course, are the very qualities she seeks to instill in those who work for Mary Kay Cosmetics.

In conclusion, role modeling is an essential element in the leader's repertoire of influence tools. It is often employed in highly visible and dramatic ways to emphasize values and actions. Just as important, the day-to-day behavior of the leader also serves as a source of modeling. Charismatic leaders' allocation of time among daily activities, their decisions concerning the deployment of resources, the people they recruit, the types of questions they ask in meetings, the actions they reward, the places and people they visit, the individuals and activities they praise and criticize, and the issues they discuss all serve to emphasize what is important and valued in the organization (Schein, 1992; Yukl, 1994).

EMPOWERMENT APPROACHES OF THE CHARISMATIC LEADER

In Chapter 3, we pointed out that a charismatic leader is concerned primarily with influencing organizational members to accept and own the vision and to work in concert toward its realization. This concern results in the leader exerting transformational influence on followers. The leader tries to bring about changes in attitudes, values, and norms of conduct among organizational members so that they can be driven by their own desire to accomplish the organizational goals encoded in the vision. In addition to role modeling, the leader achieves these outcomes through use of strategies and techniques that make followers feel empowered within the organization (Conger, 1989b). Through these activities, the leader is able to build follower self-efficacy beliefs that lead to heightened performance outcomes.

To engage in empowering strategies, charismatic leaders identify three basic conditions that characterize the empowerment of organizational members (Menon, 1995; Menon & Borg, 1995). They recognize that, in an organizational context, members feel empowered when (1) they experience perceived control over the limited organizational resources needed to accomplish their tasks (Burke, 1986), (2) they possess an enhanced sense of self-efficacy or competence in handling their tasks (Conger & Kanungo, 1988c), and (3) they show an intrinsic desire or a personal commitment that energizes or drives them to accomplish their tasks (Thomas & Velthouse, 1990). The recognition of these three conditions encourages charismatic leaders to use strategies that result in strengthening such follower beliefs as "I have control over whatever resources I need to do my job," "I can do and am competent to do my job," and "I am willing to do and committed to doing my job."

For example, Richard Branson employs a variety of means to empower members of the Virgin Group. At an organizational level, he preserves an entrepreneurial atmosphere through a Japanese-style *keiretsu* structure whereby the 500 companies under the Virgin Group operate quasi-independently but collaboratively in a global network (Kets de Vries & Dick, 1995). As we noted earlier, once a company reaches a certain size, it is split into several organizations so that employees retain their sense of identity with their organization and a small company, entrepreneurial atmosphere is preserved. At the individual level, each unit is led by a strong managing director who has considerable freedom to run the business as he or she sees fit and who is given an equity position in the company. In addition, employees with attractive ideas for new ventures are provided with seed capital and ownership. As a result, many of the Virgin companies are the product of employee ideas. A bridal service division called Virgin Bride, for example, was the idea of a Virgin Airways flight attendant whom Branson provided with "venture capital." In essence, Branson finds pleasure in providing opportunities for staff. The new ventures allow him to stretch and develop employees by creating more opportunities for upward mobility and greater responsibility (Kets de Vries & Dick, 1995). As important, he is not only rewarding innovation but also retaining talented people who might otherwise leave Virgin to start their own firms.

By empowering organizational members, four major transformational effects are achieved:

1. Organizational members internalize the leader's vision (they regard the mission of the organization as their own).
2. They demonstrate increased trust and confidence in the leader, making it easier for the leader to create and manage changes in the organization to achieve the vision.
3. They experience a stronger sense of self-efficacy while accomplishing organizational tasks (they feel more confident while handling a task, become more proactive, take initiatives on the job).
4. They develop a sense of task group solidarity or cohesion, therefore making teamwork more effective.

Three specific sets of behavioral strategies on the part of charismatic leaders can be identified, each resulting in a different empowering belief and associated transformational effects. These strategies are (1) empowerment through a visioning strategy that leads to the strengthening of follower commitment; (2) empowerment through a context-change strategy (changing organizational context factors responsible for perceived powerlessness among followers), leading to a strengthening of followers' belief in their control over resources; and (3) empowerment through a self-efficacy information strategy (providing task self-efficacy or competence information to followers), leading to a stronger belief in one's ability to accomplish tasks. These strategies are described below.

Empowerment Through Vision

First, the leader formulates a vision that represents a clear purpose or mission for the organization. For an organizational objective to be meaningful to members, it must represent a shared perspective. To achieve this shared perspective, the leader articulates the vision by anchoring it in a set of deeply held values of the members. The leader's articulation of the vision brings to the surface these deeply held values and makes the members realize that the vision is indeed a representation of their own values. The leader's articulation of the vision then is perceived not as foreign to the members but as a reflection of their own values they had never realized before. Anita Roddick's vision for The Body Shop is an illustrative example. Instead of basing her vision around profitability or market share or other common business metrics, she chose instead to fashion goals around social and environment causes: "to act as a force of social change, to continue the education of our staff, to assist development in the Third World, and above all, to help protect the environment" (Roddick, 1991, p. 24). Her employees generally are young people who are socially conscious and with whom such messages resonate powerfully. Roddick's vision allows them to transform their work into a social cause. Given the preponderance of female staff members, she also includes an emphasis on "feminine principles." She believes that the cosmetics industry has been exploitative because it is run principally by men who play on women's fears of aging and other insecurities about their self-image:

> What is wonderful about the company is that 90% of the people running the shops are female, have no formal business training, and yet are brilliant retailers and brilliant business people. . . . This is a business run by women. Policy decisions are made by women, all the words are written by women, product development is controlled by women. So our customer, our female customer, believes that we have a covert understanding of women. It gives us an extraordinary edge. It's The Body Shop's secret ingredient. (Roddick, 1991, p. 17)

This belief in the role and competence of women is remarkably empowering for Body Shop employees who see the company (much like Mary Kay Cosmetics) as an opportunity both to be their feminine selves and to be successful in a world of business dominated by men.

When organizational members perceive the vision as their own, as in the Body Shop example, they will feel internally driven to achieve the organizational objectives dictated by the vision. When the members perceive that the leader is the most articulate spokesperson of their belief and values, they also develop trust and adoration for their leader. To summarize, the first step a charismatic leader takes to empower followers is to formulate a vision with a clear purpose and to articulate its shared and idealized perspectives.

Empowerment Through Context Change

The second empowerment strategy a charismatic leader undertakes is to avoid or eliminate contextual conditions within the organization that foster a sense of powerlessness among members. For example, the leader might install structures

TABLE 6.1 Context Factors Leading to Powerlessness

Organizational Factors
> Impersonal bureaucratic climate
> Poor communications/network-forming systems
> Highly centralized organizational resources

Supervisory Style
> Authoritarian (high control)
> Negativism (emphasis on failures)
> Lack of reason for actions/consequences

Reward Systems
> Noncontingency (arbitrary reward allocation)
> Low incentive value of rewards
> Lack of competence-based rewards
> Lack of innovation-based rewards

Job Design
> Lack of role clarity
> Lack of training and technical support
> Unrealistic goals
> Lack of appropriate authority/discretion
> Low task variety
> Limited participation in programs, meetings, and decisions that have a direct impact
>   on job performance
> Lack of appropriate/necessary resources
> Lack of network-forming opportunities
> Highly established work routines
> High rule structure
> Low advancement opportunities
> Lack of meaningful goals/tasks
> Limited contact with senior management

and mechanisms that foster a sense of control over the resources needed to perform meaningful tasks required for the vision's accomplishment (Conger & Kanungo, 1988c). As described earlier, Branson's organizational initiatives that promote entrepreneurship and mitigate against bureaucracy are a prime example of this.

Charismatic leaders must be adept at detecting the organizational conditions that contribute to a sense of powerlessness among members. Some of these conditions are listed in Table 6.1. For example, organizations with high levels of formalization and impersonal control systems kill initiative and a sense of responsibility. Organizations characterized by authoritarian and patriarchal management strip control and discretion from members. Under these forms of management, the control of organizational resources is in the hands of top management.

Allocation of resources and supervision in such organizations often is perceived by the members to be unfair and arbitrary. Rewards are not allocated on the basis of members' competence or innovative behavior, but rather on their blind compliance with formalized control from the top. Routine jobs are assigned that appear isolated, repetitive, boring, and meaningless. When organizations do not provide rewards that are valued by members, and when the rewards are not based on member competence, initiative, and innovative job behavior, the members' sense of powerlessness increases (Sims, 1977; Szilagyi, 1980). Furthermore, when jobs provide very little challenge and meaning, and when they involve role ambiguity, role conflict, and role overload, members also feel a crippling sense of powerlessness.

In 1988, we argued (Conger & Kanungo, 1988c) that leaders must focus on removing these contextual factors from the organization. They must institute organizational mechanisms or structures and processes that make members feel empowered in the sense of having enough control over their environmental resources to make them effective within the organization. For example, leaders can put in place mechanisms to promote an organizational culture that values free information sharing through participation and feedback systems, meaningful jobs through enrichment and goal-setting programs, and rewards for competence and initiative. For example, Jack Welch implemented a program at General Electric titled Work Out, the purpose of which was to undermine layers of bureaucracy and other obstacles to employee empowerment at the lower levels of the organization. The program created forums for employees to speak candidly about the management of their business units without fear of retribution from senior managers. In 2- to-3-day sessions of 50 to 100 people, these forums openly critiqued the management practices in an operating group with a focus specifically on bureaucracy and unproductive behaviors that were impeding employees' effectiveness or efficacy. In essence, these forums tackled the barriers to empowerment. Their second objective was to stimulate immediate action to address the issues that were identified. At the end of each session, the unit's manager received direct feedback on the findings and recommendations for action. In response, the rules stipulated that the manager had to accept or reject recommendations "on the spot" at the meeting or else appoint a team to investigate. As the process has evolved, issues have moved on to address more complicated and structural barriers such as cross-functional processes and departmental boundaries. By the end of the first 2 years of the Work Out program, some 2,000 sessions had been conducted, with more than 90% of the suggestions acted on (Elderkin & Bartlett, 1991, pp. 10-11).

Empowerment Through
Self-Efficacy Information

The third empowerment strategy a charismatic leader pursues is to increase the sense of self-efficacy among organizational members. Some informal practices on the part of the leader can strengthen members' beliefs in their own capabilities to handle organizational tasks in innovative and effective ways. For example, in Chapter 5, we saw how leaders such as Charlotte Beers and Orit Gadiesh used personal communications to build the self-efficacy beliefs of their employees. In both these cases, the leader's behavior directly provided information to members about their task efficacy. Bandura (1977) has identified several sources of such self-efficacy information: enactive attainment, vicarious experience, verbal persuasion, and emotional arousal state. Examples of empowerment techniques under each efficacy information category are presented below.

Information in personal efficacy through enactive attainment refers to an individual's authentic mastery experience directly related to the job. When members perform complex tasks or are given more responsibility in their jobs, they have an opportunity to test their efficacy. Initial success experiences (through successively moderate increments in task complexity and responsibility along with training to acquire new skills) make one feel more capable and, therefore, empowered. Branson, for example, takes promising managers and promotes them to complete responsibility for new ventures. In other cases, leaders can structure organizational change programs in such a way that initial objectives are sufficiently attainable and so that subordinates are able to execute them successfully (Beer, 1980).

As we described at the beginning of this chapter, the feeling of being empowered also can come from the vicarious experiences of observing a leader who performs as a model. A leader's exemplary behavior with regard to taking initiative, personal risk, and unconventional tactics to achieve task objectives can empower followers to believe that they can behave in a like manner or that they can at least achieve some improvement in their performance. For example, Bennis and Nanus (1985), in their study of leaders, described how William Kieschnick, president of ARCO, learned to be an innovative risk taker through the modeling of leaders he had served under (p. 204). Similarly, we see this dynamic with the subordinates of many of the charismatic leaders described in this volume, such as Mary Kay Ash, Charlotte Beers, Richard Branson, Orit Gadiesh, and Herb Kelleher. As Bandura (1986) suggests, modeling effects can have a significant impact on efficacy expectations:

> People convinced vicariously of their inefficacy are inclined to behave in effectual ways that, in fact, generate confirmatory behavioral evidence of inability. Conversely, modeling influences that enhance perceived self-efficacy can weaken the impact of direct experiences of failure by sustaining performance in the face of repeated failures. (p. 400)

Words of encouragement, verbal feedback, and other forms of social persuasion often are used by leaders to empower followers (Conger, 1989b). According to Bandura (1986), "People who are persuaded verbally that they possess the capabilities to master given tasks are likely to mobilize greater sustained effort than if they harbor self-doubts and dwell on personal deficiencies when difficulties arise" (p. 400). For example, Mary Kay Ash, president of Mary Kay Cosmetics, uses annual sales meetings as forums largely for praising and encouraging the exceptional performance of organizational members. She opened one speech by explaining that her remarkable success was the direct result of her talented organizational members:

> Several years ago, a widely known American retired from a long career in business and public life. At a dinner held in his honor, the man made a brief address in which he reflected on the events of his life. The striking thing about his address was his claim that he could take little credit for his success. "For I am indebted to magnificent friends." I feel exactly the same way, for I am indebted to you, my magnificent friends. It is true that much of what we accomplish in life we owe to our friends, and I thank you from the bottom of a very grateful heart. (Ash, 1989)[4]

At a later point in her comments, she reflected on her greatest source of satisfaction in leading the company:

> Without a doubt, the most rewarding aspect of my life is to watch a woman come into our company like a tight little rosebud, sometimes too inhibited to even tell me who she is, and after six months of training, praise, and encouragement, and recognition by her recruiter and director friends—she blossoms into a poised beautiful woman. All because someone helped her reach down within herself and bring forth her God-given talents and abilities. (Ash, 1989)[4]

In this case, Mary Kay expounds on the empowering belief that the potential to succeed already exists within each of her representatives; it simply needs to be supported and encouraged.

Finally, one's personal competence expectations are affected by emotional arousal state. Emotional arousal states that result from stress, fear, anxiety,

TABLE 6.2 Empowering Strategies and Their Effects

Leader Behavior	Empowering Belief in Followers	Transformational Effects
1. Vision formulation and articulation: Clear and simple Shared perspective Idealized perspective	Owning the vision	Willingness and commitment to achieve the vision Confidence and trust in the leader Task group cohesion
2. Removing organizational conditions of powerlessness Promoting structure and mechanism for empowerment	Perceived control over needed resources	Self-confidence Risk taking Proactive Task group cohesion and teamwork
3. Self-efficacy information: Through modeling Risk taking Persuasion Helping in enactive attainment	Perceived task competence.	Self-confidence Risk taking Proactive Confidence and trust in the leader

depression, and so forth, both on and off the job, can lower self-efficacy expectations. Individuals are more likely to feel competent when they are not experiencing strong aversive arousal. Empowerment techniques and strategies that provide emotional support for followers and that create a supportive and trusting group atmosphere (Neilsen, 1986) can be more effective in strengthening self-efficacy beliefs. An example of such behavior is found in Kidder's *Soul of a New Machine* (1981), in which a Data General manager, Tom West, provided effective emotional and group support that ensured the completion of an extremely difficult computer project. On many occasions, employees' stress, anxiety, and tension on the job can be reduced by clearly defining task roles, reducing information overload, and offering technical assistance to accomplish tasks. The empowering strategies discussed above and their transformational effects are summarized in Table 6.2.

PROMOTING COOPERATIVE BEHAVIOR AMONG FOLLOWERS

Charismatic leaders strive to build a strong collective identity among organizational members. This is principally because cooperative behavior is essential for the mission of the charismatic leader. The demands of a lofty vision require highly effective teamwork and follower commitment that goes beyond the pursuit of individual gain. Cooperation also ensures heightened individual performance because organizational members are engaged to assist one another and to sacrifice their personal pursuits for the collective mission. The collective itself establishes norms for its members that put them under significant psychological and social forces that heighten their commitment to the mission (Kanter, 1967; Salancik, 1977).

One vehicle for the leader to build such bonds is actions that model personal sacrifices for the collective, which we discussed earlier. A second is the leader's emphasis on how the organization is unique. For example, a leader may highlight the common values and beliefs shared among all the membership and how these differ from those of other organizations. Steven Jobs has been particularly notable in this regard, as illustrated in a speech given to the Boston Computer Society in 1984, when he introduced the first Macintosh personal computer. He provided a contrast with another organization, IBM:

It is 1958. IBM passes up the chance to buy a young, fledgling company that has just invented a new technology, called xerography. Two years later Xerox is born, and IBM has been kicking themselves ever since.

It is 10 years later. The late 1960s. Digital Equipment Corporation and others invent the mini-computer. IBM dismisses the mini-computer as too small to do serious computing, and therefore unimportant to their business. DEC grows to become a multi-hundred-million-dollar corporation before IBM finally enters the mini-computer market.

It is now 10 years later. The late 1970's. In 1977, Apple, a young, fledgling company on the West Coast invents the Apple II, the first personal computer as we know it today. IBM dismisses the personal computer as too small to do serious computing and therefore unimportant to their business.

The early 1980s. 1981. Apple II has become the world's most popular computer, and Apple has grown to a $300 million corporation, becoming the fastest growing company in American business history. With over 50 companies vying for a share, IBM enters the personal computer market in November of 1981, with the IBM PC. In 1983, Apple and IBM emerge as the industry's strongest competitors, each selling approximately one billion dollars worth of personal computers in 1983. Each will invest greater than $50 million for R&D and another $50 million for television advertising in 1984. . . .

It is now 1984. It appears IBM wants it all. Apple is perceived as the only hope to offer IBM a run for its money. Dealers, initially welcoming IBM with open arms, now fear an IBM-dominated and -controlled future. They're increasingly turning back to Apple as the only force that can ensure their future freedom. IBM wants it all and is aiming its guns on the last obstacle to industry control— Apple. Will Big Blue dominate the entire computer industry? The entire information age? Was George Orwell right?[5]

Jobs portrays IBM as a slow-witted giant with little foresight whose primary advantage is to use its size to bully its way into markets. The Apple organization is described as not only the smarter of the two but also as the leader in personal computers. It also is a force for good in the marketplace. Jobs plays to the myth of David (Apple) and Goliath (IBM), the image of Orwell's all-controlling "Big Brother" (IBM), and themes surrounding the American Revolution directly suggesting that Apple employees are freedom fighters against the forces of evil and domination. They are special, and their mission is to be a powerful positive force.

The aim of such efforts is not only to heighten the sense of specialness of the organization but also to promote what are called "organizational citizenship behaviors." These are discretionary behaviors that are beyond an individual's prescribed job responsibilities. They include extra-role behavior designed to assist others in a "good citizen" manner that "in the aggregate promotes the efficient and effective functioning of the organization" (Organ, 1988, p. 4). Extra-role behaviors are critical because organizations are not able to anticipate through normal job descriptions the complete picture of behaviors required to attain their goals (George & Brief, 1992). Such extra-role behaviors would appear to be a consequence of charismatic leadership whereby followers are highly motivated to perform beyond conventional performance standards (Bass, 1985; Graham, 1988). Although these behaviors can take many forms, Organ (1988) has identified five of the more prominent:

1. Altruism—discretionary behaviors that involve helping others with an organizationally relevant problem or task;

2. Civic virtue—behavior that demonstrates that the individual is involved in and concerned about life in the organization;

3. Conscientiousness—discretionary behavior that goes significantly beyond the minimum requirements of the organization in the arenas of attendance, adherence to regulations and rules, taking of breaks, and so on;

4. Courtesy—behavior that seeks to prevent work-related problems with fellow employees from occurring; and

5. Sportsmanship—discretionary behavior that demonstrates the individual's willingness to accept less than ideal circumstances without complaining or making petty grievances.

It appears from limited research that charismatic leaders do indeed have an impact on organizational citizenship behaviors. Podsakoff and colleagues (1990) have shown that the behaviors associated with the charismatic leader build follower trust, which in turn influences citizenship behavior. In another study of employees in a manufacturing firm, Deluga (1995) found a more direct correlation between charismatic leadership using the Conger-Kanungo scale and organizational citizenship behaviors. These preliminary studies support the notion that this set of follower outcomes is a consequence of charismatic leadership.

Zaki Mustafa, the charismatic CEO and turnaround agent of Serengeti Eyewear, nicely illustrates one leader's cultivation of such cooperative behaviors (West & Garvin, 1993). He sees team building as a personal responsibility. He insists that Serengeti employees always put the team as their highest priority:

> We all pull together. Don't worry about having the brightest people; worry about the team. Trust comes from interdependence, not independence. We've made a clear statement: "The individual is secondary to the organization." There are some people who take great pride in excellent output of their own. Others take great pride in excellent output of the group. I'm always looking for people in the second category. (West & Garvin, 1993, pp. 10-11)

As a result of this philosophy, a heavy emphasis is placed on teamwork as the primary selection criterion for new recruits. In addition, Mustafa has ensured that information normally reserved for higher levels in the organization is instead widely shared. For example, financial and performance data are distributed to all employees. There are no perks to differentiate status between organizational levels: "Typical firms are like an army, with a caste system. We don't have that here. There is no reserved parking, no separate dining areas, no separate bathrooms. And everybody, including the packers, attends the annual sales meeting," explains a senior staff member (West & Garvin, 1993, p. 11).

INNOVATIVE AND UNCONVENTIONAL SOLUTIONS

Charismatic leaders are known for their use of unconventional approaches not only in terms of their behavior but also in their strategies and tactics. The aim of their unconventional *behavior* is to model innovation and risk taking as well as to heighten follower perceptions that their leader is extraordinary and possesses a special expertise. Their unconventional *strategic actions*, on the other hand, aim to catch competitors off guard or to provide "first-mover" market advantages or to overcome environmental barriers. In this section, we are concerned about the strategic side.

To illustrate the charismatic leader's capacity for unconventional approaches to environmental challenges, we return again to Herb Kelleher at Southwest Airlines. We will use an example of a regulatory barrier that Southwest faced in its early days and that Kelleher successfully overcame by unconventional means. By 1981, Southwest Airlines served only the states of Louisiana, New Mexico, Oklahoma, and Texas because of a federal ruling limiting the company to Texas and contiguous states. Kelleher, however, was determined to overcome this barrier and expand the airline to Los Angeles (Petzinger, 1995). The principal airports in California, however, had strict ceilings on the number of permissible takeoffs and landings, with only "new industry entrants" eligible for exceptions. Although young as an airline, Southwest was not a "new entrant"; it was already some 8 years old. Shortly after the Airline Deregulation Act had been approved, however, Southwest had incorporated a subsidiary company called Midway Southwest to begin service to Midway Airport in Chicago. The subsidiary never initiated service, but it existed as a legal entity. Using this paper company, Kelleher applied as a "new entrant" and received approval for the gate slots. He then traded the slots to Southwest. At some point, the Federal Aviation Agency realized what Kelleher had done and attempted to overrule the approval by decreeing that the slots could not be traded by Midway Southwest, a "paper company." In response, Kelleher sold Midway Southwest to an air charter firm that had one Learjet. The charter company then traded the slots over to Southwest. The FAA was unable this time to find sufficient reason to nullify the transaction, and Southwest now had access to California (Petzinger, 1995, p. 285).

In terms of strategy making, charismatic leaders would appear to employ frequently the strategic approaches advocated by Hamel and Prahalad (1994), in which company strategies are about rewriting industry rules rather than incremental improvements in an organization's market share and position. In contrast, most organizations and their leadership employ more incremental and conventional approaches involving strategic planning that fails to challenge existing norms and conventions. Hamel and Prahalad (1994) describe the dilemmas of this traditional approach when it comes to providing competitive advantage:

In our experience, strategic planning typically fails to provoke deeper debates about who we are as a company or who we want to be in ten years' time. . . . It seldom illuminates the new white space opportunities. It seldom uncovers the unarticulated needs of customers. It seldom provides any insight into how to rewrite industry rules. . . . It seldom forces managers to confront their potentially out-of-date conventions. Strategic planning almost always starts with "what is." It seldom starts with "what could be." Incrementalist planning in a world of profound change is unlikely to add much value. . . . To extend industry foresight and develop a supporting strategic architecture, companies need a new perspective on what it means to be "strategic." . . . They need a new process for strategy-making, one that is more exploratory and less ritualistic. (p. 282)

Furthermore, "It is a view of strategy that . . . is more concerned with creating stretch goals that challenge employees to accomplish the seemingly impossible" (p. 23).

In their research, Hamel and Prahalad (1994) found that the companies that typically went on to market leadership possessed (1) significantly greater strategic foresight into the future of their marketplaces than competitors, (2) a willingness to "unlearn" their past approaches, and (3) a capacity for challenging industry conventions and for entertaining new competitive forms. Strikingly similar notions are to be found in the strategic approaches of many charismatic leaders, who are characterized by a strong future orientation, a willingness to challenge company and industry conventions, and a propensity to set significant or "stretch" goals that force their organizations to rethink strategic approaches.

In terms of challenging the norms of existing industries, we can turn again to charismatic leaders Anita Roddick and Richard Branson as examples of a leader's unconventional expertise that led to successful marketplace opportunities. For example, many of the retailing approaches of Roddick's Body Shop were in direct contrast to the traditions of the cosmetics industry. Company advertising makes no promises of greater beauty or vitality or youthfulness, thereby suggesting an unusual level of promotional candor and therefore trustworthiness. As noted earlier, Roddick emphatically states, "You can't change your body shape. We won't use sophisticated photographic images, and we won't make exaggerated claims about our products. We just talk about the ingredients. We are quite puritanical about this" (Baker & Duncan, 1995, p. 3). This "straight talk" combined with advertising promoting social causes and simple, recyclable packaging set the company apart from its competition. It directly spoke to generations of consumers skeptical about false promises and concerned both about the environment and that their products be safe and natural.

Similarly, Branson has found opportunities in established industries by going against conventions. One of his earliest successful initiatives was in discount records. When approximately 20 years old, he observed that despite the abolition of a government policy allowing manufacturers and suppliers to "recommend" prices to retail outlets (which had ensured high prices for records), music records remained overpriced. He decided to challenge industry norms around pricing by offering records through the mail, discounting them some 15% from retail stores. When he entered the airline business in 1984, he distinguished himself from British Airways with a similar strategy—lower fares than the competition. Later, he would introduce amenities for air travelers that were completely countercultural to the entire industry, from in-flight masseurs to fashion shows to musicians to motorcycle transportation to the London airport (Kets de Vries & Dick, 1995).

In addition, many charismatic leaders are entrepreneurs. New venture contexts are particularly suitable for such leaders simply because of the opportunities they afford. In contrast, Bhide (1994) points out, mature industries are more difficult to enter successfully: "Enormous creativity, experience, and contacts are needed to take business away from competitors in a mature industry, where market forces have long shaken out weak technologies, strategies, and organizations" (p. 154). On the other hand, emerging markets are in some ways more open to new approaches and have a greater tolerance for errors: "New markets are different. There start-ups often face rough-around-the-edges rivals, customers who tolerate inexperienced vendors and imperfect products, and opportunities to profit from shortages" (p. 154).

In conclusion, charismatic leaders are strategists adept at detecting unexploited opportunities. They are also skillful at implementing their strategic vision through an ability to powerfully mobilize their organizations. At the same time, these very strengths paradoxically can become liabilities. For example, the leader after some success may fall prey to delusions about his or her strategic foresight and in turn undertake missions that are beyond the organization's capabilities. As well, the positive outcomes of empowerment may lead to strong follower dependencies on the leader. These can be manipulated and exploited by charismatic leaders who are more self-serving. Therefore, the very skills of the charismatic leaders that we have been describing throughout this volume can transform themselves into liabilities. In the next chapter, we explore this shadow side of charisma, and in the final chapter, we discuss the future of the field of charismatic leadership.

NOTES

1. The degree of self-sacrificial behavior under charismatic leadership will vary by context. For example, in religious or social movement contexts, the leader's sacrificial acts could extend even to the point of his or her own martyrdom.

2. This account is adapted from Petzinger (1995, p. 295).

3. Vicarious empowerment in this case refers to followers being empowered through observations of the leader's modeling.

4. Excerpts are from *A Festival of Friends,* a speech given by Mary Kay Ash in 1989 to the annual Mary Kay Cosmetics seminar in Dallas. Reprinted by permission.

5. Excerpt is from a speech introducing the MacIntosh computer, given by Steven Jobs in 1984 to the Boston Computer Society, Boston, Massachusetts. Reprinted with permission from Steven Jobs.

PART III

REMAINING CHALLENGES

7

The Shadow Side of Charisma

Although we have emphasized throughout this volume the positive face of charismatic leadership, it has at times produced disastrous outcomes for both followers and organizations. In this chapter, we will examine the categories of problems that are associated with it. A number of the more widespread problems associated with charismatic leaders are tied to skill deficiencies. As individuals, charismatic leaders appear to be more adept at change and innovation than at administration. As a result, they often lack the ability or desire to focus on tasks related to effective management. They may invest little of their time and attention in designing effective control systems, establishing performance standards, or structuring roles and responsibilities. These activities simply appear to hold little interest. To compensate, charismatic leaders need not only an appreciation for such activities but also an ability to seek out managerial talent that effectively addresses these activities; otherwise, both external and internal organizational demands eventually create chaos in the informally structured organizations commonly associated with the charismatic leader.

More importantly and somewhat more rarely, dramatic problems can arise because of certain character flaws. Charismatic leaders can be prone to extreme narcissism that leads them to promote highly self-serving and grandiose aims. As a result, the leader's behaviors can become exaggerated, lose touch with reality, or become vehicles for pure personal gain. In turn, they may harm the leader, followers, and the organization. An overpowering sense of self-importance and strong need to be at the center of attention can lead charismatic leaders to ignore the viewpoints of others and the development of leadership ability in followers. As Musser (1987) has suggested, we might even classify charismatic leaders as positive or negative by their orientation toward satisfying their own needs versus those of their followers. For example, negative charismatics presumably emphasize a devotion to themselves over their mission. They also are likely to promote personal identification and dependence on themselves over a more straightforward endorsement and internalization of the values and ideological goals they are promoting. Positive charismatic leaders, on the other hand, are more likely to emphasize the mission rather than themselves and to seek internalization over personal identification.

Howell and House (1993; House & Howell, 1992) have gone so far as to speculate that there is a unique set of personality characteristics and behaviors that distinguish these positive and negative forms of charismatic leadership—or as they term them, *socialized* and *personalized* charisma. Their theory holds that although the *socialized* charismatic leader has a high need for power, it is counterbalanced with high activity inhibition, low authoritarianism, an internal locus of control, high self-esteem, and low Machiavellianism. These "balancing" characteristics shape the socialized leader's behavior such that it emphasizes the collective interests of followers. The leader's tendency is to govern others through more egalitarian means, to work through established channels of authority, to address followers' needs, and to approach motivation through empowerment. In contrast, the *personalized* leader has a high need for power that is instead coupled with low activity inhibition, high authoritarianism, an external locus of control, low self-esteem, high narcissism, and high Machiavellianism. These characteristics promote leadership behavior that is largely self-serving. Such leaders govern in a totalitarian manner, discourage questioning of their decisions, advocate goals that largely benefit themselves, disregard legitimate institutional channels, and use punishments and rewards to motivate. Among their followers, they prefer to foster dependence and unquestioning obedience over independent thinking.

Our position on this typology is that it is unlikely that "pure" types exist, which Howell (1996, p. 26) similarly acknowledges. Observations of leaders in organizations suggest that their behaviors reflect varying degrees of the negative and positive forms of charismatic leadership. As observers, we often attribute negative and positive forms of charisma to leaders based on the presence of a dominant form in their behaviors. One also can perceive that both identification and internalization processes occur simultaneously among followers of both types of charismatic leaders. Follower identification results when the leader's behaviors and personal characteristics are valued and considered worthy of imitation. Follower internalization occurs when the leader's articulated vision or mission is considered an expression of the followers' own deep-seated values. Negative charismatics often are more successful in inducing identification than internalization, whereas positive charismatics are better able to induce both identification and internalization.

We find it useful to distinguish between negative and positive forms of charismatic leadership by the extent to which the leader's goals and activities are self-serving as opposed to altruistic. This distinction helps us to understand the ethical nature of charismatic leadership behavior (Kanungo & Mendonca, 1996b). The self-serving goals and activities of the negative charismatic leaders are questionable on ethical grounds, whereas the altruistic goals and behaviors of positive charismatic leaders are considered morally desirable. Such consideration of moral desirability brings out a number of additional dimensions (beyond those identified by Howell and House, 1993) on which the two charismatic leadership forms may differ. These dimensions are identified in the following section.

THE ETHICAL NATURE OF
CHARISMATIC LEADERSHIP FORMS

How can we judge the two charismatic leadership forms to be ethical or unethical? To address this question, we must first specify what we mean by the term *ethical*. The term means that which is morally good, or that which is considered morally right—as opposed to that which is legally or procedurally right. According to Thomas Aquinas, the moral goodness of behaviors should be judged on the basis of the objective *act itself*, the subjective *motive of the actor*, and the *context* in which the act is performed. The ethical nature of charismatic leadership in organizational contexts manifests itself on three dimensions: the leader's *motives*; the leader's *influence strategies*; and the leader's *character formation*. As summarized in Table 7.1, charismatic leaders exhibit ethical leadership when they (1) strive to operate with an altruistic intent, (2) utilize empowering rather than controlling strategies to influence followers, and (3) endeavor to cultivate virtues and abstain from vices to build their own inner strength. As suggested earlier, the overarching motive of the positive charismatic leaders is altruistic intent, as opposed to egotistic intent of the negative charismatic leaders. Positive charismatic leaders are truly motivated by

TABLE 7.1 Contrasting Two Forms of Charismatic Leadership

	Positive Form	Negative Form
Underlying motive	Altruistic (intent to benefit others)	Egotistic (intent to benefit self)
Manifest needs	Affiliative interest Institutional power Social achievement Self-discipline/ self-development	Affiliative assurance Personal power Personal achievement Self-aggrandizement
Influence strategy	Empowerment	Control
Leader objective in terms of behavioral outcomes in followers	Emphasis on internalization of vision by changing followers' core attitudes, beliefs, and values	Emphasis on compliance behavior and identification with the leader
Moral values and influence	Ethical	Unethical

SOURCE: Adapted from Kanungo and Mendonca (1996b).

a concern for others, and their actions invariably are guided primarily by the criterion of benefit to others even if it results in some cost to themselves.

These leaders direct and guide followers toward goals and objectives that benefit the organization and its members, as well as the society at large. The altruistic intent of these leaders is manifested in their "affiliative interest" (Boyatzis, 1982), in their high need for "institutional power" (McClelland & Burnham, 1976), and in their "social achievement motive" (Kanungo & Mendonca, 1996b).

The positive charismatic leaders' affiliative interest is expressed in their relationship with all the various stakeholders consistent with the demands of the organization. The affiliative interest stems from the leaders' recognition that the objectives of the organization can be achieved through information sharing and beliefs in the task competencies of organizational members. On the other hand, negative charismatic leaders are high on "affiliative assurance," and they emphasize relationships prompted by their deep sense of personal insecurity, which causes them to engage in behaviors that are inappropriate and improper to the demands of the situation. For example, such leaders behave in secretive ways, may not share information with their subordinates, and often reward or threaten subordinates for the sole reason of controlling them to serve their own self-interest.

Positive charismatic leaders have high institutional power needs as opposed to the high personal power needs of negative charismatic leaders (Howell & House, 1993). A leader with high personal power need clearly places the interests of self before those of others and may do so at considerable cost to others; the personal power need is the antithesis of altruism. On the other hand, a leader high in institutional power needs shows a morally desirable form of altruism by serving others even at a cost to the self.

Negative charismatic leaders are driven by personal achievement motives and engage in behaviors that benefit themselves rather than others. On the other hand, positive charismatic leaders are driven by the social achievement motive. They show a concern for others and initiate efforts "in terms of articulation of individual and collective capability, concern for a better quality of life and need to engage in meaningful organizational and social action in order to influence the environment" (Mehta, 1994, p. 171). Motivated by social achievement, these leaders generally tend toward efforts that primarily benefit others and therefore reflect real altruism.

In their efforts for personal character development, the two charismatic leadership forms also differ. The negative charismatic leaders put their efforts toward achieving the goal of self-aggrandizement, whereas the positive charismatic leaders develop self-discipline to endure the personal cost or risk of benefiting others.

Finally, negative charismatic leaders use the power of their position or office, rewards and sanctions under their control, and various impression management techniques to get followers to perform required behaviors and to demonstrate desired commitment and loyalty. They use control strategies solely to elicit follower compliance. Followers are treated as providers of knowledge, abilities, skills, and effort that enable the leaders to accomplish their own objectives. Positive charismatic leaders, on the other hand, use empowerment instead of control strategies to bring about changes in the followers' core beliefs and values as they move the organization toward its goals. In addition, positive charismatic leaders use their personal expertise and examples of personal self-discipline primarily to transform followers' beliefs and values into those consistent with the vision, rather than to elicit followers' overt compliance behavior. The use of such empowerment strategies is morally defensible because it achieves two desirable objectives. First, followers internalize the beliefs and values inherent in the vision formulated by the leader. Second, followers feel more empowered, which enhances their self-efficacy beliefs; as a result, they feel more competent to handle tasks required for the realization of the vision.

The Sources of the Shadow

At the heart of the negative form or the shadow side of charismatic leadership are two fundamental processes—follower dependence in the form of transference dynamics and the leader's own potential for narcissism. Dependence stems in large part from a strong identification with the leader (Conger, 1989a). The leader's qualities of strategic vision, dynamism, inspiration, and unconventionality are highly attractive to followers. This extraordinary figure is in essence a model to be emulated. Followers want certain of the leader's qualities and values to ensure their own growth, success, and power within the organization. In addition, the leader's abilities become the yardstick against which followers measure their own performance. Representative comments from the subordinates of charismatic leaders capture this dynamic (Conger, 1989a):

> You want to be like your leader—it's hero worship. When you look at our boss, you ask yourself: "Now why didn't I do that with such flamboyance?" We worship him because of the way that he did the common in an uncommon manner. We want to be able to do that—it's creative. I want to be like my idol so I can do it on my own. You have a basic need to learn from him. I wanted to learn. I wanted to be a good charismatic leader myself. (p. 129)

> Don is like a role model. You want to have that energy, both the physical and the intellectual. You want to have that tremendous insight—bam, just to see what he sees and have the ability to carry it out. I've grown tremendously. He's a teacher. You see what he has done, and you want to do it. You want to have the same impact. (p. 129)

What is unique about charismatic leadership in contrast to other leadership forms is the *intensity* of this identification and dependence. Drawing on concepts from psychoanalytic theory, we can best explain its depth by a process called transference. As Kets de Vries (1988) has shown, the leader in essence becomes a substitute parent of sorts. In our early years, we see our parents as all-powerful and perfect. Later, in adulthood, a strong wish still lingers—often unconsciously—to recapture this childhood state through a relationship with someone seen as omnipotent. Leaders, in their positions of authority, naturally activate this state. For followers, there is a hope or fantasy that somehow certain of the admired person's qualities will be acquired by association. Being in a relationship with someone who is admired also reaffirms followers' sense of importance, existence, and self-esteem. The interview comments of a subordinate of a highly manipulative charismatic leader capture this dynamic:

> I felt that he could make success for me. By cultivating my relationship with him, I would be raised to a higher level of success. I was looking for help and thought he could bring something for me in terms of position and challenge. He may have

been a con artist but that's not what I felt at the beginning. He liked me and was interested in me. It was a flattering kind of attention. One of his best features was that he gave you undivided attention. Since he was so powerful, it's flattering to have him give full attention to you. He would ask for my opinion. He made me feel important by accepting what I had to say. I felt like I had an impact.

This affirmation of self and resulting dependence can either then be exploited by the charismatic leader solely for his or her own personal aims or serve as a vehicle for constructive mentoring for followers' own growth. These differing outcomes provide a critical distinction between negative and positive forms of charismatic leadership.

It is important to note that the degree of identification and the leader qualities with which followers identify are likely to vary depending on the social distance between the leader and particular followers. Preliminary research by Shamir (1995) shows that identification may be more intense with close leaders. Closeness also may be related to greater emulation of the leader's traits.

On the leader's side, narcissism explains many of the shadow side problems of charisma. As House and Howell (1992) point out, narcissism is highly correlated with certain attributes of charismatic leaders. Narcissism as a disorder was advanced largely by the work of Heinz Kohut (see Kohut, 1971). As Maddi (1980) explained, Kohut argued that human beings have an essential need to "enhance and order functioning through the experience of the self. When the self has developed well, it is a consciously appreciated sense of who and what one is that lends meaning and direction to behavior" (p. 53). As children, we have two needs related to this experience—the need to be mirrored and the need to idealize. Mirroring refers to a child's desire to have his or her expressions and actions be recognized and admired. Idealizing has to do with the need to identify with others who are more capable than ourselves. When parents fail to address or provide for these twin needs, the child will grow to feel inadequate (the lack of mirroring) and aimless (the lack of idealizing). The idealizing dynamic, of course, describes our discussion about followers' needs to associate with the charismatic leader. The mirroring dynamic, on the other hand, relates to the narcissism of the leader, which is a love of self-display or the desire to get attention from others. Although this inclination is universal, leaders are more likely to experience exaggerated or extreme states of it. Kets de Vries (1988) describes the typical course:

It is very hard to imagine, unless one has the experience, what it means to be the object of excessive admiration by followers. . . . Some leaders, in being exposed to a great deal of attention, eventually may find it hard to maintain a firm grasp on reality and thus distinguish fact from fantasy. Too much admiration can have dire consequences for the leader's mind: He or she eventually may believe it all to be true—that he or she really is as perfect, as intelligent, as powerful as others think is the case—and act accordingly. Moreover, this belief may be intensified by the fact that leaders have something going for them that ordinary mortals don't have: They frequently have the power to turn some of their fantasies into reality. If this happens, we may see the beginning of a self-propelled cycle of grandiosity. (p. 115)

Narcissism can lead charismatic leaders to overestimate their capabilities and underestimate the role of critical skills, resources, and changing marketplaces. For example, they may fail to see shortcomings in their visions, to accept responsibility for bad decisions, to realize the need for managerial talent, and to develop adequate successors. Their needs for adoration and attention (or mirroring) can lead them to deny flaws or problems with their visions, manipulate followers, and exaggerate their own capabilities. In addition, we know from empirical research employing the widely used Narcissistic Personality Inventory (Raskin & Hall, 1979) that narcissism in general is correlated with the need for power (Carroll, 1987); exhibitionism and aggression (Emmons, 1984); tendencies to be autocratic, aggressive, and sadistic (Raskin & Terry, 1988); a lack of empathy (Watson, Grisham, Trotter, & Biderman, 1984); and Machiavellianism (Biscardi & Schill, 1985). Moreover, individuals who are highly narcissistic often are blind to their own dysfunctional characteristics, denying or repressing them (Emmons, 1984; Raskin & Novacek, 1989). Exhibits 7.1-7.3 identify a range of the common problems found with dysfunctional charismatic leadership. In this chapter, we will narrow our attention to four of the more major categories of problems. These include (1) the leader's goals and visions, (2) their relations with subordinates, (3) their skill sets, and (4) their ability to find and develop successors. We will examine each to discover its darker side.

FLAWS IN THE CHARISMATIC LEADER'S VISION

The very goals of the charismatic leader can produce problems if they reflect highly self-serving aims or are based on poor assessments of marketplace and organizational realities that blind the leader to barriers or resources. Three of the most common problems related to the leader's vision are (1) goals that are

---

EXHIBIT 7.1
The Sources of Flawed Vision

- The vision reflects the internal needs of the leader rather than those of the market or constituents
- The resources (e.g., financial, technological, human resource, political) needed to achieve vision are seriously miscalculated
- An unrealistic assessment or distorted perception of market and constituent needs holds sway
- A failure to recognize environmental changes prevents redirection of the vision

---

SOURCE: Adapted from Conger (1990, p. 45).

---

largely self-serving, (2) inadequate estimates of resources and political support, and (3) unrealistic assessments of the larger environment.

Visions That Reflect the Self-Serving Needs of the Leader

In earlier publications (Conger, 1989a, 1990), we have described how the pioneering products and services of charismatic leaders can essentially become

---

EXHIBIT 7.2
Potential Liabilities in the Charismatic Leader's
Communications and Impression Management Skills

- Exaggerated self-descriptions of expertise, foresight, and commitment
- Exaggerated claims for the vision's outcomes
- A technique of fulfilling positive stereotypes and images of the leader's uniqueness to manipulate audiences
- A habit of gaining commitment by restricting negative information and maximizing positive information
- Use of positive anecdotes to distract attention away from negative statistical information concerning performance outcomes
- Creation of an illusion of control through affirming information and attributing negative outcomes to external causes

---

SOURCE: Adapted from Conger (1990, p. 50).

EXHIBIT 7.3
Potential Liabilities of the
Charismatic Leader's Management Practices

- Poor management of people networks, especially superiors and peers
- Unconventional behavior that alienates
- Creation of disruptive "in group/out group" rivalries
- An autocratic, controlling management style
- An informal/impulsive style that is disruptive and dysfunctional
- Claims of responsibility for innovative products and ideas when in reality the sources are other individuals
- Alternation between idealizing and devaluing others, particularly those who report directly
- Creation of excessive dependence on themselves among subordinates
- Failure to manage essential details and to act as an effective administrator
- Attention to the superficial
- Absence from operations
- Failure to develop successors of equal ability

SOURCE: Adapted from Conger (1990, p. 52).

---

extensions of themselves. Early successes convince leaders of the infallibility of their ideas and intuition. As a result, these pioneers run the risk of becoming escapists (Miller, 1990). They essentially retire into themselves, in a world of ideals and futuristic technologies and products. Their primary concern is invention, which at some point will lose touch with marketplace realities. To support their dreams, they build organizations that have a distinct character and a distinct liability. In his analysis of these types of organizations, Miller (1990) found that

> [they] actively seek out and lionize R&D types who thrive on basic invention—useful or not. Loose, decentralized structures give these people the freedom to embark on ever more ambitious projects. Meanwhile, the marketing and production personnel who might recognize the dangers of such excesses aren't given the power or credibility to stop them. And, unfortunately, financial controls tend to be so primitive that the dangers are slow to be detected. . . . Things deteriorate further as the environment changes. Pioneers' successes often attract new competitors into the market. At the same time, as firms grow, their simple, informal structures become less and less adequate. The result is chaos. (p. 115)

Two illustrative examples are Dr. Edwin Land, the founder of Polaroid, and Steven Jobs, founder of Apple Computer. Land held a three-decade monopoly on the instant camera market. By the late 1960s, his vision was to create the ultimate instant camera—the SX-70. This camera was to be his crowning achievement—totally automatic, slim enough to fold into a pocket or purse, a focus from zero to infinity, and a single-lens reflex viewing system. A half-billion-dollar investment would produce this remarkable camera with a steep retail price of $180. Rosy projections of sales of 5 million in its first year proved illusory—only 470,000 were sold. The market was not seeking perfection. Instead, consumers wanted a relatively good instant picture at a low price. Land's dream machine was seen as prohibitively expensive and excessively sophisticated.

The failure of the SX-70, however, did not stop Land the inventor. At the company's 1976 annual shareholder's meeting, Land introduced a camera the size of a small room. Its purpose was for making instant, life-size, color copies of museum paintings, which in Land's words would "change the whole world of Art . . . make great paintings available in every high school . . . [and] bring museums into the home" (*Boston Globe*, April 28, 1976, quoted in Miller, 1990, p. 117). Needless to say, this product also proved to be too expensive to develop and as a result realized only very limited market demand. At the next year's annual meeting and some 4 years after the introduction of the SX-70, he exclaimed, "There's a rule they don't teach you at the Harvard Business School. It is, if anything is worth doing, it's worth doing to excess" (Miller, 1990, p. 126). Land clearly was Miller's pioneer driven to escapism.

Similarly, Steven Jobs was a product pioneer. After the success of the Apple II, he searched for a second product breakthrough. Borrowing technology and staff from Xerox's research center, he went on to introduce the Lisa, with its mouse, screen icons, and "friendly" user interface. At a price of $10,000, it was another expensive SX-70 with little market demand. In addition, software for it was difficult to write, and other product features proved inflexible for professionals, engineers, and businesspeople.

Jobs would follow the Lisa with the Macintosh computer. Although its price and features were attractive, Jobs had failed to understand the growing demand for open architecture in personal computing. He believed that his computer would be so "insanely great" that people would clamor for Apple's proprietary technology, but its very uniqueness proved to be its downfall. Similar to the Lisa, initially there were few software programs because of its proprietary design. At its launch, only three programs were available. Lack of "IBM compatibility" spelled the death knell over the long term for this and other Apple products as the pool of Apple-compatible software became smaller and smaller in proportion to that for IBM and its clones. Apple's market share would soon collapse. As his successor, John Sculley, observed, Jobs mistakenly believed

> that with the Macintosh he would change the way people would view the computer. He didn't see the need for anyone to be able to modify the machine—you could order any color as long as it was black, to use Ford's analogy. And what it meant was that, as Apple began to compete in a marketplace where there were lots of alternative products from competitors that offered a wide range of openness, the Macintosh became more and more isolated because it still focused on the internal vision of the founder rather than on the needs of the customers. . . . It represented a very focused vision of how Steve saw the world. (Pearlstein & Rhodes, 1987, p. 51)

Jobs's obsession with "insanely great" products would be repeated in another venture following the Macintosh—the NeXT computer. After leaving Apple, he began a new computing company to build the "next" generation of personal computers. With little evidence of strong demand for his product, he would build a highly automated, showcase factory in Fremont, California, that could produce up to $1 billion worth of computers a year. *Fortune* magazine in 1990 devoted an article to it. With the headline "The Ultimate Computer Factory," writer Mark Alpert would comment:

> Robots outnumber people 13 to five on this line. . . . Not to save money: Labor accounts for only 3% to 5% of the cost of a typical computer-manufacturing operation. Instead, the automation is meant to ensure the highest possible quality. . . . Until recently, the 40 person manufacturing staff had more Ph.D.s than the group designing the NeXT machine. (Alpert, 1990, p. 75)

The computer never approached anywhere near the $1 billion annual volume. In addition to the factory, Jobs wanted the best for his venture. A West German company would be hired to design the computer's sleek black casing made of magnesium, and $100,000 would be spent designing the company's logo (Alpert, 1990, p. 75). As had happened to Land before him, Jobs's visions became increasingly a reflection of personal obsessions rather than what the marketplace was seeking.

Resources or Political Support Necessary to
Achieve the Vision Are Underestimated

In the drive to achieve a grandiose vision, the charismatic leader may ignore the costly implications of his or her aims. Ambition and the miscalculation of necessary resources (e.g., financial, technological, human, and political) may lead to crises. Under this scenario, the leader wishes to expand or accelerate the realization of his or her vision. Initial successes reaffirm in the leader's mind the correctness of his or her judgment and in turn delude or weaken the ability to realistically assess the resources needed and the reality of market demands. The costs that must be paid for innovations or acquisitions or market share become unsustainable and threaten the long-term viability of the leader's organization. In addition, charismatic leaders within large, bureaucratic organizations may suffer from a failure to build critical networks of support outside their own division, underestimating necessary political resources.

A story widely circulated about Seymour Cray, the chief engineer of Control Data and later founder of Cray Research, is illustrative. Every spring, Cray was known for constructing a new sailboat, "sailing it over the summer, and then burning it at the end of the season so that he wouldn't be bound by that year's mistakes when he sets about designing a more perfect craft for the next year" (Miller, 1990, p. 127). He approached computer design in the same manner. As a result, his computers were infamous for their cost overruns, for significant delays in delivery, and for their complicated designs. As a result, Control Data's financial performance was like a roller coaster as cost overruns and late delivery penalties ate into the company's profitability. After leaving Control Data to found Cray Research, Cray continued his extravagant ways, undertaking high-risk supercomputing projects. Eventually, the company's CEO, John Rollwagen, convinced Cray to split the organization into two because of the financial risks. In the end, Cray's most risky and grandiose project, based on an unproved gallium arsenide semicomputer technology, was spun off into its own company with Cray and his design group. In the other company, Rollwagen retained the mainstream supercomputer business built around existing government and commercial clients. Rollwagen rightly believed that the company could not afford two major supercomputer lines at one time. He had grown concerned that Cray's project would be too costly and appeal to only a very specialized and narrow market—jeopardizing the less risky, core business of the firm (Miller, 1990).

One of the more visible change agents at AT&T during the breakup of the monopoly was Archie J. McGill, who was hired from IBM in 1975 as its director of marketing. What was unusual about his hiring was that AT&T had never before hired an outsider at such a high level. He was perceived as bringing needed expertise from an industry that the company would soon depend on—computers. He also brought with him a reputation as an achiever. At age 33, McGill had been the youngest-ever vice president at IBM. Within a decade at AT&T, he would go from managing 40 individuals to 18,000 as president of the company's new business communications division. In the process, he professionalized the sales force, introduced extensive market research programs, and restructured the organization to be more responsive.

Along the way, however, McGill would fail to cultivate the political support he would later need to succeed. Like many charismatics, he was known to be fiercely impatient with the status quo. A former colleague told us, "He's a rebel who's not averse to letting others know that he's a rebel. He deliberately fosters an image of being a shaker." This impatience with the bureaucracy at AT&T led McGill to challenge the management of the company directly in meetings. AT&T was a culture built around consensus and cooperation, and here was McGill employing direct confrontation. As head of the company's newly created business communications division, he would need political support beyond his immediate division to succeed, but he had burned numerous bridges by that point. On June 7, 1983, the company announced that McGill had handed in his resignation. Although the company's public position was that McGill had volunteered to leave, political forces, in reality, appear to have driven him from the organization. *The Wall Street Journal* would conclude,

> American Bell's first months have been marked by organizational problems and less-than-expected sales results. Some company observers said that while Mr. McGill couldn't be held accountable for many of those problems, he had upset AT&T's top management with overly optimistic business forecasts and a series of clashes with other executives. (White, 1983, p. 4)

Similarly, a charismatic leader we studied who served as president of one division of a high technology company undertook the development of a new computer product and built some $20 million of inventory without informing the company's CEO. The CEO learned of the initiative from the CEO of another company during a trade conference. The division president had chosen to go ahead with the product without the customary corporate approval because he felt the market was exploding and required quick entry. He feared that acquiring approval for the initiative through the normal channels of the corporation's new product review committee would cause untimely delay. This surprise cost the division president enormous political capital and would be one of several reasons for his later termination from the company.

In conclusion, it is not uncommon for charismatic leaders to be blinded in their quest to achieve a particular vision. When combined with extreme narcissism, they imagine their ideas to be infallible. This blindness leads them to underestimate the resources they need to succeed—whether these be political, capital, technological, or human.

The Leader's Assessment of the Environment Is Unrealistic or Distorted

It is not unusual for charismatic leaders, after a period of initial success, to begin to falter in their assessments of the environment around them. Early successes tend to reinforce a belief that they have found "the formula"—that they alone have special insight into marketplaces. Subordinates, bankers, and the press may further encourage these perceptions. The leader's own descriptions of the future become self-convincing. For example, we know from research in impression management skills that not only are one's self-descriptions effective in deceiving an audience, but they also can deceive the presenter (Schlenker, 1980). Positive responses from others can encourage individuals to internalize their own self-enhancing descriptions. This is especially true when followers' adoration reinforces the leader's image of himself or herself. The dilemma, of course, is that these perceptions are based in part on delusions. Given that the larger environment is in constant motion, the strategies and tactics of the leader eventually will be nullified by changes in marketplaces or in competitive reactions. Again, Steven Jobs, the founder of Apple Computer, nicely illustrates this predicament.

Shortly after stepping down from Apple Computer, Jobs began contemplating what would become the new venture NeXT. He spent his days reading books on science in a search for new ideas. In looking at texts on microbiology, he had become intrigued by DNA and how it replicated itself. After discussions with Paul Berg, a Nobel Prize winner in biochemistry at Stanford, he learned that the recombination of DNA in the laboratory was costly and time-consuming. Computer hardware for modeling such processes at the time was expensive, and software was primitive. Jobs saw an opportunity. He would create a company whose computing technology would permit students and faculty to model such complex processes inexpensively. As we noted earlier, NeXT had very limited success (though Jobs would succeed in selling it to Apple in 1997 for $400 million). To date, it has had little impact on the overall market for personal computers. One of the principal reasons for its lack of impact was that Jobs's supreme self-confidence apparently led him to simply replicate earlier strategies and approaches. As he explained to a reporter from *Inc.* magazine, he would succeed simply because he had succeeded before: "By the third time [referring to his two prior successes of the Apple and Macintosh personal computers], you should start to get a pretty good feeling in your gut that you understand the process" (as quoted in Nocera, 1993, p. 103). So he kept the software proprietary—just as he had done with the Macintosh and Apple computers. Meanwhile, open systems already had become the market norm. Similar to the Lisa, he would introduce the product at a price well over $6,000, versus the $3,000 he had projected—a price significantly beyond the means of the students and faculty he initially targeted. Early versions of the computer came out with a black and white screen when consumers were demanding color. The machine did not have a built-in floppy disk drive because Jobs believed that the slot would "clutter up" the design, yet floppy drives had become standard fare on PCs. His NeXT computers could not use common software products such as Lotus 1-2-3 that were enormously popular (Pitta, 1991, pp. 137-140). As one industry writer noted,

> Ultimately, Jobs believed that if he built it, they would come—simply because he was the one who built it! But even Steve Jobs could not defy the laws of the marketplace or ignore the dictates of the business he was in, no matter how passionately he viewed himself as being above such dictates. By the time he stopped trying to defy reality, it was much too late. (Nocera, 1993, p. 108)

Donald Burr, the founder of People Express Airlines, met a similar fate when he grossly underestimated his competitors. After several years of initial success and expansion, the airline began to encounter severe pricing competition from major carriers that decided to match People's low fares. As the fare wars escalated, Burr became convinced that the major carriers had confined their price-cutting tactics to the market segments that People had singled out for itself—short-haul routes (Petzinger, 1995). He believed that his competitors charged higher fares on their long-haul routes, which in turn allowed them to subsidize the short-haul ones. To undermine the major carriers' position, Burr imagined that if he could force them to cut their transcontinental fares, the profits subsidizing their short-haul flights would vanish. The major carriers, in short order, would be forced to retreat from their low-price tactics in People's markets, and his company would once again prosper. To realize this scenario, Burr had to move People Express into the transcontinental terrain of his competitors. The opportunity presented itself in the form of an airline called Frontier.

Frontier Airlines, based in Denver, had been struggling financially for several years as United and Continental airlines made inroads into the company's markets. The three airlines each had a hub in Denver despite the fact that it was not economical for more than two major airlines to operate out of a single hub. This dynamic, of course, simply exacerbated Frontier's financial difficulties. In September of 1985, Frank Lorenzo of Texas Air decided to make an offer to buy two thirds of Frontier for $250 million. Upon learning that Lorenzo had put Frontier into play, Burr decided that he needed Frontier as his vehicle to restore the market presence of People Express.

With Frontier, Burr imagined that he could build an "air bridge" between the Denver hub of Frontier and the Newark hub of People. Fifty cities in the East and 50 cities in the West would be pipelines to one another (Petzinger, 1995). Overnight, the merger would allow People to become the transcontinental carrier Burr envisaged. What he did not realize, however, was that his assumption about the subsidizing activity of the majors was incorrect. To a large extent, they were not using their long-haul routes to support fare cuts on their short-haul routes. Instead, their highly sophisticated computer systems allowed them to offer an effective mix of inexpensive seats along with high-priced ones on all routes regardless of distance. Burr had been largely oblivious to the strategic importance of such systems (Petzinger, 1995).

After bidding between Lorenzo and Burr, Frontier's board finally agreed to accept People's bid of $24 a share. Almost immediately following this victory, Burr decided to purchase Britt Airways, a commuter airline operating out of Chicago and St. Louis. Then he acquired Province-Boston Airline, the nation's largest commuter airline. His strategy was simple—he would buy his way into becoming a transcontinental airline.

By this time, Burr had grown dangerously overconfident. The media for some time had been heaping accolades on him, largely unaware of the internal problems at the company that were now growing out of control. For example, in early 1986, he would appear on the cover of *Time* magazine, and *Business Week* (as quoted in Petzinger, 1995) would call him "a new wave capitalist" who might one day become the modern equivalent of Henry Ford. A very positive case on People Express had been written by the Harvard Business School to illustrate its innovative human resources practices. The school's dean, John McArthur, had even joined the company's board of directors. By the mid-1980s, the company had become a model for academics and consultants to study. Even

Burr noted that no one ever before had created a billion dollar airline from scratch (Petzinger, 1995). All these events increased his sense of omnipotence.

Acquisitions were of course not the answer. People's competitors continued their onslaught by matching People's low fares. After a brief and failed experiment with raising People's fares to generate profits, Burr decided to cut the airline's ticket prices more deeply, hoping to increase the overall market and in doing so create enough volume to cover his operating costs and debt. The majors simply matched the new fares and made significant inroads into his home turf of Newark, New Jersey. Continental, for example, began offering fares of $99 from Newark to the West Coast. In the Newark terminal, even advertising by Continental exclaimed, "Give me your tired, your poor, your huddled masses yearning to be free of People Express" (Petzinger, 1995). By this point, People's financial problems were mounting rapidly. Losses at the end of the first quarter of 1986 reached $58 million, increasing to more than $100 million by the summer. In desperation, Burr came to the conclusion that selling the airline was the only way to salvage the company and its stock. On September 15, 1986, Frank Lorenzo of Continental Airlines acquired People Express for $300 million in stocks, notes, and a small amount of cash. Burr's vision had crashed, and his airline had become another man's airline.

DYSFUNCTIONAL RELATIONS WITH FOLLOWERS

The very strength of the charismatic relationship—deep follower identification with the leader and his or her mission—can transform itself into a liability. The dependence of followers affords charismatic leaders innumerable opportunities for manipulating the relationship. For example, leaders' communications skills often make it easy for them to mislead followers with exaggerated descriptions of future visions. They also may present information that makes their visions appear more realistic or more appealing. They may use their language skills to screen out problems or to foster an illusion of control. As Schwenk (1986) has shown, the leader may employ certain communications tactics to acquire commitment unethically. Because the human ability to process information is limited, we necessarily rely on certain simple biases and heuristics to reduce the amount of information needed to make a decision. By playing to these biases, a leader can heighten commitment to a course of action. For example, the charismatic leader may relate anecdotes designed to draw attention away from statistical information that reflects negatively on his or her plans (Schwenk, 1986).

In addition to deception, the charismatic leader may create abusive relationships with followers. The possibility for abuse is rooted in the "symbolic status" that charismatic leaders have in the eyes of their followers (Sankowsky, 1995). This type of status is derived as in our earlier discussions about *transference*, whereby the leader's status as a parental figure motivates followers to seek the personal approval of the leader. As a result, followers become more vulnerable to the messages of the leader concerning the vision, important values, courses of action, and interpretations of events. The leader is then in a far stronger position to fundamentally influence the feelings, perceptions, and actions of followers. A current example of this dynamic would be the recent exit of Jeffrey Katzenberg from the Walt Disney company (Sankowsky, 1995). Katzenberg had developed a parental relationship with company chairman Michael Eisner. Observers commented that Katzenberg had an almost singular focus on seeking Eisner's praise and approval, wishing to be Eisner's "number one son." Perhaps mirroring the aloofness of his own father, Eisner, however, rarely praised Katzenberg for his achievements—even for the outstanding success of the film *The Lion King*. In the end, the two had a falling-out over a senior executive position at the company that was at first promised (by Eisner) and then later denied to Katzenberg.

Transference is more likely to occur under charismatic leadership because the leader is so often seen as someone who is quite extraordinary and "omnipotent"—an individual who will fulfill followers' needs. Followers therefore are more willing to relinquish healthy skepticism because their leader is seen as highly competent and trustworthy. What pushes the charismatic leader into abusing status or symbolic power is narcissism. Although all individuals have a measure of narcissism, it can become pathological in certain leaders as their sense of self-importance grows beyond reasonable boundaries. As a personality disorder, narcissism takes the form of exhibitionism, fantasies of unlimited power and success, grandiose visions, and expectations that others will defer to the individual (Sankowsky, 1995). Kohut comments that the combination of narcissism and charisma is a particularly potent and dangerous one: "[These individuals] have the uncanny ability to exploit, not necessarily in full awareness, the unconscious feelings of their subordinates" (Sankowsky, 1995, p. 65). Over time, the leader's symbolic power causes followers to accept without questioning the leader's views and commands. As a *Forbes* writer noted, narcissistic leaders often surround themselves with "believers," as was the case with Steven Jobs: "On his own, Jobs has a tendency to surround himself with people who, though talented, aren't likely to question his vision" (Pitta, 1991, p. 140). Similarly, the values and ideology of the leader go unquestioned. At The Body Shop, a 1993 internal report found that

> the staff does not know how much they can say or to whom; . . . Staff are unable to speak out because they are expected to "be positive and toe the Company line." . . . Some feel that the Company indulges in emotional blackmail and tries to indoctrinate staff to take on beliefs and values held by the Company. (Baker & Duncan, 1995, p. 17)

In the worst of cases, followers end up seeing the leader's grandiosity and demands not as foolhardy or abusive but as justifiable. As they buy into the leader's belief system, they increasingly put themselves at risk. Sankowsky (1995) outlines the steps that then unfold.

First, the charismatic leader promotes a grandiose vision and requires that followers put forth tremendous efforts to achieve the vision. Followers who accept the leader's mandate, however, soon find themselves in a double bind. The leader's grandiose vision has caused them to misread and underestimate the existing internal and external barriers to realizing the vision. Followers soon find themselves lacking the resources necessary to implement the mission. In spite of their desire to realize the leader's vision and demands, they can only partially meet the organization's goals. Their performance then falls short and appears substandard. At first, the highly narcissistic leader may blame external sources, but he or she will sooner or later turn internally and blame the followers. They become responsible for shortcomings. Because followers have been conditioned to accept unquestioningly the leader's viewpoints, they accept the blame placed on themselves. As Sankowsky (1995) notes, the leader may even question their commitment, using poor performance as proof: "If you were really committed, you would have found a way to make this work." The scenario is more complex, however, in that certain followers may indeed achieve the unrealistic demands of the leader. These "achievers" provide further rationale for the leader to single out as flawed any others who have not been successful. From the standpoint of organizational learning, this scenario precludes the possibility of objectively reexamining the tenets of the leader's vision or understanding resource constraints. In the end, followers become the scapegoat for the leader's own follies.

A second dilemma for the followers of the highly narcissistic leader is that these leaders often claim credit for others' ideas. John DeLorean at General

Motors and Lee Iaccoca at Chrysler are both recognized for automotive innovations, yet the source of their ideas was a team of individuals. Steven Jobs's claim to the Macintosh was captured in the unveiling ceremonies of the personal computer when the machine itself announced in a digital voice: "I would like to thank a man who has been a father to me—Steven Jobs." In reality, Jef Raskin appears to have been the original champion of the Macintosh. Bucher (1988) has documented that in 1979 Raskin had worked on the forerunner to the Macintosh, the Lisa:

> Lisa was originally started as a character generated machine, like the IBM PC. I was the one who changed it to being a bit more graphic. I changed it single-handedly to a graphics computer connected to a Xerox machine to make the print-outs. I was the one who put it all together, but Jobs told everyone that he had done it. It made me very annoyed, because it took me two years to negotiate the deal with Xerox. (Bucher, 1988, p. 136)

Raskin believed that the public wanted a computer that would require no significant expertise to operate. He would name it the Everyman's Computer because of its ease of use. He claims that initially Jobs thought the Macintosh was a dead-end idea:

> Jobs hated the idea. He ran around saying, "No! No! It will never work." He was one of the Macintosh's hardest critics and he was always putting it down at board meetings. When he became convinced that it would work, and that it would be an exciting product, he started to take over. (Bucher, 1988, p. 87)

By 1980, Jobs was unofficially running the Macintosh division. By 1982, he had taken over hardware design, then a week later, documentation; shortly thereafter, he assumed responsibility for software. By that point, the Macintosh was Jobs's creation and no longer Raskin's (Bucher, 1988, p. 136).

SHORTCOMINGS IN THE SKILL MIX
OF THE CHARISMATIC LEADER

Nadler and Tushman (1990) have argued that charismatic leadership in itself is insufficient in the majority of change situations. From an analysis of successful turnarounds, they identify a second form of leadership they call instrumental leadership. They conclude:

It appears that effective organizational re-orientation requires both charismatic and instrumental leadership. Charismatic leadership is needed to generate energy, create commitment, and direct individuals towards new objectives, values, and aspirations. Instrumental leadership is required to ensure that people really do act in a manner consistent with their new goals. Either one alone is insufficient for the achievement of change. (p. 129)

Instrumental leadership concerns itself with three key activities: structuring, controlling, and rewarding. In *structuring*, the leader actively builds management teams that possess the ability to execute and implement. The leader also is involved in creating structures that effectively convey throughout the company the types of behaviors required for the organization to succeed. This activity revolves around detailed planning about roles and responsibilities, standards, and goals. The second element, *controlling*, concerns the creation of systems to measure and assess both performance outcomes and behavior. Finally, *rewarding* involves the administration of rewards and punishments so that performance and behavior match the requirements of the change effort. As readers can discern, Nadler and Tushman's instrumental leadership is based largely around a set of managerial roles that we identified in earlier chapters. Nevertheless, they correctly note that these are activities uncharacteristic of many charismatic leaders.

The surface manifestations of a lack of instrumental leadership can be seen in the informality that characterizes the organizations of charismatic leaders. As leaders, they themselves are often loosely organized individuals, and this trait is mirrored in their organizations. As their organizations grow, this informality discourages the use of effective control systems and clear lines of responsibility and coordination. There is a failure to appreciate and cultivate professional management. For example, while at Control Data, Seymour Cray had a cardinal rule to avoid formal meetings. On one occasion, he was asked by a vice president to provide both a 1-year and a 5-year plan. On the next day, the executive found on his desk two binders. Inside each was a single page. The page in the first binder simply stated: "Five year plan: To build the world's fastest computer." A single page in the second binder had written on it: "To complete one-fifth of the five year plan" (Miller, 1990, p. 129). Charismatic leaders often encourage an atmosphere of innovation over a more disciplined, managerial focus. For example, after taking over from Steven Jobs at Apple, John Sculley found an organizational culture that was antithetical to coordinated and focused efforts:

We used to celebrate the fact that you had the freedom to do anything you wanted at Apple, if you thought it was a better idea. That was fine when the company was a handful of people trying to invent new things. But it became very destructive when there was no focus or process for people to work together. (Pearlstein & Rhodes, 1987, p. 59)

From our own observations of successful change efforts, we generally concur with Nadler and Tushman that the two forms of charismatic and instrumental leadership (or effective managing) are needed together to effectively address change. The dilemma is that charismatic leaders may not see the necessity of such a complement to their skills. They may even have ideological biases against "professional management," fearing that it may stifle creativity or the company's values or the free flow of information. This often is the case in companies run by charismatic entrepreneurs such as Anita Roddick of The Body Shop. For example, Roddick's early hiring criteria were based around friendships. She felt that business skills were relatively easily acquired by simply possessing a curious personality: "We hired friends. To run a business you literally don't need to know too much. You need to learn, understand, listen, ask questions . . . it wasn't rocket science . . . it was just trading" (Baker & Duncan, 1995, p. 11). Only in 1994 would she realize that management skills were of equal importance: "We should have had a bit more of a professional management or more professional skills than we did [early on]. But instead we brought in people with passion: ex-teachers, people like me" (Baker & Duncan, 1995, p. 11). Similarly, the company long neglected basic human resources practices. An internal investigation in the 1990s revealed pay inequities, an absence of succession or career plans, and inadequate management skills training.

Nowhere, however, was the lack of instrumental leadership more apparent than at People Express. Its absence would surface visibly only several years after its founding. By 1984, People Express had expanded service to 50 cities. As the passenger numbers grew, the company's service levels began to break down—specifically in reservations (the controlling and structuring dimensions of the Nadler and Tushman framework). The company had largely neglected investments in up-to-date reservations systems (Petzinger, 1995). Instead, it employed a crude mix of mechanical and electronic systems that resembled an airline of the 1950s. Burr also had refused to pay transaction fees to the national airline reservation systems of Sabre and Apollo, which meant that customers had to call People Express directly to book a seat. For many, their first experience with the company was an endless series of busy signals on the telephone line. It was estimated that by 1984 some 6,000 potential passengers failed to connect by telephone per day. By 1983, with service levels declining, Burr decided to invest in an in-house reservation system. An initial contract with NCR, however, would collapse a year later because of implementation disputes. American Express was then invited to design a new system. By the end of 1984, the reservation system was still not up and running (Petzinger, 1995).

The company at that point had become notorious for "overbooking" its flights. Because People Express customers could pay for their tickets on the day of their flight, there was little incentive to cancel one's reservations if plans changed (Petzinger, 1995). As a result, no-shows were increasingly common-place. People Express, in turn, responded to the problem by overselling flights, sometimes by as much as 100%. Numerous times, the expected "no-show" passengers appeared, and many unhappy clients with reservations were left without a flight (Petzinger, 1995).

The clearest example of where an absence of instrumental leadership had an impact on Burr and People Express was in fare pricing. A competitor, American Airlines, and its CEO, Robert Crandall, powerfully demonstrated the vital role that sophisticated information systems would play in ensuring the success of the larger carriers. In an earlier career as data processing manager at Hallmark Cards, Crandall had developed a sophisticated restocking system for the company's greeting card sales. The system was so sophisticated that a mainframe computer carefully tracked trends down to the individual card display slot at each store location. On joining American, Crandall believed that he could apply a similar procedure to the airline industry. He experimented with a system (named Sabre) that would vary the proportion of full-fare and discount seats on a daily basis and by departure, depending on whether bookings were ahead or behind their predicted levels. In essence, prices would vary precisely with the flow of supply and demand (Petzinger, 1995).

The Sabre reservation system contained an enormous amount of historical information on sales trends. For example, the data allowed American to deduce how many days in advance travelers typically booked trips to Atlanta, in December versus June, on Mondays versus Fridays, on afternoons versus evenings. Crandall established a special department to monitor the rate of bookings in the different fare categories. Bookings were in turn compared with a forecasted rate. As they varied, rates were adjusted accordingly to take full advantage of changes in supply and demand. By 1984, Crandall and his staff had largely perfected the process they termed "yield management." This would soon prove to be a powerful competitive tool to minimize the inroads of People Express's cheap fares. It allowed American to match fares but to do so selectively on its total seat inventory. For example, if People offered a $59 fare on a southwestern route, American could do the same but sell only as many of these inexpensive seats as the Sabre system suggested. The additional seats would be held in reserve for full-fare passengers who were booking close to the date of departure. On the same southwestern route, American's average fare on a particular flight might be $199 as a result, whereas People's would be only $59. American could offer inexpensive seats while maintaining a healthier level of overall revenues per planeload (Petzinger, 1995).

American discovered, like People, that no-shows were a greater problem at the low fare, so in January of 1985, Crandall introduced a new pricing strategy. Passengers would have to purchase their seats at the time of their reservation. Nonrefundable tickets would alleviate the no-show problem. More important, the guaranteed revenue stream would allow American to subsidize even deeper discounts than had been possible for the larger carriers. With the power of Sabre's information systems and the nonrefundable ticket, American could outprice People Express. As Donald Carty, American's planning director, would later explain, "We have devised the fare structure that put them [People Express] out of business" (Petzinger, 1995, p. 272). Soon American was offering fares up to 70% off across its system. This act of instrumental leadership eventually would drive People Express into the hands of Frank Lorenzo. Because Donald Burr had no computer systems and no capability at yield management, People Express could respond to Crandall's price moves only by offering every one of its seats at Crandall's lowest fare (Petzinger, 1995).

In contrast to both Burr and Roddick, other charismatic leaders such as Jack Welch at General Electric, Herb Kelleher at Southwest Airlines, and Richard Branson at Virgin have been very adept at finding complementary expert or managerial talent. For example, Colleen Barrett, the executive vice president of Southwest, is the managerial complement to Kelleher's loosely organized style: "She is a stickler for detail and provides the organizational counterweight to Kelleher's sometimes chaotic style" (O'Reilly & Pfeffer, 1995, p. 10).

Similarly, as he began his music recording business, Richard Branson found the "golden ears" for his venture in a cousin, Simon Draper, who had come to England looking for a job. Draper was an avid fan of popular music. Although he began as a record buyer, he soon earned a reputation for a remarkable ability to spot and develop music talent. For example, he persuaded Branson to back a young musician who already had been rejected by the major recording studios. Draper was convinced that this particular artist, Mike Oldfield, had potential. After a year's effort, Oldfield produced a piece called *Tubular Bells*, released in 1973, that went on to sell more than 5 million copies worldwide—a remarkable success. Branson, on the other hand, was known to be almost tone-deaf. Later, as Virgin grew, Branson brought on board a professional manager to oversee operations, Don Cruickshank, a Scottish accountant with an MBA and a career in consulting at McKinsey and Company (Kets de Vries, 1986). Throughout his business career, Branson's talent has been finding complementary skills to run the various enterprises so that he can do what he does best—work on new business ventures and public relations.

SUCCESSION CHALLENGES

Given the strength of character of many charismatic leaders, it is not uncommon that problems arise in succession. Because of the dependence the charismatic leader can cultivate, followers may never develop similar leadership capabilities. Although these leaders may mentor their subordinates, we suspect that it is difficult for them to develop others to be leaders of equal power to themselves. They simply enjoy the limelight too much to share it. In addition, their need to be *the leader* may drive more junior leaders to other organizations, where they are able to flourish, out from under the shadow of their charismatic superior. A leader's need to be the principal decision maker within the organization encourages him or her to centralize important decisions under his or her jurisdiction. This type of arrangement, however, weakens the authority structures that are normally dispersed throughout an organization.

In other situations, charismatic leaders may have found complementary successors who provide the operational excellence at which they themselves are often weak or have limited interest in, but these individuals may be lacking in the leadership qualities demanded by their new position. The charismatic leader's track record also may create untenable expectations for his or her successors. One potential example of this is at Lockheed Martin. Norman R. Augustine, who recently stepped down as CEO, was a charismatic leader who transformed Martin Marietta Corporation through his masterful skills at deal making. He orchestrated a $5 billion merger with Lockheed, a $9 billion acquisition of Loral, and a $11.3 billion purchase of Northrop Grumman Corporation, along with other acquisitions of smaller defense companies. In total, these deals created a $30 billion manufacturer of rockets, missiles, jet fighters, and satellites. His successor, Vance Coffman, who assumed the CEO position in August of 1997, has been an inside-operations executive with a straightforward, "no frills" manner. His career track has been in managing complex technological projects and in implementing many of the company's mergers (Crock, 1997). The challenge for Coffman is to develop the complementary skills possessed by his predecessor, the charismatic Augustine. As a leading business journal recently commented:

> To succeed, Coffman—an engineer by training—must transform himself into an outspoken strategist and cheerleader. "He made a name for himself operating at deck level," says one Lockheed Martin insider. "Now, he's operating at 25,000 feet, following a guy who operated at 50,000 feet." (Crock, 1997, p. 103)

The dilemma, then, for the successor of the charismatic leader becomes one of expectations and of new skill requirements. For example, organizational members and shareholders expect their senior leader or chief executive officer to be strategic and visionary, and to a large extent these are indeed the skills required for such positions. The charismatic leader's second-in-command who assumes the leader's role, however, may have had few opportunities to develop a more strategic capacity—having been rewarded repeatedly for operational skills. As a result, the successor continues to focus on the internal operating challenges of the organization, neglecting to an important degree external strategic challenges. Conversely, successors are active in strategy formulation, but their lack of sufficient experience leads to poor strategic choices. In other cases, they may inherit from the charismatic leader an organization whose activities and businesses reflect an overly ambitious and visionary agenda—in essence, inadvertently setting the new leader up for extremely demanding organizational challenges that in the end will result in poorer performance or even failure. Returning to the Lockheed Martin example, Coffman's challenge, for example, is to meld Augustine's broad vision of diverse and far-flung acquisitions (which have been termed "a defense industry archaeological dig" by Crock [1997, p. 103]) into an integrated organization. This is an enormous task for anyone, no matter how talented.

To address dilemmas such as these, charismatic leaders must be prepared to recognize their own "organizational mortality," to actively prepare for succession, and to ensure that the grooming of others includes developmental experiences that enhance new skill sets. One recent example of a charismatic leader who has been highly effective in this regard is Henry Schacht, the recently retired CEO of Lucent Technologies (Nadler, 1997). Lucent is a spin-off company from AT&T. Four of AT&T's least successful, least profitable businesses, along with Bell Labs, were lumped together to create Lucent, a $23 billion venture with

130,000 employees worldwide. Leadership of the spin-off fell to Henry Schacht and Richard McGinn. The charismatic Henry Schacht was 61 years old at the time and the retired CEO of Cummins Engine. He also had been a board member of AT&T for a considerable length of time. Rich McGinn, on the other hand, was a company insider and the operating head of one of the divisions that AT&T had merged to create Lucent. Schacht was appointed by AT&T's chairman, Robert Allen, to be Lucent's CEO, and McGinn was appointed the company's COO. In contrast to many CEOs, Schacht knew that his time horizon in the position would be limited, given his age and a prevailing assumption that he would stay on for only a few years. As Schacht explained, "We were into management succession the day I walked in here" (Nadler, 1997, p. 16). Wisely, Schacht decided to make it very clear to McGinn that he was the uncontested heir to the CEO position. Schacht consciously positioned his role as a partner with McGinn and then actively prepared McGinn and the rest of the senior team to assume control of the company on his retirement (Nadler, 1997):

> We started off saying, "Rich, there is no alternative in this company to you to be the next CEO. My job is to do everything I can to make sure you are the next CEO. We're not going to hire somebody else to make this a horse race." And I told everybody else in the company, "Look, Rich is my guy. I'm here to help him lead this group." (p. 20)

To reinforce this dynamic, Schacht avoided designing a corporate structure that viewed him as the centerpiece (Nadler, 1997). Instead, he assumed the principal roles of teaching and coaching, helping McGinn and his team to be more effective in building the senior team's collective identity and in managing the board. They worked together on developing the company's strategy and shared in external responsibilities for managing the press, customers, and financial analysts. In essence, they avoided the traditional division of CEO-COO activities into strategy versus operations. During the transition period, the company itself performed remarkably, with both revenue and profit growth up substantially. In October of 1997, Henry Schacht passed the CEO title on to McGinn, with Schacht remaining as chairman. McGinn already has begun a process for sharing leadership with the next generation. With four other senior executives, he has established plans for assigning primary responsibilities for major executive functions within the new team to prepare for his succession (Nadler, 1997).

In conclusion, charismatic leadership is a double-edged sword. The forces that produce the very strengths of the leader may also give rise to the shadow side of charisma. For example, the qualities of vision and foresight, when coupled with the leader's natural tendencies toward narcissism, can lead to personal goals that are detached from marketplace realities. Similarly, the forces that attract followers to charismatic leaders and engender remarkable levels of commitment and performance can become the forces that lead to excessive dependency and blind acceptance of the leader's wishes. To counter such dysfunctional outcomes, organizations, their boards of directors, and leaders themselves must assume far greater responsibility for self-monitoring. In the ideal case, charismatic leaders need to become more objective observers of their behavior and actions, especially in response to negative signals from the environment and followers (Sankowsky, 1995). They must endeavor to develop a greater reflective capacity as well as becoming more consultative. Sankowsky (1995) has succinctly outlined the qualities that these leaders must develop in themselves to avoid highly dysfunctional outcomes for themselves and their organizations:

> Like psychotherapists, leaders who care about the psychological well-being of their followers can work to prevent abuse by developing commitment, awareness, responsibility, and self-evaluation. Commitment includes honoring both agreed-upon external values and an inner sense of morality and fairness—and not allowing moral expediency and convenience to determine decision-making. Leaders must be aware—they must develop the ability to distinguish between personal issues and an organizationally based vision in driving the mission and its implementation. Likewise, they must be responsible, making the time and effort to assist the followers' development, separate from the mission. Self-evaluation is important; leaders should assess their own contributions to successful and unsuccessful outcomes in a fair and honest way, through self-monitoring—and by addressing follower discomfort and poor performance, seeing these as signals to re-evaluate their management of various functions, particularly the communication process. (p. 70)

At the same time, it is important to be realistic. Many who are charismatic leaders may simply lack the desire or discipline to become truly reflective. The strength of their own egos, their own passion, or the multiple and never-ending demands on their time may prevent many of these leaders from undertaking active self-examination and self-monitoring. In such cases, we can only hope that their superiors or their boards of directors or the media draw attention in time to avert organizational tragedies.

8

Looking to the Future

In our introductory chapter, we pointed out that the interest of management scholars in charismatic leadership has grown considerably in recent years. This trend has resulted from the realization that charismatic leadership is well suited to meet the demands of today's competitive business environment on a global scale. Our present business environment also provides us with signals as to the challenges that corporations might expect in the future. With this in mind, we conclude this volume with an examination of the major environmental challenges that lie ahead and why charismatic leadership is needed to meet these challenges. In addition, this chapter identifies a number of areas related to charismatic leadership where further research is needed.

As we stand at the doorstep of the next century, it is prudent to examine the environmental challenges that organizations will face in the next decade or two. Such an examination can help us identify the capabilities organizations need to develop to respond successfully to the challenges that lie ahead. Identification of these capabilities naturally leads to several other questions. How can such capabilities be built into organizations? What types of managerial and leadership roles will executives have to play to build organizations that can meet the environmental challenges of the 21st century? What types of adaptive changes will executives have to bring about in their own behaviors to reshape organizational missions, goals, structures, and operating procedures? What should be the nature of their leadership influence as they seek to direct and control members of their organizations to achieve company missions and goals? Given these challenges, what directions should leadership research and theory follow in the future?

These questions are addressed in the sections to follow. The first section describes four ongoing major changes in the corporate environment that pose future challenges. We then identify the organizational capabilities and leadership strategies needed to meet these challenges successfully. Specific charismatic leadership behaviors and influence processes that are conducive to building the appropriate capabilities are highlighted. The concluding section provides direction for future research by drawing attention to a number of emerging trends in leadership research that will have significant effects on future management practices.

CHANGES IN THE CORPORATE ENVIRONMENT

Compared with 1970s and 1980s, the business environment of the 1990s is experiencing more radical changes at an accelerated pace. Specifically, changes can be seen in four areas that will have an increasing impact on business in the 21st century. These changes are taking place in (1) the economic environment, (2) information technology, (3) the sociocultural environment, and (4) demands for social responsibility in business.

The Changing Economic Environment

As noted in Chapter 1, the economic environment of business has transformed itself, with increasing trade liberalization and the globalization of economies all across the world. Recent developments such as the Canada-U.S. Free Trade Agreement, the formulation of the North American Free Trade Agreement (NAFTA) and the European Economic Union as trade blocs, the emergence of the Pacific Rim as a powerful influence in manufacturing and international trade, and the presence of strong emerging markets in developing countries such as China and India are all exerting increasing pressure on business to build organizational capabilities for gaining competitive advantage in world markets (Cohen, 1995).

To respond to these changes in the environment, corporations will have to expand, diversify, and integrate globally through new investments, acquisitions, and joint ventures. This implies that there should be new business formation, with an emphasis on new process and new product development as well as new marketing strategies. There is a need for considerable investment in information gathering to identify special customer needs and the competitive moves of rivals.

Responses to competition and market changes must be quick and unconventional, through frequent product/service redesigns and new process and product introductions. To build such competitive capabilities in an organization, corporate leaders will need to develop entrepreneurial and innovative strategies. D'Aveni (1995) has proposed a framework for coping with hypercompetition that involves (1) changing the status quo and (2) having a vision for identifying opportunities by creating new ways to serve existing customers and finding new customers that no one else serves. In the same vein, one could argue that improving competitive position in global markets will continue to require organizations to adopt quality improvement practices consistent with a total quality management (TQM) philosophy (Dean & Evans, 1994). The leadership practices necessary for promoting TQM are characterized by a vision for the future that understands customer and other stakeholder needs, emphasizes innovation and continuous product and service improvements, and empowers workers to develop self-efficacy and team spirit (Puffer & McCarthy, 1996).

The Changing World of Information Technology

The explosion in the use and sophistication of information technology in recent years has created new opportunities and challenges for business organizations. For example, the creation of electronic information highways is opening up opportunities to enter global markets. By the same token, such changes are posing new challenges to win over customers or increase market share. Increasingly, customers are demanding better quality products while looking for customized services to meet their special needs. Thus, business organizations have higher growth potential but simultaneously must face stiffer competition. To remain competitive, they must utilize the integrative power of information and communications technology. As Howard (1995) points out, in this "post-industrial information age, the balance of work has tipped from hand to head, from brawn to brain. Workers don't just run machines and push papers, they control information. And information is displacing capital as the essential resource for industrial success" (p. 23).

Managing and utilizing information will be a major task for future organizational leaders. A wide range of organizational mechanisms will need to be developed for information acquisition and processing relating to both the external and internal environments of the organization. Organizational capabilities for quick learning from information feedback and for adaptation to rapid change have to be developed. This will require leaders to be change oriented and to develop a readiness to abandon the status quo and any practices that are obsolete or untenable. Furthermore, leaders will need to promote decentralized decision making. At the same time, they will need to centralize coordination within their organizations so that information technology can facilitate the exchange of information and foster teamwork among all functional units. An integrated decision support system is needed at the corporate level. Whereas decentralization implies participatory decision making with a free flow of information, ideas, and expertise across functional lines, coordination implies synthesizing and integrating various decisions in terms of the shared vision and core values advocated by leaders for the organization. Leaders can accomplish this by being visionary and developing a broad generalist orientation. In popular terms, "they should have their head in the clouds and their feet on the ground" (Kouzes & Posner, 1996, p. 103).

The Changing Sociocultural Environment

The sociocultural environment of an organization influences its internal work culture and its human resource and marketing management practices (Kanungo & Jaeger; 1990, Mendonca & Kanungo, 1994). In recent years, business organizations have experienced changes in their sociocultural environment, in both domestic and international contexts. Such changes are going to affect their future management practices. These changes can be noticed on three fronts. First, the inflow of immigrants from all parts of the world is reshaping both the labor force and the consumers of products and services into an increasingly multicultural and multiethnic pool. As a result, business organizations are finding their workforces and their customers to be culturally diverse. Second, there is a steady increase in the participation of women in the workforce. This has added another dimension to the workforce and to customer diversity. Managing labor diversity and gender issues within organizations, and marketing products and services to meet diverse ethnic customer needs, are becoming major challenges for business organizations. Third, the task of managing diversity is becoming critical in the context of the global economy as business has become more and more international and transnational. In a global context, it is highly important to understand how the underlying cultural values of a society determine organizational forms, managerial practices, and employee behavior. Corporations that operate in different countries will find that the workforces and customers in those countries are diverse and culturally different. To manage such diversity, one must not only ensure the culture fit of the state-of-the-art, home-grown management practices, but also adapt management practices that "fit" the cultural norms and values of the countries in which these organizations operate (Mendonca & Kanungo, 1994).

Sociocultural and gender heterogeneity in organizations can cause negative feelings among members, social stress, and turnover (Miliken & Martins, 1996; Morrison, 1992). On the other hand, there are potential benefits of such diversity. It can result in better decision making, higher levels of creativity and innovation, and increased job performance (Cox, 1991; Watson, Kumar, & Michaelsen, 1993). To manage diversity, organizations need to develop capabilities for recognizing cultural differences as a strength rather than as a weakness of people. Organizations should promote perceptions of fairness and equity among all members by designing and implementing equitable hiring, promotion, performance appraisal, supervision, and reward systems. Leaders can help build such capabilities by developing strategies that demonstrate sensitivity, flexibility, and understanding of ethnic, cultural, and gender differences. These strategies should reflect a global mind-set and a global vision that values "diversity and multicultural teamwork and team play as the basic form within which to accomplish their personal, professional and organizational objectives" (Rhinesmith, 1993, p. 3). Leaders must be capable of bringing "people of diverse backgrounds and interests together in ways that provide fair and equitable opportunities to contribute their best, achieve personal goals, and realize their full potential" (Work, 1996, p. 79).

Changing Demands for Social Responsibility in Business

Business and industry are gaining a commanding role in the nation's economic life. Business is expected to provide employment and income, as well as goods and services for consumption. In exchange for providing these benefits, business organizations are permitted greater access to common resources with minimal government control. This situation often leads many organizations to engage in resource exploitation for short-run economic gains at the cost of community and consumer interests. Concurrent with the increasing influence of business organizations, the public's awareness of many adverse effects of business is also increasing. Incidents of media reporting on environmental pollution, contaminated blood banks, adulterated products, false advertising, bribery, and so on are commonplace. Citizens are increasingly demanding greater accountability from both business and government organizations. There is a growing realization that profitability in business must go hand in hand with a socially responsible and ethical code of conduct in business.

At the corporate level, the ethical issues of governance will become more of a concern for leaders. Already, environmental protection and human rights standards are being enforced in international trade negotiations. Organizations are beginning to consider such ethical issues as a part of their total business strategy. With respect to their external environment, corporations must develop the capacity to be sensitive and committed to environmental protection. With respect to their internal environment, corporations should provide codes of ethics for promoting actions "needed to map a high road to economic and ethical performance—and to mount guardrails to keep corporate wayfarers on track" (Andrews, 1989, p. 99).

To achieve organizational capabilities that can deal effectively with ethical issues, leaders need to become sensitive to their moral obligations, not only to stockholders but also to other stakeholders—consumers, employees, suppliers, government, and local communities. They need to develop a culture of workplace ethics within organizations that is morally defensible, one that empowers employees to practice such ethics in their day-to-day work behavior (Kanungo & Mendonca, 1996b). At a personal level, a leader's intelligence, hard work, technical competence, and knowledge might fail to achieve organizational objectives if the leader is "perceived as arrogant, vindictive, untrustworthy, selfish, emotional, compulsive, over-controlling, insensitive, abrasive . . ." (Hogan, Curphy, & Hogan, 1994, p. 499). To avoid such failures, a leader has to develop as a moral person with an ethical and principle-governed mind-set (see Kanungo & Mendonca, 1996b, for a description of such qualities) as well as exhibit characteristics of the positive charismatic as outlined in Chapter 7.

To sum up, four significant changes in the environment are under way that pose major challenges for business organizations of the future. These, in turn, pose leadership challenges for developing the appropriate organizational capabilities to meet such environmental demands. The leadership strategies necessary for each of the tasks are summarized in Table 8.1.

FUTURE RESEARCH AGENDA

The new paradigm for the study of charismatic and transformational leadership, as outlined in this book, has raised issues that require research exploration in the future (Conger & Kanungo, 1988d). The first area for exploration concerns the process and content of the activity of visioning. Studies that identify mental representations and processes underlying the visioning activity of a leader

TABLE 8.1 Environmental Changes and Adaptive Leadership Strategies for Business Organizations

Environmental Changes	Major Tasks	Building Organizational Capabilities	Leadership Strategies
1. Globalization of business	Managing competition	New businesses New products New processes Total quality	Entrepreneurial Innovative
2. Explosion of information technology	Managing information/ knowledge	Rapid and timely change Free information flow Decentralized decision making Coordinated clearinghouses	Change oriented Visionary Environmental scanning oriented Participatory
3. Diverse labor force and consumer markets	Managing diversity and gender issues	Sociocultural sensitivity Employment and reward system equity	Culture sensitive Sensitive to members and customer needs Global mind-set

clearly are needed. Because the formulation of a vision implies an activity that is both novel or original and useful or adaptive, future research in this area will benefit from the creativity literature (Sternberg & Lubart, 1996). What triggers the visioning activity and what sustains it over a period of time are questions that call for answers. What predispositional, motivational, and contextual variables may be responsible for the initiation and maintenance of visioning is an equally important question that needs to be answered.

Another aspect of the visioning activity that needs to be studied is the structure and content of the vision itself (Larwood et al., 1995). What are the components of a vision? Are there different types of visions based on unique configurations of various contents (such as corporate values, missions, specific goals or purposes, etc.), their scope, time frame, specificity, and complexity? Knowing how to structure a vision and what aspects of the vision (e.g., risk propensity, degree of detail) are universally important can help corporate executives in their leadership role.

A third aspect of the visioning activity that requires researchers' attention is the use of language that gives shape to the vision for the organization. The issue is how to frame and articulate the vision for maximum impact (Conger, 1991; Fairhurst & Sarr, 1996).

Finally, although there is agreement on the significance of visioning activity (see, e.g., Conger & Kanungo, 1988b; Nutt & Backoff, 1997), strategic visioning as a behavioral process is poorly understood. Earlier, we identified the two polar positions that exist. One argues that the process is deliberate, rational, and therefore trainable (Sashkin, 1988). The other sees visioning by the leader as a more complex, emergent process (Conger, 1989a; Westley & Mintzberg, 1988). These distinct positions raise several interesting questions for future research: (1) whether strategic visioning is indeed deliberate or emergent or both, (2) whether it might be possible for both deliberate and emergent visioning processes to occur simultaneously, and (3) whether under certain contextual conditions one process is more appropriate and feasible than the other.

Another area for exploration is the manner in which leaders' behavioral characteristics such as articulation skills, high activity level, or exemplary modeling facilitate trust, provide direction, and stimulate motivation in followers to achieve the vision for the organization. Our own study (Study 6 in Chapter 3), the study by Kirkpatrick and Locke (1996), and the work of Podsakoff and colleagues (1990) are examples of efforts in this direction. Generally, however, our knowledge of how and when these leader behaviors influence followers' attitudes and behaviors is poorly understood and requires further research attention.

Explorations are needed into the dynamics of how *context* acts as a contingency for leadership effectiveness. Both theoretical development and empirical verification of how, why, and when leaders identify and articulate crises and deficiencies in their environment need to be on the agenda for future research. Besides "crisis" in the task context, leadership effectiveness can be influenced by the leader's perception of unexplored positive opportunities in the larger environment. Depending on the emphasis the leader places while relating to the context (either on the crisis in the status quo or on the opportunity inherent in the vision), his or her influence could be characterized as a crisis or ideological influence. Future research attention should be directed toward exploring the extent to which crisis and opportunities in the context are used by leaders to foster their influence.

The identification of dispositional attributes of followers that may enhance their receptivity and commitment to a leader has been a largely neglected area of research. Various researchers have suggested that certain follower predispositions such as submissiveness and low self-esteem (Downton, 1973; Galanter, 1982) may in part be responsible for behavioral outcomes such as a high level of emotional commitment to the leader, heightened motivation, willing obedience to the leader, greater group cohesion, and a sense of empowerment (Conger

& Kanungo, 1988a). Besides their dispositions, followers' perceptions of the context may act as possible contingencies of charismatic leadership effectiveness. For example, when the context evokes feelings of high uncertainty, helplessness, powerlessness, and alienation among followers, conditions become ripe for a leader's influence within an organization. The psychological processes underlying helplessness (Garber & Seligman, 1980) and alienation (Kanungo, 1982) and the identification of specific organizational conditions (Martinko & Gardner, 1982) that promote such psychological states among followers have received little attention in leadership research. Future studies need to explore such issues in greater depth.

Analysis of culture as a contingency variable in leadership effectiveness is an important area for future exploration. Innumerable cultural dynamics influence the leadership process (Kanungo & Mendonca, 1996a). Followers are more likely to attribute leadership to an individual when they perceive his or her leadership behavior to be culturally appropriate and in congruence with their own cultural values. Culture sensitivity is a part of the global mind-set required of leaders operating in a global environment (Adler, 1997). Because different cultures have different beliefs, values, modes of articulation and vision formulation, and so on, explorations of these variations is critical for identifying sources of leadership effectiveness in different cultural contexts.

The final area of research exploration has to do with the mechanisms of the transformational effects of charismatic leadership on followers. Our understanding of these influence dynamics remains at a speculative level and requires both theoretical development and empirical validation in future research. For example, the process of empowerment is used to explain the charismatic/transformational influence process (Kanungo & Mendonca, 1996b). Traditionally, empowerment has been viewed more as a transactional process of sharing power and resources. Several researchers, however, have argued that the empowerment process should be viewed as a process of enabling followers through the enhancement of their personal self-efficacy beliefs and intrinsic task motivation (Conger & Kanungo, 1988c; Thomas & Velthouse, 1990). Viewed in this way, leadership influence is a process of transforming followers' self-concepts and attitudes toward the task and goal set for the organization. Thomas and Velthouse's (1990) model of empowerment, defined around increased intrinsic task motivation, suggests that critical to the process of empowerment is an understanding of workers' interpretive styles and global beliefs. Implications of this cognitive perspective on empowerment need further exploration, as has been recently done by Spreitzer (1995, 1996). Likewise, the nature of and mechanisms underlying the empowerment process as suggested by the self-efficacy model proposed by

Conger and Kanungo (1988c) need to be validated empirically. Furthermore, it has been argued that the transformation of followers achieved through empowerment is very much influenced by leaders' altruistic motives and conduct (Kanungo & Conger, 1993; Kanungo & Mendonca, 1996b) in organizational contexts. Future research must explore the roles of altruism and ethical conduct of leaders as the basis of their transformational influence in organizations.

CONCLUSION

To have relevance for corporations of the future, leadership practice and research need to shift their emphasis from managerial behavior (e.g., consideration, task, participation) to charismatic and transformational leadership behavior. When organizations are overmanaged but underled, they often fail in their adaptive capability. To meet the challenges of the future, corporate executives must take on the responsibility to lead for change rather than simply to manage. This book provides a framework as well as examples of how this can be done. In addition, the attention of management researchers must be redirected from the exclusive preoccupation with specific task characteristics in small groups to the study of the larger global context within which organizations accomplish their mission. This should include the in-depth study of specific charismatic leadership behaviors and their interaction with contextual and cultural variables as possible contingencies influencing leadership effectiveness. Furthermore, past research largely has emphasized the transactional influence process, but future research must be directed toward exploring the basis of transformational influence in the context of the management of change, innovation, diversity, and business ethics. Reflecting on future leaders, Beckhard (1996) states:

> Truly effective leaders in the years ahead will have personas determined by strong values and belief in the capacity of individuals to grow. They will have an image of the society in which they would like their organizations and themselves to live. They will be visionary, they will believe strongly that they can and should be shaping the future, and they will act on these beliefs through their personal behaviour. (p. 129)

The Conger-Kanungo Charismatic Leadership Questionnaire

INSTRUCTIONS

In your work experience you may have come across several individuals whom you considered to have leadership abilities. Pick one with whom you are most familiar and assess him or her on the basis of the statements in the questionnaire.

Indicate the extent to which each of the following items is characteristic of the person by circling the appropriate category next to the item.

The response categories are numbered 6 to 1 to represent the categories in the following way:

6 = Very Characteristic	3 = Slightly Uncharacteristic
5 = Characteristic	2 = Uncharacteristic
4 = Slightly Characteristic	1 = Very Uncharacteristic

1. Influences others by developing mutual   6   5   4   3   2   1
   liking and respect

2. Readily recognizes barriers/forces within the organization that may block or hinder achievement of his/her goals   6   5   4   3   2   1

3. Engages in unconventional behavior in order to achieve organizational goals   6   5   4   3   2   1

4. Entrepreneurial; seizes new opportunities in order to achieve goals   6   5   4   3   2   1

5. Shows sensitivity for the needs and feelings of the other members in the organization   6   5   4   3   2   1

6. Uses nontraditional means to achieve organizational goals   6   5   4   3   2   1

7. In pursuing organizational objectives, engages in activities involving considerable self-sacrifice   6   5   4   3   2   1

8. Readily recognizes constraints in the physical environment (technological limitations, lack of resources, etc.) that may stand in the way of achieving organizational objectives   6   5   4   3   2   1

9. Advocates following non-risky, well-established courses of action to achieve organizational goals   6   5   4   3   2   1

10. Provides inspiring strategic and organizational goals   6   5   4   3   2   1

11. Readily recognizes constraints in the organization's social and cultural environment (cultural norms, lack of grassroots support, etc.) that may stand in the way of achieving organizational objectives   6   5   4   3   2   1

12. Takes high personal risks for the sake of the organization   6   5   4   3   2   1

13. Inspirational; able to motivate by articulating effectively the importance of what organizatinal members are doing   6   5   4   3   2   1

14. Consistently generates new ideas for the   6   5   4   3   2   1
future of the organization

15. Exciting public speaker   6   5   4   3   2   1

16. Often expresses personal concern for   6   5   4   3   2   1
the needs and feelings of other
members of the organization

17. Tries to maintain the status quo or the   6   5   4   3   2   1
normal way of doing things

18. Often exhibits very unique behavior   6   5   4   3   2   1
that surprises other members of the
organization

19. Recognizes the abilities and skills of   6   5   4   3   2   1
other members in the organization

20. Often incurs high personal costs for the   6   5   4   3   2   1
good of the organization

21. Appears to be a skillful performer when   6   5   4   3   2   1
presenting to a group

22. Has vision; often brings up ideas about   6   5   4   3   2   1
possibilities for the future

23. Readily recognizes new environmental   6   5   4   3   2   1
opportunities (favorable physical and
social conditions) that may facilitate
achievement of organizational
objectives

24. Recognizes the limitations of other   6   5   4   3   2   1
members in the organization

25. In pursuing organizational objectives,   6   5   4   3   2   1
engages in activities involving
considerable personal risk

References

Adler, N. J. (1997). *International dimensions of organizational behavior* (3rd ed.). Cincinnati, OH: Northwestern College Publishing.

Agle, B. R. (1993). *Charismatic chief executive officers. Are they more effective? An empirical test of charismatic leadership.* Unpublished doctoral dissertation, University of Washington.

Agle, B. R., & Sonnenfeld, J. A. (1994). Charismatic chief executive officers: Are they more effective? An empirical test of charismatic leadership theory. *Academy of Management Best Papers Proceedings*, 2-6.

Alpert, M. (1990, February 26). The ultimate computer factory. *Fortune*, pp. 75-79.

Alcoholics Anonymous World Services. (1953). *Twelve steps and twelve traditions.* New York: Alcoholics Anonymous.

Alexander, L. D. (1985). Successfully implementing strategic decisions. *Long Range Planning, 18*, 91-97.

Anderson, J. C., & Gerbing, D. W. (1988). An updated paradigm for scale development incorporating unidimensionality and its assessment. *Journal of Marketing Research, 25*(2), 186-187.

Andrews, K. R. (1989, September-October). Ethics in practice. *Harvard Business Review*, pp. 99-104.

Andriessen, E. J. H., & Drenth, P. J. D. (1984). Leadership: Theories and models. In P. J. D. Drenth, H. Theirry, et al. (Eds.), *Handbook of work and organizational psychology.* New York: Wiley.

Ash, M. K. (1989, Summer). *A festival of friends.* Speech given at the annual Mary Kay sales convention, Dallas.

Atwater, L. E., Camobreco, J. F., Dionne, S. D., Avolio, B. J., & Lau, A. (1997). Effects of rewards and punishments on leader charisma, leader effectiveness and follower reactions. *Leadership Quarterly, 8*(2), 133-152.

Avolio, B., & Bass, B. M. (1988). Transformational leadership, charisma and beyond. In J. G. Hunt, B. R. Baliga, H. P. Dachler, & C. A. Schriesheim (Eds.), *Emerging leadership vistas* (pp. 29-49). Lexington, MA: D. C. Heath.

255

Avolio, B., & Gibbons, T. C. (1988). Developing transformational leaders: A lifespan approach. In J. A. Conger & R. N. Kanungo (Eds.), *Charismatic leadership: The elusive factor in organizational effectiveness* (pp. 267-308). San Francisco: Jossey-Bass.

Avolio, B., & Yammarino, F. J. (1990). Operationalizing charismatic leadership using a levels-of-analysis framework. *Leadership Quarterly, 1*, 193-208.

Bacharach, S. B., & Lawler, E. J. (1980). *Power and politics in organizations.* San Francisco: Jossey-Bass.

Baker, J., & Duncan, R. (1995). *The Body Shop: A case study.* Unpublished manuscript, Evanston, IL, Kellogg School, Northwestern University.

Balakrishnan, S., Gopakumar, K., & Kanungo, R. (in press). Entreprenuerial development: Concept and context. In R. N. Kanungo (Ed.), *Entrepreneurship and innovation: Models for development.* New Delhi: Sage.

Bales, R. F., & Slater, P. E. (1955). Role differentiation in small decision-making groups. In T. Parsons & R. F. Bales (Eds.), *Family, socialization and interaction process* (pp. 259-306). New York: Free Press.

Bandura, A. (1977). Self-efficacy: Toward a unifying theory of behavioral change. *Psychological Review, 84*(2), 191-215.

Bandura, A. (1986). *Social foundations of thought and action: A social-cognitive view.* Englewood Cliffs, NJ: Prentice Hall.

Bartlett, C. (1989). *Komatsu: Ryoichi Kawai's leadership.* Boston: Harvard Business School.

Bartlett, C., Elderkin, K., & McQuade, K. (1991). *The Body Shop International.* Boston: Harvard Business School.

Bass, B. M. (1970). When planning for others. *Journal of Applied Behavioral Science, 6*, 151-171.

Bass, B. M. (1985). *Leadership and performance beyond expectations.* New York: Free Press.

Bass, B. M. (1990). *Bass and Stogdill's handbook of leadership: Theory, research and managerial expectations* (3rd ed.). New York: Free Press.

Bass, B. M. (1997). Does the transactional-transformational leadership paradigm transcend organizational and national boundaries? *American Psychologist, 52,* 130-139.

Bass, B. M., & Avolio, B. (1993). Transformational leadership: A response to critiques. In M. M. Chemers & R. Ayman (Eds.), *Leadership theory and research: Perspectives and directions* (pp. 49-80). New York: Academic Press.

Bass, B. M., & Yammarino, F. J. (1988). *Leadership: Dispositional and situational* (ONR Technical Report No. 1). Binghamton: State University of New York, Center for Leadership Studies.

Beckhard, R. (1969). *Organizational development: Strategies and models.* Reading, MA: Addison-Wesley.

Beckhard, R. (1996). On future leaders. In F. Hesselbein, M. Goldsmith, & R. Beckhard (Eds.), *The leader of the future: New visions, strategies and practices for the new era* (pp. 125-129). San Francisco: Jossey-Bass.

Beer, M. (1980). *Organizational change and development: A systems view.* Santa Monica, CA: Goodyear.

Bellah, R. N., Madsen, R., Sullivan, W. M., Swidler, A., & Tipton, S. M. (1985). *Habits of the heart: Individuals and commitment in American life.* New York: Harper & Row.

Bem, D. J. (1970). *Beliefs, attitudes, and human affairs.* Belmont, CA: Brooks/Cole.

Bennis, W. G., & Nanus, B. (1985). *Leaders: The strategies for taking charge.* New York: Harper & Row.

Bentler, P. M. (1980). Multivariate analysis with latent variables: Causal modeling. *Annual Review of Psychology, 31*, 419-456.

Bentler, P. M., & Chou, C. P. (1987). Practical issues in structural modeling. *Sociological Methods and Research, 16*, 78-117.

Berger, P. L. (1963). Charisma and religious innovation: The social location of the Israelite Prophecy. *American Sociological Review, 28*, 940-950.

Berlew, D. E. (1974). Leadership and organizational excitement. *California Management Review, 17*, 21-30.

Bhide, A. (1994, March-April). How entrepreneurs craft strategies that work. *Harvard Business Review*, pp. 150-161.

Biggart, N. W. (1989). *Charismatic capitalism: Direct selling organizations in America.* Chicago: University of Chicago Press.

Biscardi, D., & Schill, T. (1985). Correlations of narcissistic traits with defensive style, Machiavellianism, and empathy. *Psychological Reports, 57*, 354.

Blake, R. R., & Mouton, J. S. (1964). *The managerial grid.* Houston: Gulf.

Blau, P. M. (1974). *Exchange and power in social life.* New York: Wiley.

Bourgeois, L. J. (1985). Strategic goals, perceived uncertainty, and economic performance in volatile environments. *Academy of Management Journal, 3*, 548-573.

Bower, J. L., & Doz, Y. (1979). Strategy formulation: A social and political process. In D. E. Schrendel & C. E. Hofer (Eds.), *Strategic management* (pp. 152-166). Boston: Little, Drown.

Boyatzis, R. E. (1982). *The competent manager.* New York: John Wiley.

Bradley, R. T. (1987). *Charisma and social structure: A study of love and power, wholeness and transformation.* New York: Paragon House.

Brislin, R. W., Lonner, W. J., & Thorndike, R. M. (1973). *Cross-cultural research methodology.* New York: Wiley.

Brooke, P. P., Russell, D. W., & Price, J. L. (1988). Discriminant validation of measures of job satisfaction, job involvement, and organizational commitment. *Journal of Applied Psychology, 73*, 139-145.

Bryman, A. (1986). *Leadership and organizations.* London: Routledge & Kegan Paul.

Bryman, A. (1992). *Charisma and leadership in organizations.* London: Sage.

Bryman, A. (1993). Charismatic leadership in business organizations: Some neglected issues. *Leadership Quarterly, 4*(3/4), 289-304.

Bucher, L. (1988). *Accidental millionaire.* New York: Paragon House.

Burgelman, R. A. (1988). Strategy making as a social learning process: The case of internal corporate venturing. *Interfaces, 18*(3), 74-85.

Burgelman, R. A. (1991). Intraorganizational ecology of strategy making and organizational adaption: Theory and field research. *Organizational Science, 2*(3), 239-262.

Burke, W. (1986). Leadership as empowering others. In S. Srivastra (Ed.), *Executive power* (pp. 51-77). San Francisco: Jossey-Bass.

Burlingham, B. (1988, June 1). This woman has changed business forever. *Inc.*, pp. 34-47.

Burns, J. M. (1978). *Leadership.* New York: Harper & Row.

Burns, T., & Stalker, G. M. (1961). *The management of innovation.* London: Tavistock.

Butler, J. K. (1991). Toward understanding and measuring conditions of trust: Evolution of a condition of trust inventory. *Journal of Management, 17*(3), 643-663.

Byrne, D. (1977). *The attraction paradigm.* New York: Academic Press.

Calder, B. J. (1977). An attribution theory of leadership. In B. M. Staw & G. R. Salancik (Eds.), *New directions in organizational behavior* (pp. 179-204). Chicago: St. Clair.

Campbell, D. T., & Fiske, D. W. (1959). Convergent and discriminant validation by the multitrait-multimethod matrix. *Psychological Bulletin, 56,* 81-105.

Carlzon, J. (1987). *Moments of truth.* Cambridge, MA: Ballinger.

Carroll, L. (1987). A study of narcissism, affiliation, intimacy, and power motives among students in business. *Psychological Reports, 61,* 355-358.

Cartwright, D. (1965). Leadership, influence, and control. In J. G. March (Ed.), *Handbook of organizations.* Chicago: Rand McNally.

Cartwright, D., & Zander, A. (1968). *Group dynamics: Research and theory* (3rd ed.). New York: Harper & Row.

Cell, C. P. (1974). Charismatic heads of state: The social context. *Behavioral Science Research, 4,* 255-305.

Chemers, M. M., & Ayman, R. (Eds.). (1993). *Leadership theory and research: Perspectives and directions.* New York: Academic Press.

Chen, C. C., & Meindl, J. R. (1991). The construction of leadership images in the popular press: The case of Donald Burr and People Express. *Administrative Science Quarterly, 36,* 521-551.

Coch, L., & French, J. R. P., Jr. (1948). Overcoming resistance to change. *Human Relations, 1,* 512-532.

Cohen, M. G. (1995). Economic restructuring through trade: Implications for people. In G. N. Ramu & V. P. Govitrikat (Eds.), *Liberalization: Indian and Canadian perspectives* (pp. 95-110). New Delhi: Allied Publishers.

Conger, J. A. (1985). *Charismatic leadership in business: An exploration study.* Unpublished doctoral dissertation, School of Business Administration, Harvard University.

Conger, J. A. (1988). Theoretical foundations of charismatic leadership. In J. A. Conger & R. N. Kanungo (Eds.), *Charismatic leadership: The elusive factor in organizational effectiveness.* San Francisco: Jossey-Bass.

Conger, J. A. (1989a). *The charismatic leader: Behind the mystique of exceptional leadership.* San Francisco: Jossey-Bass.

Conger, J. A. (1989b). Leadership: The art of empowering others. *Academy of Management Executive, 3*(1), 17-24.

Conger, J. A. (1990). The dark side of leadership. *Organizational Dynamics, 19*(2), 44-55.

Conger, J. A. (1991). Inspiring others: The language of leadership. *Academy of Management Executive, 5*(1), 31-45.

Conger, J. A. (1993). Max Weber's conceptualization of charismatic authority: Its influence on organizational research. *Leadership Quarterly, 4*(3/4), 277-288.

Conger, J. A., & Kanungo, R. N. (1987). Toward a behavioral theory of charismatic leadership in organizational settings. *Academy of Management Review, 12,* 637-647.

Conger, J. A., & Kanungo, R. N. (1988a). Behavioral dimensions of charismatic leadership. In J. A. Conger & R. N. Kanungo (Eds.), *Charismatic leadership: The elusive factor in organizational effectiveness* (pp. 78-97). San Francisco: Jossey-Bass.

Conger, J. A., & Kanungo, R. N. (Eds.). (1988b). *Charismatic leadership: The elusive factor in organizational effectiveness.* San Francisco: Jossey-Bass.

Conger, J. A., & Kanungo, R. N. (1988c). The empowerment process: Integrating theory and practice. *Academy of Management Review, 13,* 471-482.

Conger, J. A., & Kanungo, R. N. (1988d). Patterns and trends in studying charismatic leadership. In J. A. Conger & R. N. Kanungo (Eds.), *Charismatic leadership: The elusive factor in organizational effectiveness* (pp. 324-336). San Francisco: Jossey-Bass.

Conger, J. A., & Kanungo, R. N. (1992). Perceived behavioral attributes of charismatic leadership. *Canadian Journal of Behavioral Science, 24,* 86-102.

Conger, J. A., & Kanungo, R. (1994). Charismatic leadership in organizations: Perceived behavioral attributes and their measurement. *Journal of Organizational Behavior, 15,* 439-452.

Conger, J. A., Kanungo, R. N., Menon, S. T., & Mathur, P. (1997). Measuring charisma: Dimensionality and validity of the Conger-Kanungo scale of charismatic leadership. *Canadian Journal of Administrative Sciences, 14*(3), 290-302.

Cooper, A. C., & Schendel, D. E. (1976, February). Strategic responses to technological threats. *Business Horizons,* pp. 61-63.

Cowley, W. H. (1928). Three distinctions in the study of leaders. *Journal of Abnormal and Social Psychology, 23,* 144-157.

Cox, T., Jr. (1991). The multicultural organization. *Academy of Management Executive, 5*(2), 34-47.

Crock, S. (1997, October 27). Can this farm boy keep Lockheed in orbit? *Business Week,* pp. 103-107.

Csikszentmihalyi, M., & Rochberg-Halton, E. (1981). *The meaning of things: Domestic symbols and self.* New York: Cambridge University Press.

Curphy, G. J. (1990). *An empirical study of Bass's (1985) theory of transformational and transactional leadership.* Unpublished doctoral dissertation, University of Minnesota.

Dahl, R. A. (1957). The concept of power. *Behavioral Science, 2,* 201-218.

D'Aveni, R. A. (1995). Coping with hypercompetition: Utilizing the new 7S's framework. *Academy of Management Executive, 9,* 45-57.

Davies, J. C. (1954). Charisma in the 1952 campaign. *American Political Science Review, 48,* 1083-1102.

Dean, J. W., Jr., & Evans, J. R. (1994). *Total quality: Management, organization and strategy.* St. Paul, MN: West.

Deluga, R. J. (1995). The relationship between attributional charismatic leadership and organizational citizenship behavior. *Journal of Applied Psychology, 25*(18), 1652-1669.

Dorfman, P. (1994, July). *Cross-cultural leadership research: Issues and assumptions.* Paper presented at the SIOP Conference Symposium, Nashville, TN.

Dow, T. E. (1969). A theory of charisma. *Social Quarterly, 10,* 306-318.

Downton, J. V., Jr. (1973). *Rebel leadership.* New York: Free Press.

Earley, P. C., Wojnaroski, P., & Prest, W. (1987). Task planning and energy expended: Exploration of how goals influence performance. *Journal of Applied Psychology, 72,* 107-114.

Eden, D. (1990). *Pygmalion in management: Productivity as a self-fulfilling prophecy.* Lexington, MA: Lexington Books.

Eisenstadt, S. N. (1968). *Max Weber: On charisma and institution building.* Chicago: University of Chicago Press.

Elderkin, K., & Bartlett, C. (1991). *General Electric: Jack Welch's second wave.* Boston: Harvard Business School.

Emmons, R. A. (1984). Factor analysis and construct validity of the narcissistic personality inventory. *Journal of Personality Assessment, 48,* 291-300.

Ericsson, K. A., & Charness, N. (1994). Expert performance. *American Psychologist, 49*(8), 725-747.

Erikson, E. (1968). *Identity, youth, and crisis.* New York: Norton.

Evans, M. G. (1970). The effects of supervisory behavior on the path-goal relationship. *Organizational Behavior and Human Performance, 5,* 277-298.

Fairhurst, G. T., & Sarr, R. A. (1996). *The art of training: Managing the language of leadership.* San Francisco: Jossey-Bass.

Fiedler, F. E. (1967). *A theory of leadership effectiveness.* New York: McGraw-Hill.

Fiedler, F. E., & Chemers, M. M. (1982). *Improving leadership effectiveness: The leader match concept* (2nd ed.). New York: Wiley.

Fleishmann, E. A., Harris, E. F., & Burtt, H. E. (1955). *Leadership and supervision in industry.* Columbus: Ohio State University, Bureau of Educational Research.

Freemesser, G. F., & Kaplan, H. B. (1976). Self-attitudes and deviant behavior: The case of the charismatic religious movement. *Journal of Youth and Adolescence, 5*(1), 1-9.

French, J. R., Jr., & Raven, B. H. (1959). The bases of social power. In D. Cartwright (Ed.), *Studies in social power* (pp. 150-167). Ann Arbor: University of Michigan Press.

Friedland, W. H. (1964). For a sociological concept of charisma. *Social Forces, 43,* 18-26.

Gabarro, J. J. (1985, May-June). When a new manager takes charge. *Harvard Business Review,* pp. 110-123.

Galanter, M. (1982). Charismatic religious sects and psychiatry: An overview. *American Journal of Psychiatry, 139*(2), 1539-1548.

Garber, J., & Seligman, M. E. P. (Eds.). (1980). *Human helplessness: Theory and applications.* Orlando, FL: Academic Press.

George, J. M., & Brief, A. P. (1992). Feeling good—doing good: A conceptual analysis of the mood at work-organizational spontaneity relationship. *Psychological Bulletin, 112,* 310-329.

Gibbs, J. (1972). *Sociology theory construction.* Hinsdale, IL: Dryden.

Ginter, P. M., & Duncan, W. J. (1990). Macroenvironmental analysis for strategic management. *Long Range Planning, 23,* 91-100.

Goffman, E. (1974). *Frame analysis.* Cambridge, MA: Harvard University Press.

Graen, G., & Cashman, J. F. (1975). A role making model of leadership in formal organizations. In J. G. Hunt & L. L. Larson (Eds.), *Leadership frontiers* (pp. 143-165). Carbondale: Southern Illinois University Press.

Graen, G., & Scandura, T. (1987). Toward a psychology of dyadic organizing. In B. M. Staw & L. L. Cummings (Eds.), *Research in organizational behavior* (Vol. 9, pp. 125-208). Greenwich, CT: JAI Press.

Graham, J. W. (1988). Chapter 3 commentary. Transformational leadership: Fostering follower autonomy, not automatic followership. In J. G. Hunt, B. R. Baliga, H. P. Dachler, & C. A. Schriesheim (Eds.), *Emerging leadership vistas* (pp. 73-79). Lexington, MA: D. C. Heath.

Greiner, L. (1967). Antecedents of planned organization change. *Journal of Applied Behavioral Science, 3,* 202-216.

Grinyer, P. H., Mayes, D., & McKiernan, P. (1990). The sharpbenders: Achieving a sustained improvement in performance. *Long Range Planning, 23,* 116-125.

Hage, J. (1972). *Techniques and problems of theory construction in sociology.* New York: Wiley.

Halpin, A. W., & Winer, B. J. (1957). A factorial study of the leader behavior descriptions. In R. M Stogdill & A. E. Coons (Eds.), *Leader behavior: Its description and measurement* (pp. 39-51). Columbus: Ohio State University, Bureau of Business Research.

Hambrick, D. C., & Fukutomi, G. D. S. (1991). The seasons of a CEO's tenure. *Academy of Management Review, 16,* 719-742.

Hamel, G., & Prahalad, C. K. (1994). *Competing for the future.* Cambridge, MA: Harvard Business School Press.

Harris, M. M. (1991). Role conflict and role ambiguity as substance versus artifact: A confirmatory factor analysis of House, Schuler and Leranoni's (1983) scales. *Journal of Applied Psychology, 76,* 122-126.

Harris, M. M., & Schaubroeck, J. (1990). Confirmatory modeling in organizational behavior/human resource management: Issues and applications. *Journal of Management, 16*(2), 337-360.

Hater, J. J., & Bass, B. M. (1988). Superiors' evaluations and subordinates' perceptions of transformational and transactional leadership. *Journal of Applied Psychology, 73,* 695-702.

Hauser, G. A. (1986). *Introduction to rhetorical theory.* New York: Harper Books.

Heller, F. (1971). *Managerial decision making: A study of leadership style and power sharing among senior managers.* London: Tavistock,

Hersey, P., & Blanchard, K. H. (1977). *Management of organizational behavior* (3rd ed.) Englewood Cliffs, NJ: Prentice Hall.

Hickman, C. R. (1990). *Mind of a manager, soul of a leader.* New York: Wiley.

Hogan, R., Curphy, G. J., & Hogan, J. (1994). What we know about leadership: Effectiveness and personality. *American Psychologist, 49,* 493-504.

Hollander, E. P. (1958). Conformity, status, and idiosyncrasy credit. *Psychological Review, 65,* 117-127.

Hollander, E. P. (1979). Leadership and social exchange processes. In K. Gergen, M. S. Greenberg, & R. H. Willis (Eds.), *Social exchange: Advances in theory and research* (pp. 103-118). New York: Winston-Wiley.

Hollander, E. P. (1986). On the central role of leadership of process. *International Review of Applied Psychology, 35,* 39-53.

Hollander, E. P., & Offermann, L. R. (1990). Power and leadership in organizations. *American Psychologist, 45,* 179-189.

House, R. J. (1971). A path-goal theory of leader effectiveness. *Administrative Science Quarterly, 16,* 321-339.

House, R. J. (1977). A 1976 theory of charismatic leadership. In J. G. Hunt & L. L. Larson (Eds.), *Leadership: The cutting edge* (pp. 189-207). Carbondale: Southern Illinois University Press.

House, R. J. (1988). Power and personality in complex organizations. In L. L. Cummings & B. M. Staw (Eds.), *Research in organizational behavior: An annual review of critical essays and reviews* (Vol. 10, pp. 305-357). Greenwich, CT: JAI Press.

House, R. J. (1995). Leadership in the twenty-first century: A speculative inquiry. In A. Howard (Ed.), *The changing nature of work* (pp. 411-450). San Francisco: Jossey-Bass.

House, R. J., & Dessler, G. (1974). The path-goal theory of leadership: Some post hoc and a priori tests. In J. G. Hunt & L. L. Larson (Eds.), *Contingency approaches to leadership* (pp. 29-55). Carbondale, IL: Southern Illinois University Press.

House, R., & Howell, J. M. (1992). Personality and charismatic leadership. *Leadership Quarterly,* *3*(2), 81-108.

House, R. J., & Mitchell, T. R. (1974). Path-goal theory of leadership. *Contemporary Business, 3,* 81-98.

House, R., & Shamir, B. (1993). Toward the integration of transformational, charismatic, and visionary theories. In M. Chemmers & R. Ayman (Eds.), *Leadership theory and research perspectives and directions* (pp. 577-594). Orlando, FL: Academic Press.

House, R. J., Spangler, W. D., & Woycke, J. (1991). Personality and charisma in the U.S. presidency: A psychological theory of leader effectiveness. *Administrative Science Quarterly, 36,* 364-396.

Hovland, C. I., Janis, I. L., & Kelley, H. H. (1953). *Communication and persuasion.* New Haven, CT: Yale University Press.

Hovland, C. I., & Pritzker, H. A. (1957). Extent of opinion change as a function of amount of change advocated. *Journal of Abnormal Psychology, 54,* 257-261.

Howard, A. (1995). A framework for work change. In A. Howard (Ed.), *The changing nature of work* (pp. 3-44). San Francisco: Jossey-Bass.

Howell, J. M. (1988). Two faces of charisma: Socialized and personalized leadership in organizations. In J. A. Conger & R. N. Kanungo (Eds.), *Charismatic leadership: The elusive factor in organizational effectiveness* (pp. 213-236). San Francisco: Jossey-Bass.

Howell, J. (1996). *Organization contexts, charismatic and exchange leadership.* Unpublished manuscript, University of Western Ontario, London, Ontario.

Howell, J. M., & Avolio, B. J. (1993). Transformational leadership, transactional leadership, loss of control, and support for innovation: Key predictors of consolidated business unit performance. *Journal of Applied Psychology, 78,* 891-902.

Howell, J. M., & Frost, P. (1989). A laboratory study of charismatic leadership. *Organizational Behavior and Human Decision Processes, 43,* 243-269.

Howell, J. M., & Higgins, C. A. (1990). Champions of technological innovation. *Administrative Science Quarterly, 35,* 317-341.

Howell, J. M., & House, R. (1993). *Specialized and personalized charisma: A theory of the bright and dark sides of leadership.* Unpublished manuscript, University of Western Ontario, London, Ontario.

Hunt, J. G. (1991). *Leadership: A new synthesis.* Newbury Park, CA: Sage.

Hunt, J. G., Baliga, B. R., & Peterson, M. F. (1988). Strategic apex leadership scripts and an organizational life cycle approach to leadership. *Journal of Management Development, 7*(5), 61-83.

Iacocca, L., & Novak, W. (1984). *Iacocca: An autobiography.* New York: Bantam.

James, W. (1958). *Varieties of religious experiences.* New York: Mentor.

Jenster, P. V. (1987). Using critical success factors in planning. *Long Range Planning, 20,* 102-109.

Johnson, G. (1992). Managing strategic change—Strategy, culture and action. *Long Range Planning, 25,* 28-36.

Johnson, K. E., & Mervis, C. (1994). Microgenetic analysis of first steps in children's acquisition of expertise on shorebirds. *Developmental Psychology, 30*(3), 418-435.

Jöreskog, K. G., & Sörbom, D. (1989). (2nd ed.). *LISREL 7: A guide to the program and applications.* Chicago: SPSS, Inc.

Kanter, R. M. (1967). Commitment and social organization: A study of commitment mechanisms in utopian communities. *American Sociological Review, 33*(4), 499-517.

Kanungo, R. N. (1982). *Work alienation: An integrative approach.* New York: Praeger.

Kanungo, R. N., & Conger, J. A. (1993). Promoting altruism as a corporate goal. *Academy of Management Executive, 7*(3), 37-48.

Kanungo, R. N., & Jaeger, A. M. (1990). Introduction: The need for indigenous management in developing countries. In R. N. Kanungo & A. M. Jaeger (Eds.), *Management in developing countries* (pp. 1-19). London: Routledge.

Kanungo, R. N., & Mendonca, M. (1996a). Cultural contingencies and leadership in developing countries. In P. A. Bamberger, M. Erez, & S. B. Bacharach (Eds.), *Research in the sociology of organizations* (Vol. 14, pp. 263-295). Greenwich, CT: JAI Press.

Kanungo, R. N., & Mendonca, M. (1996b). *Ethical dimensions of leadership.* Thousand Oaks, CA: Sage.

Kanungo, R. N., & Mendonca, M. (1997). *Fundamentals of organizational behavior.* Dubuque, IA: Kendall/Hunt.

Katz, J., & Kahn, R. L. (1978). *The social psychology of organizations.* New York: Wiley.

Kelman, H. C. (1958). Compliance, identification, and internalization: Three processes of attitude change. *Journal of Conflict Resolution, 2*, 51-56.

Kenny, P. A., & Zacarro, S. J. (1983). An estimate of variance due to traits in leadership. *Journal of Applied Psychology, 68*, 678-685.

Kerr, S., & Jermiar, J. M. (1978). Substitutes for leadership: Their meaning and measurement. *Organizational Behavior and Human Performance, 22,* 375-403.

Kets de Vries, M. F. R. (1986). *Richard Branson and the Virgin Group.* Fontaineblcau, France: INSEAD.

Kets de Vries, M. F. R. (1988). Origins of charisma: Ties that bind the leader and the led. In J. A. Conger & R. N. Kanungo (Eds.), *Charismatic leadership: The elusive factor in organizational effectiveness* (pp. 237-252). San Francisco: Jossey-Bass.

Kets de Vries, M. F. R. (1994). The leadership mystique. *Academy of Management Executive, 8*(3), 73-92.

Kets de Vries, M. F. R., & Dick, R. J. (1995). *Branson's Virgin: The coming of age of a counter-cultural enterprise.* Fontainebleau, France: INSEAD.

Kidder, T. (1981). *Soul of a new machine.* New York: Little, Brown.

Kinder, P. R., & Sears, P. O. (1985). Public opinion and political action. In G. Lindzey & E. Aronson (Eds.), *Handbook of social psychology* (pp. 659-742). New York: Random House.

Kirkpatrick, S. A. (1992). *Decomposing charismatic leadership: The effects of leader content and procession follower performance, attitudes, and perceptions.* Unpublished doctoral dissertation, University of Maryland, College Park.

Kirkpatrick, S. A., & Locke, E. A. (1996). Direct and indirect effects of three core charismatic leadership components on performance and attitudes. *Journal of Applied Psychology, 81*(1), 36-51.

Koene, H., Pennings, H., & Schrender, M. (1991). *Leadership, culture, and organizational effectiveness.* Boulder, CO: Center for Creative Leadership.

Koh, W. L., Terborg, J. R., & Steers, R. M. (1991). *The impact of transformational leaders on organizational commitment, organizational citizenship behavior, teacher satisfaction and student performance in Singapore.* Miami, FL: Academy of Management Meetings.

Kohut, H. (1971). *The analysis of the self.* New York: International Universities Press.

Komaki, J. (1986). Toward effective supervision: An operant analysis and comparison of managers at work. *Journal of Applied Psychology, 71,* 270-278.

Kotter, J. P. (1982). *The general managers.* New York: Free Press.

Kotter, J. P. (1988). *The leadership factor.* New York: Free Press.

Kotter, J. (1990). *A force for change.* New York: Free Press.

Kouzes, J. M., & Posner, B. Z. (1987). *The leadership challenge.* San Francisco: Jossey-Bass.

Kouzes, J. M., & Posner, B. Z. (1996). Seven lessons for leading the voyage to the future. In F. Hesselbein, M. Goldsmith, & R. Beckhard (Eds.), *The leader of the future: New visions, strategies, and practices for the next era* (pp. 99-110). San Francisco: Jossey-Bass.

Larwood, L., Falbe, C. M., Kriger, M. P., & Miesing, P. (1995). Structure and meaning of organizational vision. *Academy of Management Journal, 38*(3), 740-769.

Lawler, E. E. (1973). *Motivation in work organizations.* Monterey, CA: Brooks/Cole.

Levering, R., Moskowitz, M., & Katz, M. (1984). *The 100 best companies to work for in America.* New York: Plume.

Lewin, K., Lippitt, R., & White, R. K. (1939). Patterns of aggressive behavior in experimentally created social climates. *Journal of Social Psychology, 10,* 271-301.

Likert, R. (1961). *New patterns of management.* New York: McGraw-Hill.

Lindholm, C. (1988). Lovers and leaders: Comparative models of romance and charisma. *Social Science Information, 27*(1), 3-45.

Lippitt, R., & White, R. K. (1947). An experimental study of leadership and group life. In E. E. Maccoby, T. M. Newcomb, & E. C. Hartley (Eds.), *Readings in social psychology* (pp. 495-511). New York: Holt, Rinehart, & Winston.

Locke, E. A. (in press). The role of individual consideration, vision, and egoism in effective leadership. In F. Dansereau & F. Yammarino (Eds.), *Leadership: A multiple level analysis.* Greenwich, CT: JAI Press.

Locke, E. A., & Henne, D. (1986). Work motivation theories. In C. L. Cooper & I. Robertson (Eds.), *International review of industrial and organizational psychology* (pp. 1-36). Chichester, UK: Wiley.

Locke, E., Kirkpatrick, S., Wheeler, J. K., Schneider, J., Niles, K., Goldstein, H., Welsh, K., & Chau, D-Ok. (1991). *The essence of leadership.* New York: Lexington Books.

Locke, E. A., & Latham, G. P. (1990). *Goal setting: A motivational technique that works.* Englewood Cliffs, NJ: Prentice Hall.

Lodahl, A. (1982). *Crisis in values and the success of the Unification Church.* Unpublished doctoral dissertation, Cornell University, Ithaca, NY.

Lord, R. G., & Maher, K. J. (1991). *Leadership and information processing: Linking perceptions and performance.* Cambridge, MA: Unwin Hyman.

Luthans, F., & Kreitner, R. (1975). *Organizational behavior modification.* Glenview, IL: Scott, Foresman.

Maddi, S. (1980). *Personality theories.* Homewood, IL: Dorsey.

Marcus, J. T. (1961, March). Transcendence and charisma. *Western Political Quarterly, 14,* 236-241.

Marsh, H. W., & Hocevar, D. (1985). Application of confirmatory factor analysis to the study of self concept: First and higher order factor models and their invariance across groups. *Psychological Bulletin, 97,* 562-582.

Martin, J., & Siehl, C. (1983). Organizational culture and counterculture: An uneasy symbiosis. *Organizational Dynamics, 12*(2), 52-64.

Martinko, M. H., & Gardner, W. L. (1982). Learned helplessness: An alternative explanation for performance deficits. *Academy of Management Review, 7,* 195-204.

Maslow, A. H. (1968). *Towards a psychology of being* (2nd ed.). Princeton, NJ: Van Nostrand Reinhold.

McClelland, D. C. (1987). Characteristics of successful entrepreneurs. *Journal of Creative Behavior, 21,* 219-233.

McClelland, D. C., & Burnham, D. H. (1976, March-April). Power is the great motivator. *Harvard Business Review,* pp. 100-110.

McGregor, D. (1960). *The human side of enterprise.* New York: McGraw-Hill.

Medsker, G. J., Williams, L. J., & Holahan, P. J. (1994). A review of current practices for evaluating casual models in organizational behavior and human resource management. *Journal of Management, 20*(2), 439-464.

Mehta, P. (1994). Empowering the people for social achievement. In R. N. Kanungo & M. Mendonca (Eds.), *Work motivation: Models for developing countries* (pp. 161-183). New Delhi: Sage.

Meindl, J. R. (1990). On leadership: An alternative to the conventional wisdom. In B. M. Staw & L. L. Cummings (Eds.), *Research in organizational behavior* (Vol. 12, pp. 159-203). Greenwich, CT: JAI.

Meindl, J. R., Ehrlich, S. B., & Dukerich, J. M. (1985). The romance of leadership. *Administrative Science Quarterly, 30,* 521-551.

Meindl, J., & Lerner, M. J. (1983). The heroic motive: Some experimental demonstrations. *Journal of Experimental Social Psychology, 19,* 1-20.

Mendonca, M. J., & Kanungo, R. N. (1994). Managing human resources: The issue of cultural fit. *Journal of Management Inquiry, 3,* 189-205.

Menon, S. T. (1995). *Employee empowerment: Definition, measurement, and construct validation.* Unpublished doctoral dissertation, McGill University, Montreal.

Menon, S. T., & Borg, I. (1995). Facets of subjective empowerment. In J. Hox & P. Swanborn (Eds.), *Facet analyses and design* (pp. 129-140). Zeist, The Netherlands: Zeist Press.

Miliken, F. H., & Martins, L. L. (1996). Searching for common threads: Understanding the multiple effects of diversity in organizational change. *Academy of Management Review, 21,* 402-433.

Miller, A. B. (1974). Aristotle on habit and character: Implications for the rhetoric. *Speech Monographs, 41,* 309-316.

Miller, D. (1990). *The Icarus paradox.* New York: Harper.

Milliken, F. J., & Vollrath, D. A. (1991). Strategic decision-making tasks and group effectiveness: Insights from theory and research on small group performance. *Human Relations, 44,* 1229-1253.

Mintzberg, H. (1973). *The nature of managerial work.* New York: Harper & Row.

Mintzberg, H. (1979). *The structuring of organizations.* Englewood Cliffs, NJ: Prentice Hall.

Mintzberg, H., & Waters, J. A. (1985). Of strategies, deliberate and emergent. *Strategic Management Journal, 6,* 257-272.

Misumi, J. (1985). *The behavioral science of leadership: An interdisciplinary Japanese research program.* Ann Arbor: University of Michigan Press.

Mitchell, T. R. (1982). Expectancy-value models in organizational psychology. In N. T. Feather (Ed.), *Expectations and actions: Expectancy-value models in psychology* (pp. 293-312). Hillsdale, NJ: Erlbaum.

Morris, C. W. (1949). *Signs, language, and behavior.* New York: Prentice Hall.

Morrison, A. M. (1992). *The new leaders: Guidelines on leadership diversity in America.* San Francisco: Jossey-Bass.

Musser, S. J. (1987). *The determination of positive and negative charismatic leaders.* Unpublished manuscript, Messiah College, Grantham, PA.

Nadler, D. A. (1997). *Leadership and change: The case of Lucent Technologies.* New York: Delta Consulting Group.

Nadler, D. A., & Tushman, M. L. (1990). Beyond the charismatic leader: Leadership and organizational change. *California Management Review, 32,* 77-97.

Nanus, B. (1992). *Visionary leadership.* San Francisco: Jossey-Bass.

Narchal, R. M., Kittappa, K., & Bhattacharya, P. (1987). An environmental scanning system for business planning. *Long Range Planning, 20,* 96-105.

Neilsen, E. (1986). Empowerment strategies: Balancing authority and responsibility. In S. Srivastra (Ed.), *Executive power* (pp. 78-110). San Francisco: Jossey-Bass.

Nocera, J. (1993, October). Stevie Wonder. *Gentlemen's Quarterly,* pp. 105-111.

Nutt, P. C., & Backoff, R. W. (1997). Crafting vision. *Journal of Management Inquiry, 6*(4), 308-328.

Oldham, G. R. (1976). The motivational strategies used by supervisors: Relationships to effectiveness indicators. *Organizational Behavior and Human Performance, 15,* 66-86.

O'Reilly, C., & Pfeffer, J. (1995). *Southwest Airlines.* Palo Alto, CA: Stanford Graduate School of Business.

Organ, D. W. (1988). *Organizational citizenship behavior: The good soldier syndrome.* Lexington, MA: Lexington Books.

Pascale, R. T. (1989). *Managing on the edge.* New York: Simon & Schuster.

Pawar, B. S., & Eastman, K. K. (1997). The nature and implications of contextual influences on transformational leadership: A conceptual examination. *Academy of Management Review, 22,* 80-109.

Pearlstein, S., & Rhodes, L. (1987, October). Corporate antihero: John Sculley. *Inc.,* pp. 49-59.

Peters, T., & Austin, N. (1985). *A passion for excellence.* New York: Random House.

Peters, T. J., & Waterman, R. H., Jr. (1982). *In search of excellence: Lessons from America's best-run companies.* New York: Harper & Row.

Pettigrew, A. M. (1987). Context and action in the transformation of the firm. *Journal of Management Studies, 24,* 649-670.

Petty, R. E., & Cacioppo, J. T. (1981). *Attitudes and persuasion: Classic and contemporary approaches.* Dubuque, IA: Brown.

Petzinger, T. (1995). *Hard landing.* New York: Times Books.

Pfeffer, J. (1977). The ambiguity of leadership. *Academy of Management Review, 2,* 104-112.

Pierce, J. L., Gardner, D. G., Cummings, L. L., & Dunham, R. (1989). Organization-based self-esteem: Construct definition, measurement, and validation. *Academy of Management Journal, 32*(3), 622-648.

Pitta, J. (1991, April). The Steven Jobs reality distortion field. *Forbes,* pp. 137-140.

Podsakoff, P. M., MacKenzie, S. B., Moorman, R. H., & Fetter, R. (1990). Transformational leader behaviors and their effects on followers' trust in leader, satisfaction, and organizational citizenship behaviors. *Leadership Quarterly, 1,* 107-142.

Podsakoff, P. M., Todor, W. D., & Skov, R. (1982). Effects of leader contingent and noncontingent reward and punishment behaviors on subordinate performance and satisfaction. *Academy of Management Journal, 25*, 810-821.

Pondy, L. (1978). Leadership as a language game. In M. W. McCall, Jr., & M. M. Lombardo (Eds.), *Leadership: Where else can we go?* (pp. 87-99). Durham, NC: Duke University Press.

Prentice, D. A. (1987). Psychological correspondence of possessions, attitudes and values. *Journal of Personality and Social Psychology, 53*(6), 993-1003.

Puffer, S. M. (1990). Attributions of charismatic leadership: The impact of decision style, outcome, and observer characteristics. *Leadership Quarterly, 1*, 177-192.

Puffer, S. M., & McCarthy, D. J. (1996). A framework for leadership in a TQM context. *Journal of Quality Management, 1*, 109-130.

Quigley, J. V. (1993). *Vision.* New York: McGraw-Hill.

Quinn, J. B. (1980). Formulating strategy one step at a time. *Journal of Business Strategy, 1*, 42-63.

Raskin, R., & Hall, S. C. (1979). A narcissistic personality inventory. *Psychological Reports, 45*, 55-60.

Raskin, R., & Novacek, J. (1989). A MMPI description of the narcissistic personality. *Journal of Personality Assessment, 53*, 66-80.

Raskin, R., & Terry, H. (1988). A principal-component analysis of the narcissistic personality inventory and further evidence of its construct validity. *Journal of Personality and Social Psychology, 54*, 890-902.

Reynolds, L. D. (1971). *A primer in theory construction.* New York: Bobbs-Merrill.

Rhinesmith, S. H. (1993). Global mindsets for global managers. *OD Practitioner, 25*(2), 2-9.

Roberts, N. C. (1985). Transforming leadership: A process of collective action. *Human Relations, 38*, 1023-1046.

Roberts, N. C., & Bradley, R. T. (1988). Limits of charisma. In J. A. Conger & R. N. Kanungo (Eds.), *Charismatic leadership: The elusive factor in organizational effectiveness* (pp. 253-275). San Francisco: Jossey-Bass.

Roddick, A. (1991). *Body and soul.* New York: Crown.

Rokeach, M. (1973). *The nature of human values.* New York: Free Press.

Rose, R. (1989). *West of Eden: The end of innocence at Apple Computer.* London: Business Books.

Ross, L. (1977). The intuitive psychologist and his shortcomings: Distortions in the attribution process. In L. Berkowitz (Ed.), *Advances in experimental social psychology, 10* (pp. 174-220). New York: Academic Press.

Rothbard, N., & Conger, J. A. (1993). *Orit Gadiesh: Pride at Bain & Co.* Boston: Harvard Business School.

Rubin, Z. (1973). *Liking and loving: An invitation to social psychology.* New York: Holt, Rinehart, and Winston.

Sackley, N., & Ibarra, H. (1995). *Charlotte Beers at Ogilvy & Mather Worldwide.* Boston: Harvard Business School.

Salancik, G. R. (1977). Commitment and the control of organizational behavior and belief. In B. M. Staw & G. R. Salancik (Eds.), *New directions in organizational behavior* (pp. 1-54). Chicago: St. Clair.

Sankowsky, D. (1995). The charismatic leader as narcissist: Understanding the abuse of power. *Organizational Dynamics, 23*(4), 57-71.

Sashkin, M. (1988). The visionary leader. In J. A. Conger & R. N. Kanungo (Eds.), *Charismatic leadership: The elusive factor in organizational effectiveness* (pp. 122-160). San Francisco: Jossey-Bass.

Schein, E. H. (1992). *Organizational culture and leadership* (2nd ed.). San Francisco: Jossey-Bass.

Schlender, B. (1997, May 26). On the road with Chairman Bill. *Fortune*, p. 81.

Schlenker, B. R. (1980). *Impression management*. Monterey, CA: Brooks/Cole.

Schwenk, C. R. (1986). Information, cognitive bias and commitment to a course of action. *Academy of Management Review, 11*(2), 298-310.

Sears, D. O., Freedman, L., & Peplau, L. A. (1985). *Social psychology* (5th ed.). Englewood Cliffs, NJ: Prentice Hall.

Selznick, P. (1948). Foundations of a theory of organizations. *American Sociological Review, 13*, 25-35.

Selznick, P. (1957). *Leadership in administration*. New York: Harper & Row.

Shamir, B. (1992). Attribution of influence and charisma to the leader: The romance of leadership revisited. *Journal of Applied Social Psychology, 22*(5), 386-407.

Shamir, B. (1995). Social distance and charisma: Theoretical notes and an exploratory study. *Leadership Quarterly, 6*(1), 19-47.

Shamir, B., Arthur, M. B., & House, R. J. (1994). The rhetoric of charismatic leadership: A theoretical extension, a case study, and implications for research. *Leadership Quarterly, 5*(1), 25-42.

Shamir, B., House, R., & Arthur, M. B. (1993). The motivational effects of charismatic leadership: A self-concept based theory. *Organization Science, 4*(4), 577-594.

Shore, L. M., Barksdale, K., & Shore, T. H. (1995). Managerial perceptions of employee commitment to the organization. *Academy of Management Journal, 38*, 1593-1615.

Sims, H. P., Jr. (1977). The leader as a manager of reinforcement contingencies: An empirical example and a model. In J. G. Hun & L. L. Larson (Eds.), *Leadership: The cutting edge* (pp. 121-137). Carbondale: Southern Illinois University Press.

Sims, H. P., & Lorenzi, P. (1992). *The new leadership paradigm*. Newbury Park, CA: Sage.

Sinha, J. B. P. (1984). A model of effective leadership styles in India. *International Studies of Management and Organization, 14*, 86-98.

Snow, D. A., Rochford, E. B., Worden, S. K., & Benford, R. D. (1986). Frame alignment processes, micromobilization, and movement participation. *American Sociological Review, 51*, 464-481.

Snyder, M., & Ickes, W. (1985). Personality and social behavior. In G. Lindzey & E. Aronson (Eds.), *Handbook of social psychology* (pp. 883-947). New York: Random House.

Spreitzer, G. M. (1995). Individual empowerment in the workplace: Dimensions, measurement, validation. *Academy of Management Journal, 38*(5), 1442-1465.

Spreitzer, G. M. (1996). Social structural levels for workplace empowerment. *Academy of Management Journal, 39*(2), 483-504.

Staw, B., Sandelands, L. E., & Dutton, J. E. (1981). Thrust-rigidity effects in organizational behavior: A multi-level analysis. *Administrative Science Quarterly, 26*, 147-160.

Sternberg, R. J., & Lubart, T. I. (1996). Investing in creativity. *American Psychologist, 51*(7), 677-688.

Stinchecombe, A. (1968). *Constructing social theories*. New York: Harcourt, Brace, Jovanovich.

Student, K. R. (1968). Supervisory influence and work-group performance. *Journal of Applied Psychology, 52*, 188-194.

Sullivan, J. J. (1988). Three roles of language in motivation. *Academy of Management Review,* *13*(1), 104-115.

Szilagyi, A. D. (1980). Causal inferences between leader reward behavior and subordinate goal attainment, absenteeism, and work satisfaction. *Journal of Occupational Psychology, 53,* 195-204.

Tannenbaum, R., & Schmidt, W. H. (1958, March-April). How to choose a leadership pattern. *Harvard Business Review*, pp. 95-101.

Taylor, A. (1991, April). Can Iacocca fix Chrysler—again? *Fortune*, pp. 40-44.

Terry, P. T. (1977). Mechanisms for environmental scanning. *Long Range Planning, 10,* 2-9.

Thomas, K. (1976). Conflict and conflict management. In M. D. Dunnette (Ed.), *Handbook of industrial and organizational psychology* (pp. 889-935). Chicago: Rand McNally.

Thomas, K. W., & Velthouse, B. A. (1990). Cognitive elements of empowerment: An interpretive model of intrinsic task motivation. *Academy of Management Review, 15,* 666-681.

Thompson, J. D. (1967). *Organizations in action.* New York: McGraw-Hill.

Tichy, N. M., & Devanna, M. A. (1986). *The transformational leader.* New York: Wiley.

Tichy, N., & Sherman, S. (1993). *Control your destiny, or someone else will.* New York: Currency Doubleday.

Toth, M. A. (1981). *The theory of two charismas.* Washington, DC: University Press of America.

Trice, H. M., & Beyer, J. M. (1986). Charisma and its routinization in two social movement organizations. *Journal of Occupational Behavior, 7,* 125-138.

Turner, R. H., & Killian, L. M. (1972). *Collective behavior.* Englewood Cliffs, NJ: Prentice Hall.

Tushman, M. L., & Anderson, P. (1986). Technological discontinuities and organizational environments. *Administrative Science Quarterly, 31,* 439-465.

Vroom, V. H., & Yetton, P. W. (1973). *Leadership and decision-making.* Pittsburgh: University of Pittsburgh Press.

Waldman, D. A., & Ramirez, G. G. (1992). *CEO leadership and organizational performance: The moderating effect of environmental uncertainty* (Working paper 92-10-37). Montreal: Concordia University.

Waller, M. J., Huber, G. P., & Glick, W. H. (1995). Functional background as a determinant of executives' selective perception. *Academy of Management Journal, 38*(4), 943-974.

Walster, E., Aronson, D., & Abrahams, D. (1966). On increasing the persuasiveness of a low prestige communicator. *Journal of Experimental Social Psychology, 2,* 325-342.

Watson, P. J., Grisham, S. O., Trotter, M. V., & Biderman, M. D. (1984). Narcissism and empathy: Validity evidence for the narcissistic personality inventory. *Journal of Personality Assessment, 48,* 301-305.

Watson, W. E., Kumar, K., & Michaelsen, L. (1993). Cultural diversity's impact on interaction process and performance: Comparing homogeneous and diverse task groups. *Academy of Management Journal, 36,* 590-602.

Weber, M. (1947). *The theory of social and economic organizations* (A. M. Henderson & T. Parsons, Trans.; T. Parsons, Ed.). New York: Free Press.

Weber, M. (1968). *Economy and society* (3 vols., R. Guenther & C. Wittich, Eds.). New York: Bedminster. (Original work published 1925)

Welch, J. J. (1989, April 26). *Speed, simplicity, self-confidence: Keys to leading in the 1990's.* Speech given at the General Electric Annual Shareholders Meeting, Greenville, SC.

Welch, J. J. (1990, April 25). *A boundary-less company in a decade of change.* Speech given at the General Electric Annual Shareholders Meeting, Erie, PA.

West, J., & Garvin, D. A. (1993). *Serengeti: Entrepreneurship with Corning Inc.* Boston: Harvard Business School.

Westley, F. (1992). Vision Worlds: Strategic visions as social interaction. *Advances in Strategic Management, 8,* 271-305.

Westley, F. R., & Mintzberg, H. (1988). Profiles of strategic vision: Levesque and Iacocca. In J. A. Conger & R. N. Kanungo (Eds.), *Charismatic leadership: The elusive factor in organizational effectiveness* (pp. 161-212). San Francisco: Jossey-Bass.

Westley, F. R., & Mintzberg, H. (1989). Visionary leadership and strategic management. *Strategic Management Journal, 10,* 17-32.

White, J. A. (1983). AT & T's McGill expected to quit as head of unregulated business unit. *The Wall Street Journal,* June 7, p. 4.

Whitestone, D., & Schlesinger, L. (1983). *People Express.* Boston: Harvard Business School.

Wilkins, A. L., & Ouchi, W. G. (1983). Efficient cultures: Exploring the relationships between culture and organizational performance. *Administrative Science Quarterly, 28,* 468-481.

Willner, A. R. (1984). *The spellbinders: Charismatic political leadership.* New Haven, CT: Yale University Press.

Wilson, B. R. (1975). *The noble savages: The primitive origins of charisma and its contemporary survival.* Berkeley: University of California Press.

Work, J. W. (1996). Leading a diverse work force. In F. Hesselbein, M. Goldsmith, & R. Beckhard (Eds.), *The leader of the future: New vision, strategies, and practices for the next era* (pp. 71-79). San Francisco: Jossey-Bass.

Yammarino, F. J., & Bass, B. M. (1990). Long-term forecasting of transformational leadership and its effects among naval officers. In K. E. Clark & M. B. Clark (Eds.), *Measures of leadership* (pp. 151-170). West Orange, NJ: Leadership Library of America.

Yukl, G. A. (1988). *Development of a validation of the Managerial Practices Questionnaire* (Technical Report). Albany: State University of New York at Albany.

Yukl, G. (1989). *Leadership in organizations* (2nd ed.). Englewood Cliffs, NJ: Prentice Hall.

Yukl, G. (1994). *Leadership in organizations* (3rd ed.). Englewood Cliffs, NJ: Prentice Hall.

Zaleznik, A. (1990). The leadership gap. *The Executive, 4,* 7-22.

Zaleznik, A., & Kets de Vries, M. (1975). *Power and the corporate mind.* Boston: Houghton Mifflin.

Zetterberg, H. (1965). *On theory and verification in sociology.* Totowa, NJ: Bedminster.

Index

Acceptance, latitude of, 54, 66, 66 (table), 158
Achievement motives, in ethical vs unethical leadership, 213-214, 214 (table), 215
Achievement. *See* Success
Active learning:
　and environmental assessments, 127
　expertise acquired through, 140
Adaptation:
　efficiency vs., 24-25, 26
　rapidity of change forcing, 243-244, 247 (table)
　tradition vs., 30-31
　See also Change
Adhocracy structure, receptivity to change, 25-26
Administrators:
　charismatic leaders lacking skills as, 32, 211, 220 (exhibit), 232-236
　leadership roles separate from task roles, 81
　maintenance of status quo by, 8, 53, 66 (table)
　See also Managers
Affiliative interest, of ethical vs. unethical leadership, 214, 214 (table)
Agents of change:
　as role of leadership, 8, 9 (table), 24, 46, 51 (table), 52, 66 (table), 121-122, 132-133
　supervisors as moderate, 53, 66 (table), 133
　validity test (Study 1), 72, 74, 75 (table), 79-80 (tables), 81
Air Southwest, 145
Airlines:
　information systems, 234
　mergers, 190-191

See also Burr, Donald; Kelleher, Herb; Southwest Airlines, Texas International Airlines
Alcoholics Anonymous, 28
Alienation, 249
　from class distinctions, 136-137, 170, 191
Alpert, Mark, 222
Altruism:
　as discretionary behavior in followers, 203
　balancing personality quirks of leader, 134
　gaining trust through, 56, 66 (table)
　identification with leader through, 60
　in ethical vs. nonethical leadership, 213-215, 214 (table)
　research needs, 250
　See also Sacrifices; Self-interests of leaders
American Airlines, 234
Amway, 30
"A 1976 Theory of Charismatic Leadership" (House), 16
Appearance, as impression management device, 55
Apple Computer Company. *See* Jobs, Steven
Approval, measuring self-worth through, 20, 216-217
ARCO, 199
Arthur, M. B., 16, 17, 18, 20, 137, 191-192
Articulation:
　aiding implementation of vision, 159, 164-165, 166-167, 168-169, 187 (n1), 247, 248
　aligning values through, 180-183
　building credibility through, 183-187

271

About the Authors

Jay A. Conger is Chairman and Executive Director of The Leadership Institute at the University of Southern California. As the author of more than 60 articles and seven books, he researches executive leadership, corporate boards, the management of organizational change, and the training and development of leaders and managers. His articles have appeared in the *Academy of Management Review, Academy of Management Executive Boards and Directors, Business and Strategy, Harvard Business Review, Journal of Organizational Behavior, Leadership Quarterly*, and *Organizational Dynamics*. His books include *The Leader's Change Handbook* (1998), *Winning 'Em Over: A New Model for Management in the Age of Persuasion* (1998), *Spirit at Work* (1994), *Learning to Lead* (1992), *The Charismatic Leader* (1989), and *Charismatic Leadership* (1988). An outstanding teacher, he has been selected by *Business Week* as the pick of business school professors to teach leadership to executives.

In recognition of his work on leadership education, Professor Conger was invited 3 years ago to join the Harvard Business School as a visiting professor to assist in redesign of the school's organizational behavior course around leadership issues. While a professor at McGill University in Montreal, he twice received McGill's Distinguished Teaching Award. He received his BA from Dartmouth College, his MBA from the University of Virginia, and his DBA from the Harvard Business School.

Rabindra N. Kanungo is Professor of Organizational Behavior and holds the Faculty of Management Chair at McGill University, Montreal, Canada. His work experience as a university professor, researcher, and consultant spans both East (India) and West (Canada and the United States). He has published widely in both the basic and applied areas of psychology and management. His publications include more than 100 professional articles in such journals as *Experimental Psychology*, *Journal of Applied Psychology*, *Journal of Personal and Social Psychology*, *Academy of Management Review*, *California Management Review*, and *Psychological Bulletin*. He has written several books, including *Memory and Affect* (1975), *Biculturalism and Management* (1980), *Work Alienation* (1982), *Compensation: Effective Reward Management: The Canadian Context* (1977), *Management of Work and Personal Life* (1984), *Charismatic Leadership* (1988), and *Management in Developing Countries* (1990). His most recent books include *Compensation: Effective Reward Management* (1996, with M. Mendonca), *Work Motivation* (Sage, 1994, edited with M. Mendonca), and *Ethical Dimensions of Leadership* (Sage, 1996, with M. Mendonca). For his contributions to psychology and management, Professor Kanungo was elected a Fellow of the Canadian Psychological Association and has won Commonwealth and Seagram Senior Faculty Fellowships and Best Paper Awards. He received his PhD from McGill University in 1962.